Frank Moore

Spirit of the Pulpit

With Reference to the present Crisis. Part 1

Frank Moore

Spirit of the Pulpit
With Reference to the present Crisis. Part 1

ISBN/EAN: 9783337379582

Printed in Europe, USA, Canada, Australia, Japan

Cover: Foto ©Lupo / pixelio.de

More available books at **www.hansebooks.com**

SPIRIT OF THE PULPIT,

WITH REFERENCE TO THE PRESENT CRISIS.

PART I.

☞ *The Second Part of the* "Spirit of the Pulpit" *will include Sern preached on Thanksgiving-Day, November* 28, 1861.

CONTENTS.

1. SLAVERY A DIVINE TRUST. The Duty of the South to preserve and perpetuate it. A Sermon preached in the First Presbyterian Church of New Orleans, La., Nov. 29, 1860. By B. M. PALMER, D. D., . . . 1

2. THE DEMORALIZATION OF THE NATIONAL SOUL. Preached in All Souls' Church, N. Y., Jan. 25, 1861. By HENRY W. BELLOWS, ... 9

3. THE BIBLE VIEW OF SLAVERY. A Sermon delivered in the Greene Street Hebrew Synagogue, New York City, Jan. 4, 1861. By Rev. Dr. M. J. RAPHALL, Rabbi, 14

4. SERMON, delivered in St. George's Church, New York, on the day of the National Fast, Sept. 26, 1861. By STEPHEN H. TYNG, D. D., 21

5. SERMON, preached in the Hall of the House of Representatives, at Washington, D. C., Sunday, April 28, 1861. By BYRON SUNDERLAND, D. D., ... 27

6. LOYALTY AND RELIGION. A Discourse for the Times: delivered in the Church of the Messiah, St. Louis, Mo., Aug. 18, 1861. By W. G. ELIOT, D. D., . . . 31

7. INCENTIVES TO PRAYER AND HOPE. A Discourse delivered in the First Baptist Church, before the Baptist Churches of the City of New York, on the occasion of the National Fast, Sept. 26, 1861. By HENRY G. WESTON, ... 41

8. THANKSGIVING SERMON. Preached in Christ's Church, New Orleans, on Thanksgiving Day. By Rev. Dr. W. T. LEACOCK, 50

9. OUR NATIONAL SINS. A Sermon preached in the Presbyterian Church, Columbia, S. C., on the day of the State Fast, Nov. 21, 1860. By Rev. J. H. THORNWELL, D. D., 54

10. THE PENTECOST OF THE NATION. A Sermon preached in the Church of the Messiah, Broadway, New York, Whit-Sunday Morning, May 19, 1861. By SAMUEL OSGOOD, D. D., ... 71

11. THE RE-UNION OF THE STATES. A Sermon preached at Boston, Mass., Sept. 26, 1861. By Rev. NEHEMIAH ADAMS, D. D., 73

12. SERMON ON THE DIVINE ORIGIN OF CIVIL GOVERNMENT, AND THE SINFULNESS OF REBELLION. Delivered in the Ebenezer M. E. Church, at Philadelphia, Pa., Sabbath, June 30, 1861. By Rev. P. COOMBE, . . . 85

13. SERMON delivered in the Second Baptist Church, at St. Louis, Mo.; on the evening of April 21, 1861. By Rev. GALUSHA ANDERSON, ... 96

14. GOD'S CONTROVERSY WITH THE PEOPLE OF THE UNITED STATES. A Sermon delivered in St. Stephen's Church, Baltimore, on National Fast Day, Sept. 26, 1861. By Rev. JOHN N. McJILTON, D. D., 101

15. OBEDIENCE TO THE CIVIL AUTHORITY. A Sermon preached in the South Presbyterian Church, Brooklyn, N. Y., April 28, 1861. By Rev. SAMUEL T. SPEAR, D. D., 113

16. THE CHRISTIAN'S BEST MOTIVE FOR PATRIOTISM. A Sermon preached in the College Church, Hampden, Sidney, Va., on General Fast Day, Nov. 1, 1860. By ROBERT L. DABNEY, D. D., . . . 125

17. GOD'S PRESENCE WITH THE CONFEDERATE STATES. A Sermon preached in Christ Church, Savannah, Ga., on Thursday, the 13th of June, being the day appointed, at the request of Congress, by the President of the Confederate States as a day of solemn humiliation, fasting, and prayer. By the Rt. Rev. STEPHEN ELLIOTT, 130

18. OUR PERIL AND OUR DELIVERANCE. A Sermon preached Sunday, October 20, 1861, in the South Reformed Dutch Church, New York. By Rev. ROSWELL D. HITCHCOCK, D. D., . . . 138

19. ABSALOM'S REBELLION. A Sermon preached in Christ Church, Philadelphia, Thursday, Sept. 26, 1861, on occasion of the National Fast, recommended by the President of the United States, at the request of both Houses of Congress. By BENJAMIN DORR, D. D., ... 145

20. THE NATIONAL WEAKNESS. A Discourse delivered in the First Church, Brookline, Mass., on Fast Day, Sept. 26, 1861. By Rev. F. H. HEDGE, D. D., . 152

21. NATIONAL LAWLESSNESS, AND ITS CURE. A Sermon preached in the Madison Square Presbyterian Church, New York, the Sunday after the Fourth of July, 1861. By WILLIAM ADAMS, D. D., . 157

SPIRIT OF THE PULPIT.

SLAVERY A DIVINE TRUST.

THE DUTY OF THE SOUTH TO PRESERVE AND PERPETUATE IT.

A Sermon preached in the First Presbyterian Church of New Orleans, La., November 29, 1860,

BY REV. B. M. PALMER, D. D.

Shall the throne of iniquity have fellowship with thee, which frameth mischief by a law?—*Psalm* xciv. 20.
All the men of thy confederacy have brought thee even to the border; the men that were at peace with thee have deceived thee, and prevailed against thee; they that ate thy bread have laid a wound under thee; there is none understanding in him.—*Obadiah* vii.

THE voice of the Chief Magistrate has summoned us to-day to the house of prayer. This call, in its annual repetition, may be, too often, only a solemn state-form; nevertheless, it covers a mighty and a double truth.

It recognizes the existence of a personal God, whose will shapes the destiny of nations, and that sentiment of religion in man which points to Him as the needle to the pole. Even with those who grope in the twilight of natural religion, natural conscience gives a voice to the dispensations of Providence. If in autumn "extensive harvests hang their heavy head," the joyous reaper, "crowned with the sickle and the wheaten sheaf," lifts his heart to the "Father of lights, from whom cometh down every good and perfect gift." Or, if pestilence and famine waste the earth, even pagan altars smoke with bleeding victims, and costly hecatombs appease the divine anger which flames out in such dire misfortunes. It is the instinct of man's religious nature, which, among Christians and heathen alike, seeks after God—the natural homage which reason, blinded as it may be, pays to a universal and ruling Providence. All classes bow beneath its spell, especially in seasons of gloom, when a nation bends beneath the weight of a general calamity, and a common sorrow falls upon every heart. The hesitating skeptic forgets to weigh his scruples, as the dark shadow passes over him and fills his soul with awe. The dainty philosopher, coolly discoursing of the forces of nature and her uniform laws, abandons for a time his atheistical speculations, abashed by the proofs of a supreme and personal will.

Thus the devout followers of Jesus Christ, and those who do not rise above the level of mere theism, are drawn into momentary fellowship; as, under the pressure of these inextinguishable convictions, they pay a public and united homage to the God of nature and grace.

In obedience to this great law of religious feeling, not less than in obedience to the civil ruler who represents this Commonwealth in its unity, we are now assembled. Hitherto, on similar occasions, our language has been the language of gratitude and song. "The voice of rejoicing and salvation was in the tabernacles of the righteous." Together we praised the Lord "that our garners were full, affording all manner of store; that our sheep brought forth thousands and tens of thousands in our streets; that our oxen were strong to labor, and there was no breaking in nor going out, and no complaining was in our streets." As we together surveyed the blessings of Providence, the joyful chorus swelled from millions of people, "Peace be within thy walls, and prosperity within thy palaces." But, to-day, burdened hearts all over this land are brought to the sanctuary of God. We "see the tents of Cushan in affliction, and the curtains of the land of Midian do tremble." We have fallen upon times when there are "signs in the sun, and in the moon, and in the stars; upon the earth distress of nations, with perplexity; the sea and the waves roaring men's hearts failing them for fear, and for looking after those things which are coming" in the near, yet gloomy, future. Since the words of this proclamation were penned by which we are convened, that which all men dreaded, but against which all men hoped, has been realized; and in the triumph of a sectional majority, we are compelled to read the probable doom of our once happy and united confederacy. It is not to be concealed, that we are in the most fearful and perilous crisis which has occurred in our history as a nation. The cords which, during four-fifths of a century, have bound together this growing Republic, are now strained to their utmost tension—they just need the touch of fire to part asunder forever. Like a ship laboring in the storm, and suddenly grounded upon some treacherous shoal, every timber of this vast confederacy strains and groans under the pressure. Sectional divisions, the jealousy of rival interests, the lust of political power, a bastard ambition, which looks to personal aggrandizement rather than to the public weal, a reckless radicalism, which seeks for the subversion of all that is ancient and stable, and a furious fanaticism, which drives on its ill-considered conclusions with utter disregard of the evil it engenders—all these combine to create a portentous crisis, the like of which we have never known before, and which puts to a crucifying test the virtue, the patriotism, and the piety of the country.

You, my hearers, who have waited upon my public ministry, and have known me in the intimacies of pastoral intercourse, will do me the justice to testify that I have never intermeddled with political questions. Interested as I might be in the progress of events, I have never obtruded, either publicly or privately, my opinions upon any of you; nor can a single man arise and say that, by word or sign, have I ever sought to warp his sentiments or control his judgment upon any political subject whatsoever. The party questions which have hitherto divided the political world, have seemed to me to involve no issue sufficiently momentous to warrant my turning aside, even for a moment, from my chosen calling. In this day of intelligence, I have felt there were thousands around me more competent to instruct in statesmanship; and thus, from considerations of modesty no less than prudence, I have preferred to move among you as a preacher of righteousness belonging to a kingdom not of this world.

During the heated canvass which has just been brought to so disastrous a close, the seal of a rigid and religious silence has not been broken. I deplored the divisions amongst us as being, to a large extent, impertinent in the solemn crisis which was too evidently impending. Most clearly did it appear to me that but one issue was before us; an issue soon to be presented in a form which would compel the attention. That crisis might make it imperative upon me, as a Christian and a divine, to speak in language admitting no misconstruction. Until then, aside from the din and strife of parties, I could only mature with solitary and prayerful thought the destined utterance. That hour has come. At a juncture so solemn as the present, with the destiny of a great people waiting upon the decision of an hour, it is not lawful to be still. Whoever may have influence to shape public opinion at such a time must lend it, or prove faithless to a trust as solemn as any to be accounted for at the bar of God.

Is it immodest in me to assume that I may represent a class whose opinions in such a controversy are of cardinal importance—the class which seeks to ascertain its duty in the light simply of conscience and religion, and which turns to the moralist and the Christian for support and guidance? The question, too, which now places us upon the brink of revolution, was, in its origin, a question of morals and religion. It was debated in ecclesiastical councils before it entered legislative halls. It has riven asunder the two largest religious communions in the land; and the right determination of this primary question will go far toward fixing the attitude we must assume in the coming struggle. I sincerely pray God that I may be forgiven if I have misapprehended the duty incumbent upon me to-day; for I have ascended this pulpit under the agitation of feeling natural to one who is about to deviate from the settled policy of his public life. It is my purpose—not as your organ, compromitting you, whose opinions are for the most part unknown to me, but on my sole responsibility—to speak upon the one question of the day; and to state the duty which, as I believe, patriotism and religion alike require of us all. I shall aim to speak with a moderation of tone and feeling almost judicial, well befitting the sanctities of the place and the solemnities of the judgment-day.

In determining our duty in this emergency, it is necessary that we should first ascertain the nature of the trust providentially committed to us. A nation often has a character as well-defined and intense as that of the individual. This depends, of course, upon a variety of causes, operating through a long period of time. It is due largely to the original traits which distinguish the stock from which it springs, and to the providential training which has formed its education. But however derived, this individuality of character alone makes any people truly historic, competent to work out its specific mission, and to become a factor in the world's progress. The particular trust assigned to such a people becomes the pledge of Divine protection, and their fidelity to it determines the fate by which it is finally overtaken. What that trust is must be ascertained from the necessities of their position, the institutions which are the outgrowth of their principles, and the conflicts through which they preserve their identity and independence. If, then, the South is such a people, what, at this juncture, is their providential trust? I answer, that it is *to conserve and to perpetuate the institution of slavery as now existing.* It is not necessary here to inquire whether this is precisely the best relation in which the hewer of wood and drawer of water can stand to his employer; although this proposition may perhaps be successfully sustained by those who choose to defend it. Still less are we required, dogmatically, to affirm that it will subsist through all time. Baffled as our wisdom may now be in finding a solution of this intricate social problem, it would, nevertheless, be the height of arrogance to pronounce what changes may or may not occur in the distant future. In the grand march of events, Providence may work out a solution undiscoverable by us. What modifications of soil and climate may hereafter be produced, what consequent changes in the products on which we depend, what political revolutions may occur among the races which are now enacting the great drama of history,—all such inquiries are totally irrelevant, because no prophetic vision can pierce the darkness of that future. If this question should ever arise, the generation to whom it is remitted will doubtless have the wisdom to meet it, and Providence will furnish the lights in which it is to be resolved. All that we claim for them and for ourselves is liberty to work out this problem, guided by nature and God, without obtrusive interference from abroad. These great questions of providence and history must have free scope for their solution; and the race whose fortunes are distinctly implicated in the same is alone authorized, as it is alone competent, to determine them. It is just this impertinence of human legislation, setting bounds to what God only can regulate, that the South is called this day to resent and resist. The country is convulsed simply because "the throne of iniquity frameth mischief by a law." Without, therefore, determining the question of duty for future generations, I simply say that for us, as now situated, the duty is plain of conserving and transmitting the system of slavery with the freest scope for its natural development and extension. Let us, my brethren, look our duty in the face. With this institution assigned to our keeping, what reply shall we make to those who say that its days are numbered? My own conviction is that we should at once lift ourselves, intelligently, to the highest moral ground, and proclaim to all the world that we hold this trust from God, and in its occupancy we are prepared to stand or fall as God may appoint. If the critical moment has arrived at which the great issue is joined, let us say that, in the sight of all perils, we will stand by our trust: and God be with the right!

The argument which enforces the solemnity of this providential trust is simple and condensed. It is bound upon us, then, by the *principle of self-preservation,* that "first law" which is continually asserting its supremacy over others. Need I pause to show how this system of servitude underlies and supports our material interests? That our wealth consists in our lands, and in the serfs who till them? That from the nature of our products they can only be cultivated by labor which must be controlled in order to be certain? That any other than a tropical race must faint and wither beneath a tropical sun? Need I pause to show how this system is interwoven with our entire social fabric? That these slaves form par's of our households, even as our children;

that, too, through a relationship recognized and sanctioned in the Scriptures of God even as the other? Must I pause to show how it has fashioned our modes of life, and determined all our habits of thought and feeling, and moulded the very type of our civilization? How, then, can the hand of violence be laid upon it without involving our existence? The so-called free States of this country are working out the social problem under conditions peculiar to themselves. These conditions are sufficiently hard, and their success is too uncertain, to excite in us the least jealousy of their lot. With a teeming population, which the soil cannot support—with their wealth depending upon arts, created by artificial wants—with an eternal friction between the grades of their society—with their labor and their capital grinding against each other like the upper and nether millstones—with labor cheapened and displaced by new mechanical inventions, bursting more asunder the bonds of brotherhood; amid these intricate perils we have ever given them our sympathy and our prayers, and have never sought to weaken the foundations of their social order. God grant them complete success in the solution of all their perplexities! We, too, have our responsibilities and our trials; but they are all bound up in this one institution, which has been the object of such unrighteous assault through five and twenty years. If we are true to ourselves we shall, at this critical juncture, stand by it and work out our destiny.

This duty is bound upon us again *as the constituted guardians of the slaves themselves.* Our lot is not more implicated in theirs, than is their lot in ours; in our mutual relations we survive or perish together. The worst foes of the black race are those who have intermeddled on their behalf. We know better than others that every attribute of their character fits them for dependence and servitude. By nature, the most affectionate and loyal of all races beneath the sun, they are also the most helpless; and no calamity can befall them greater than the loss of that protection they enjoy under this patriarchal system. Indeed, the experiment has been grandly tried of precipitating them upon freedom, which they know not how to enjoy; and the dismal results are before us, in statistics that astonish the world. With the fairest portions of the earth in their possession, and with the advantage of a long discipline as cultivators of the soil, their constitutional indolence has converted the most beautiful islands of the sea into a howling waste. It is not too much to say, that if the South should, at this moment, surrender every slave, the wisdom of the entire world, united in solemn council, could not solve the question of their disposal. Their transportation to Africa, even if it were feasible, would be but the most refined cruelty; they must perish with starvation before they could have time to relapse into their primitive barbarism. Their residence here, in the presence of the vigorous Saxon race, would be but the signal for their rapid extermination before they had time to waste away through listlessness, filth, and vice. Freedom would be their doom; and equally from both they call upon us, their providential guardians, to be protected. I know this argument will be scoffed abroad as the hypocritical cover thrown over our own cupidity and selfishness; but every Southern master knows its truth and feels its power. My servant, whether born in my house or bought with my money, stands to me in the relation of a child. Though providentially owing me service, which, providentially, I am bound to exact, he is, nevertheless, my brother and my friend; and I am to him a guardian and a father. He leans upon me for protection, for counsel, and for blessing; and so long as the relation continues, no power, but the power of almighty God, shall come between him and me. Were there no argument but this, it binds upon us the providential duty of preserving the relation that we may save him from a doom worse than death.

It is a duty which we owe, further, *to the civilized world.* It is a remarkable fact, that during these thirty years of unceasing warfare against slavery, and while a lying spirit has inflamed the world against us, that world has grown more and more dependent upon it for sustenance and wealth. Every tyro knows that all branches of industry fall back upon the soil. We must come, every one of us, to the bosom of this great mother for nourishment. In the happy partnership which has grown up in providence between the tribes of this confederacy, our industry has been concentrated upon agriculture. To the North we have cheerfully resigned all the profits arising from manufacture and commerce. Those profits they have, for the most part, fairly earned, and we have never begrudged them. We have sent them our sugar, and bought it back when refined; we have sent them our cotton, and bought it back when spun into thread or woven into cloth. Almost every article we use, from the shoe-latchet to the most elaborate and costly article of luxury, they have made and we have bought; and both sections have thriven by the partnership, as no people ever thrived before since the first shining of the sun. So literally true are the words of the text, addressed by Obadiah to Edom, "All the men of our confederacy, the men that were at peace with us, have eaten our bread at the very time they have deceived and laid a wound under us." Even beyond this—the enriching commerce which has built the splendid cities and marble palaces of England as well as of America, has been largely established upon the products of our soil; and the blooms upon Southern fields, gathered by black hands, have fed the spindles and looms of Manchester and Birmingham not less than of Lawrence and Lowell. Strike now a blow at this system of labor, and the world itself totters at the stroke. Shall we permit that blow to fall? Do we not owe it to civilized man to stand in the breach and stay the uplifted arm? If the blind Samson lays hold of the pillars which support the arch of the world's industry, how many more will be buried beneath its ruins than the lords of the Philistines? "Who knoweth whether we are not come to the kingdom for such a time as this?"

Last of all, in this great struggle, *we defend the cause of God and religion*. The Abolition spirit is undeniably atheistic. The demon which erected its throne upon the guillotine in the days of Robespierre and Marat, which abolished the Sabbath, and worshipped reason in the person of a harlot, yet survives to work other horrors, of which those of the French revolution are but the type. Among a people so generally religious as the American, a disguise must be worn; but it is the same old threadbare disguise of the advocacy of human rights. From a thousand Jacobin clubs here, as in France, the decree has gone forth which strikes at God by striking at all subordination and law. Availing itself of the morbid and misdirected sympathies of men, it has entrapped weak consciences in the meshes of its treachery; and now, at last, has seated its high-priest upon the throne, clad in the black garments of discord and schism, so symbolic of its ends. Under this specious cry of reform, it demands that every evil shall be corrected, or society become a wreck—the sun must be stricken from the heavens, if a spot is found on his disk. The Most High, knowing his own power, which is infinite, and his own wisdom, which is unfathomable, can afford to be patient. But these self-constituted reformers must quicken the activity of Jehovah, or compel his abdication. In their furious haste, they trample upon obligations sacred as any which can bind the conscience. It is time to reproduce the obsolete idea that Providence must govern man, and not that man should control Providence. In the imperfect state of human society, it pleases God to allow evils which check others that are greater. As in the physical world, objects are moved forward, not by a single force, but by the composition of forces; so in his moral administration, there are checks and balances whose intimate relations are comprehended only by himself. But what reck they of this—these fierce zealots who undertake to drive the chariot of the sun? working out the single and false idea which rides them like a nightmare, they dash athwart the spheres, utterly disregarding the delicate mechanism of Providence; which moves on wheels within wheels, with pivots, and balances, and springs, which the great designer alone can control. This spirit of atheism, which knows no God who tolerates evil, no Bible which sanctions law, and no conscience that can be bound by oaths and covenants, has selected us for its victims, and slavery for its issue. Its banner-cry rings out already upon the air—"Liberty, equality, fraternity," which, simply interpreted, mean bondage, confiscation, and massacre. With its tricolor waving in the breeeze, it waits to inaugurate its reign of terror. To the South the highest position is assigned, of defending, before all nations, the cause of all religion, and of all truth. In this trust, we are resisting the power which wars against constitutions, and laws, and compacts, against Sabbaths and sanctuaries, against the family, the State, and the Church; which blasphemously invades the prerogatives of God, and rebukes the Most High for the errors of his administration, which, if i‘

cannot snatch the reins of empire from his grasp, will lay the universe in ruins at his feet. Is it possible that we shall decline the onset?

This argument, then, which sweeps over the entire circle of our relations, touches the four cardinal points of duty *to ourselves, to our slaves, to the world, and to Almighty God.* It establishes the nature and solemnity of our present trust to *preserve and transmit our existing system of domestic servitude, with the right, unchanged by man, to go and root itself wherever Providence and nature may carry it.* This trust we will discharge in the face of the worst possible peril. Though war be the aggregation of all evils, yet, should the madness of the hour appeal to the arbitration of the sword, we will not shrink even from the baptism of fire. If modern crusaders stand in serried ranks upon some plain of Esdraelon, there shall we be in defence of our trust. Not till the last man has fallen behind the last rampart, shall it drop from our hands; and then only in surrender to the God who gave it.

Against this institution a system of aggression has been pursued through the last thirty years. Initiated by a few fanatics, who were at first despised, it has gathered strength from opposition until it has assumed its present gigantic proportions. No man has thoughtfully watched the progress of this controversy without being convinced that the crisis must at length come. Some few, perhaps, have hoped against hope that the gathering imposthume might be dispersed and the poison be eliminated from the body politic by healthful remedies. But the delusion has scarcely been cherished by those who have studied the history of fanaticism in its path of blood and fire through the ages of the past. The moment must arrive when the conflict must be joined, and victory decide for one or the other. As it has been a war of legislative tactics, and not of physical force, both parties have been manœuvring for a position, and the embarrassment has been, while dodging amidst constitutional forms, to make an issue that should be clear, simple, and tangible. Such an issue is at length presented in the result of the recent Presidential election. Be it observed, too, that it is an issue made by the North, not by the South; upon whom, therefore, must rest the entire guilt of the present disturbance. With a choice between three national candidates, who have more or less divided the vote of the South, the North, with unexampled unanimity, have cast their ballot for a candidate who is sectional, who represents a party that is sectional, and the ground of that sectionalism, prejudiced against the established and constitutional rights, and immunities, and institutions of the South. What does this declare—what can it declare—but that from henceforth this is to be a government of section over section; a government using constitutional forms only to embarrass and divide the section ruled, and as fortresses through whose embrasures the cannon of legislation is to be employed in demolishing the guaranteed institutions of the South? What issue is more direct, concrete, intelligible, than this? I thank God that, since the conflict must be joined, the responsibility of this issue rests not with us, who have ever acted upon the defensive; and that it is so disembarrassed and simple that the feeblest mind can understand it.

The question with the South to-day is not what issue shall *she* make, but how shall she meet that which is prepared for her? Is it possible that we can hesitate longer than a moment? In our natural recoil from the perils of revolution, and with our clinging fondness for the memories of the past, we may perhaps look around for something to soften the asperity of this issue, for some ground on which we may defer the day of evil, for some hope that the gathering clouds may not burst in fury upon the land.

It is alleged, for example, that the President elect has been chosen by a fair majority, under prescribed forms. But need I say to those who have read history, that no despotism is more absolute than that of an unprincipled democracy, and no tyranny more galling than that exercised through constitutional formulas? But the plea is idle, when the very question we debate is the perpetuation of that Constitution now converted into an engine of oppression, and the continuance of that Union which is henceforth to be our condition of vassalage. I say it with solemnity and pain, this Union of our forefathers is already gone. It existed but in mutual confidence, the bonds of which were ruptured in the late election. Though its form should be preserved, it is, in fact, destroyed. We may possibly entertain the project of reconstructing it; but it will be another Union, resting upon other than past guarantees. "In that we say a new covenant, we have made the first old, and that which decayeth and waxeth old is ready to vanish away"—"as a vesture it is folded up." For myself, I say, that under the rule which threatens us, I throw off the yoke of this Union as readily as did our ancestors the yoke of King George III., and for causes immeasurably stronger than those pleaded in their celebrated Declaration.

It is softly whispered, too, that the successful competitor for the throne protests and avers his purpose to administer the Government in a conservative and national spirit. Allowing him full credit for personal integrity in these protestations, he is, in this matter, nearly as impotent for good as he is competent for evil. He is nothing more than a figure upon the political chess-board—whether pawn, or knight, or king, will hereafter appear—but still a silent figure upon the checkered squares, moved by the hands of an unseen player. That player is the party to which he owes his elevation; a party that has signalized its history by the most unblushing perjuries. What faith can be placed in the protestations of men who openly avow that their consciences are too sublimated to be restrained by the obligation of covenants or by the sanctity of oaths? No: we have seen the trail of the serpent five and twenty years in our Eden; twined now in the branches of the forbidden tree, we feel the pangs of death already begun, as its hot breath is upon our cheek, hissing out the original falsehood, "Ye shall not surely die."

Another suggests, that even yet the electors, alarmed by these demonstrations of the South, may not cast the black ball which dooms their country to the executioner. It is a forlorn hope. Whether we should counsel such breach of faith in them, or take refuge in their treachery—whether such a result would give a President chosen by the people according to the Constitution—are points I will not discuss. But that it would prove a cure for any of our ills, who can believe? It is certain that it would, with some show of justice, exasperate a party sufficiently ferocious—that it would doom us to four years of increasing strife and bitterness—and that the crisis must come at last, under issues possibly not half so clear as the present. Let us not desire to shift the day of trial by miserable subterfuges of this sort.

The issue is upon us; let us meet it like men, and end this strife forever.

But some quietist whispers, yet further, this majority is accidental, and has been swelled by accessions of men simply opposed to the existing Administration; the party is utterly heterogeneous, and must be shivered into fragments by its own success. I confess, frankly, this suggestion has staggered me more than any other, and I sought to take refuge therein. Why should we not wait and see the effect of success itself upon a party whose elements might devour each other in the very distribution of the spoil? Two considerations have dissipated the fallacy before me. The first is, that, however mixed the party, Abolitionism is clearly its informing and actuating soul; and fanaticism is a bloodhound that never bolts its track when it has once lapped blood. The elevation of their candidate is far from being the consummation of their aims; it is only the beginning of that consummation; and, if all history be not a lie, there will be cohesion enough till the end of the beginning is reached, and the dreadful banquet of slaughter and ruin shall glut the appetite. The second consideration is a principle which I cannot blink. It is nowhere denied that the first article in the creed of the new dominant party is the restriction of slavery within its present limits. It is distinctly avowed by their organs, and in the name of their elected chieftain, as will appear from the following extract from an article written to pacify the South, and to reassure its fears:—

"There can be no doubt whatever in the mind of any man, that Mr. Lincoln regards slavery as a moral, social, and political evil, and that it should be dealt with as such by the Federal Government, in every instance where it is called upon to deal with it at all. On this point there is no room for question—and there need be no misgivings as to his official action. The whole influence of the Executive Department of the Government, while in his hands, will be thrown against the extension of slavery into the new territories of the Union, and the reopening of the African slave trade. On these points he will make no compromise, nor yield one hair's breadth to coercion from any quarter or in any shape. He does not accede to the alleged decision of the Supreme Court, that the Constitution places slaves upon the footing of other property, and protects them as such wherever its jurisdiction extends; nor will he be, in the least degree, governed or controlled by it in his executive action. He will do all in his power personally and officially, by the direct exercise of the powers of his office, and the indirect influence inseparable from it, to arrest the tendency to make slavery national and perpetual, and to place it in precisely the same position which it held in the early days of the Republic, and in the view of the founders of the Government."

Now, what enigmas may be couched in this last sentence, the sphinx which uttered them can perhaps resolve; but the sentence in which they occur is as big as the belly of the Trojan horse which laid the city of Priam in ruins.

These utterances we have heard so long, that they fall stale upon the ear; but never before have they had such significance. Hitherto they have come from Jacobin conventicles and pulpits, from the rostrum, from the hustings, and from the halls of our national Congress; but always as the utterances of irresponsible men, or associations of men. But now the voice comes from the throne; already, before clad with the sanctities of office, ere the anointing oil is poured upon the monarch's head, the decree has gone forth that the institution of Southern slavery shall be constrained within assigned limits. Though nature and Providence should send forth its branches like the banyan tree, to take root in congenial soil, here is a power superior to both, that says it shall wither and die within its own charmed circle.

What say you to this, to whom this great providential trust of conserving slavery is assigned? "Shall the throne of iniquity have fellowship with thee which frameth the mischief by a law?" It is this that makes the crisis. Whether we will or not, this is the historic moment when the fate of this institution hangs suspended in the balance. Decide either way, it is the moment of our destiny—the only thing affected by the decision is the complexion of that destiny. If the South bows before this throne, she accepts the decree of restriction and ultimate extinction, which is made the condition of her homage.

As it appears to me, the course to be pursued in this emergency is that which has already been inaugurated. Let the people in all the Southern States, in solemn council assembled, reclaim the powers they have delegated. Let those conventions be composed of men whose fidelity has been approved—men who bring the wisdom, experience, and firmness of age to support and announce principles which have long been matured. Let these conventions decide firmly and solemnly what they will do with this great trust committed to their hands. Let them pledge each other, in sacred covenant, to uphold and perpetuate what they cannot resign without dishonor and palpable ruin. Let them, further, take all the necessary steps looking to separate and independent existence, and initiate measures for framing a new and homogeneous confederacy Thus, prepared for every contingency, let the crisis come. Paradoxical as it may seem, if there be any way to save, or rather to reconstruct, the Union of our forefathers, it is this.

Perhaps, at the last moment, the conservative portions of the North may awake to see the abyss into which they are about to plunge. Perchance they may arise and crush out forever the Abolition hydra, and cast it into a grave from which there shall never be a resurrection.

Thus, with restored confidence, we may be rejoined a united and happy people. But, before God, I believe that nothing will effect this but the line of policy which the South has been compelled in self-preservation to adopt. I confess frankly I am not sanguine that such an auspicious result will be reached. Partly, because I do not see how new guarantees are to be grafted upon the Constitution, nor how, if grafted, they can be more binding than those which have already been trampled under foot; but, chiefly, because I do not see how such guarantees can be elicited from the people at the North. It cannot be disguised that, almost to a man, they are anti-slavery where they are not Abolition. A whole generation has been educated to look upon the system with abhorrence as a national blot. They hope, and look, and pray, for its extinction within a reasonable time, and cannot be satisfied unless things are seen leading to that conclusion. We, on the contrary, as its constituted guardian, can demand nothing less than that it should be left open to expansion, subject to no limitations save those imposed by God and nature. I fear the antagonism is too great, and the conscience of both parties too deeply implicated to allow such a composition of the strife. Nevertheless, since it is within the range of possibility in the providence of God, I would not shut out the alternative.

Should it fail, what remains but that we say to each other, calmly and kindly, what Abraham said to Lot: "Let there be no strife, I pray thee, between me and thee, and between my herdmen and thy herdmen, for we be brethren. Is not the whole land before thee? Separate thyself, I pray thee, from me—if thou wilt take the left hand, then I will go to the right, or if thou depart to the right hand, then I will go to the left." Thus, if we cannot save the Union, we may save the inestimable blessings it enshrines; if we cannot preserve the vase, we will preserve the precious liquor it contains.

In all this, I speak for the North no less than for the South; for on our united and determined resistance at this moment depends the salvation of the whole country—in saving ourselves we shall save the North from the ruin she is madly drawing down upon her own head.

The position of the South is at this moment sublime. If she has grace given her to know her hour, she will save herself, the country, and the world. It will involve, indeed, temporary prostration and distress; the dikes of Holland must be cut to save her from the troops of Philip. But I warn my countrymen, the historic moment, once passed, never returns. If she will arise in her majesty, and speak now as with the voice of one man, she will roll back for all time the curse that is upon her. If she succumbs now, she transmits that curse as an heir-loom to posterity.

We may, for a generation, enjoy comparative ease, gather up our feet in our beds, and die in peace; but our children will go forth beggared from the homes of their fathers. Fishermen will cast their nets where your proud commercial navy now rides at anchor, and dry them upon the shore now covered with your bales of merchandise. Sapped, circumvented, undermined, the institutions of your soil will be overthrown; and within five and twenty years, the history of St. Domingo will be the record of Louisiana. If dead men's bones can tremble, ours will move under the muttered curses of sons and daughters, denouncing the blindness and love of ease which hath left them an inheritance of woe.

I have done my duty under as deep a sense of responsibility to God and man as I have ever felt. Under a full conviction that the salvation of the whole country is depending upon the action of the South, I am impelled to deepen the sentiment of resistance in the Southern mind, and to strengthen the current now flowing toward a union of the South in defence of her chartered rights. It is a duty which I shall not be recalled to repeat, for such awful junctures do not occur twice in a century.

Bright and happy days are yet before us; and before another political earthquake shall shake the continent, I hope to be "where the wicked cease from troubling, and where the weary are at rest."

It only remains to say that, whatever be the fortunes of the South, I accept them for my own. Born upon her soil, of a father thus born before me—from an ancestry that occupied it while yet it was a part of England's possessions, she is, in every sense, my mother. I shall die upon her bosom; she shall know no peril but it is my peril—no conflict but it is my conflict—and no abyss of ruin into which I shall not share her fall. May the Lord God cover her head in this her day of battle!

THE DEMORALIZATION OF THE NATIONAL SOUL.

Preached in All Souls' Church, Jan. 25, 1861,

BY HENRY W. BELLOWS.

"Give me understanding, that I may know Thy testimonies."—*Psalm* 119 : 125.

GOD'S testimonies, my brethren, are nothing more nor less than all the signs and indications by which His holy and perfect will is made known to us. The laws of nature, the constitution of our minds, the revelations of Scripture, the evidences of experience, the fruits of patient meditation, and the accumulations of past wisdom, these are all God's testimonies. The Almighty love and wisdom is a perpetual respondent to human appeal for guidance; the Universe is the permanent stand of this sublime Witness to His own perfect and ever-blessed will! Human life—which in its sum we call history—is the record of the answers God is giving in ever greater distinctness and fulness to the questionings of man's soul, touching the Divine purposes, and the right methods of furthering them. There is nothing arbitrary, uncertain, or changeable in God's character or designs. "The law of the Lord is perfect, converting the soul; the testimony of the Lord is sure, making wise the simple; the statutes of the Lord are right, rejoicing the heart; the commandment of the Lord is sure, enlightening the eyes."

We must not mistake our imperfect acquaintance with this law, our vacillating theories and speculations respecting it; our misrenderings and false positiveness, and as false uncertainty about parts and portions of it, for any variableness or shadow of turning in the Law itself— or in any jot or tittle of it. The commandment of God abideth sure. He who is "without beginning of days, or end of years" changeth not. There is a frame of law governing alike the physical, the moral, the social universe— the fixed expression of the Divine will—which all our blunderings, misconceptions, and contradictions do nothing to dislocate or alter. We run against these laws in our ignorance, wilfulness, and folly. We deny them; assert other laws; attribute purposes and motives to the Divine Being in all sincerity and faith, which do not belong to Him. But the effect is only to injure us—not Him—and at last by our painful experiences to *convert* our souls to His way and will, not to amend His perfect law. "The law of the Lord is perfect, converting the soul."

This is now pretty well understood in regard to that part of God's law which is embodied in the works of nature. Most people in our generation understand that the laws of nature are steadfast, immovable, self-executing, and do not depend in the least on our account of them. They act on through all false theories of astronomy, geology, chemistry, upon their own true and perfect theory—and man's stupid ignorance, and false knowledge, and ingenious errors, though hurtful enough to them, do not, and cannot in the slightest degree, touch the calm and benignant operation of the stable laws of God in nature. We no longer expect through any supplications or propitiations, to have the light and the rain and the dew accommodated to our special wishes or circumstances. In agriculture, for instance, we study the laws of nature, and find out what conditions and circumstances are already appointed and unchangeably fixed, and carefully accommodate our sowing and planting to these laws. It will take us how much longer to believe in the fixity of moral laws as practically as we already believe in the stability of physical laws? And yet there is no more caprice about the government of the moral universe than the physical universe. We cannot make one hair white or black in the moral world by all our asseverations. The moral universe, originated in perfect holiness, moves on in its own sublime path of justice, truth, and righteousness. It crushes wrong; it wheels all immorality and unrighteousness out of its track. Because men have leave to err, sin, and dispute within their own petty spheres of independence, we are sometimes tempted to think that the great morality of God is imperilled—that the moral plan of history is likely to be defeated—that the regular unfolding of the conscience of the race can be delayed. But really there is no more danger of this than of the repeal of seed-time and harvest through our poor agriculture. Individual farmers ruin themselves by bad husbandry; but spring, and summer, and autumn, and early and later rains do not fail; nor with all the sins and follies of society, and all the wickedness of individuals, do the great moral laws of the universe fail to vindicate perfectly their eternal and perfect sway. Private independence, free will, is a part of God's moral law. There can be no morality without freedom of action; but freedom of action in imperfect moral beings leads to disobedience. But God's moral law ordains that peace, wellbeing, happiness, shall follow only obedience to righteousness; and this law is honored as much in the misery and wretchedness of the sinful as in the felicity and contentment of the obedient. But more than this, the moral law tends to convert the soul, and although it fails to do so in this, that, or the other case, it does not fail on the whole; nay, it succeeds to the fullest possible extent—that is to say, succeeds, as it was meant to succeed, and according to its nature, by gradual, but sure and steadily accumulating triumphs. I venture to say that ignorance and immorality obey one law, and preserve a strict analogy in the rate of their disappearance; that the knowledge of God's laws, as the author of nature, and obedience to them, has not advanced with greater rapidity or certainty than the knowledge of His laws as the God of conscience, and obedience to these laws.

It is high time, therefore, that we should understand that we cannot have things as we will, or otherwise than as they are, in this moral world of which we form a part. There are certain great moral principles running through it which do not and cannot change, and which every now and then bring us up in our ignorance or disobedience squarely against the Divine commandments, and then we are compelled to pause and reverse our steps. It is not only the physical universe that is under law. Human nature has Divine laws which cannot be defied or trampled on with impunity. Society has Divine laws which we cannot evade or materially change. God's providence has Divine laws of which the soul is the prophecy, and history the fulfilment.

At certain periods in human affairs we are brought to a dead lock. The wisest are at fault. None know what to advise. The difficulties that involve us are unexpected. They arise suddenly, and yet they are as desperate and deep as though they were the culmination of some long-ripening disaster. What is it that has happened at such periods in history? It is always that some great moral law of God has been set aside, overlooked, resisted, until it has accumulated a vast resentment, and with the last drop of disobedience added to the unseen cloud, its wrath has burst in sudden and disastrous fury on a nation's head. It was so in England, when the levity of the court and the people had, in two licentious reigns, almost extinguished private morality and public virtue, and the revolution of 1640 burst on that people with Cromwellian indignation. It was so in France, when pampered pride, and vain magnificence, and royal debauchery were trampling on an oppressed people's honor, rights, and consciences, corrupting the Church and the State, and all with the gravity of saintly authority and a most punctilious decorum. Then it was that a slow-gathering cloud of terrible witnesses broke and let loose the furious bigots of blood, who drenched the corruption of France in retributive gore, and testified for God with axe and fagot; while statesmen, nobles, poets, lovely women, and innocent children mingled their ashes on the sacrificial pyre of a nation's outraged morality. It is likely enough to be so in our country now. I do not know that it will be. I cannot even say that it ought to be; for I am, just as most of you are, so much a partaker in the national life and ideas, so accommodated to the prevailing habits of thought and feeling, that I do not really know how far my judgment is demoralized and corrupted by the atmosphere I breathe. I distrust my own opinions, as navigators justly distrust their own reckoning in new seas, where unkown currents prevail. We may be all of us much more seriously off the track of right than we suspect.

We may have slowly and almost unconsciously, but yet for so long a time, been departing from the fixed conditions of well-being, as to have laid up a vast offence against that righteousness to which meanwhile God has perfectedly adhered; and the period of His retribution may have drawn nigh. A whisper, you know, finally brings down the Alpine avalanche, which every added snow-flake has been ripening to its fall. Because vengeance tarrieth, the wicked say there is no God. But moral laws act precisely as physical laws do. Canker and rust do not develop themselves in an hour; but they are none the less sure in their action for that. The consequences of unrighteousness, public or private, do not precipitate themselves upon offenders with furious haste; but the dungeon and the chain never held the condemned man more certainly to the day and hour of his execution than the inexorable laws of God hold the wrong-doer to his final account, whatever delays or postponements may stand between him and the judgment-day.

I am afraid, I confess, that we have been laying up wrath against the day of wrath more recklessly and more threateningly than our haste to be rich and our desire to develop the resources of the country, and our partisan schemes and ambitions have allowed us to recognize, or even now permit us to acknowledge. It is not, I repeat, that I affect to be wiser than you, and pretend clearly to see this. I only suspect it, I fear that it is so. I fear it, because I cannot account for the state of things in which we are involved on any other hypothesis. I venture to say that the world itself, let alone our own country, is taken with immense surprise at the terrible evils that suddenly threaten our national existence. Never less in anger and more in sorrow did all other nations look upon the afflictions of a mighty rival, than the states of the civilized world stand tearful and astonished looking on the sudden suicide of a young, and wealthy, and proud, and prosperous country—with expectations before it of the utmost magnificence, yet secretly too unhappy and remorseful to be able or willing to support existence longer.

What can have wrought this sudden frenzy? Violent diseases do not break out in constitutions in which long preparation for their sudden devastation has not been making. People do not go mad in a month, who have been observing the conditions of sanity all their previous lives. Panic does not seize those who are prudent and self-governed in their affairs. Sedition, rebellion, secession, revolution, however instantaneously developed, are like the lightning which leaps from clouds that have been gathering slowly, and owe all their power to harm to the accumulated wrath they represent. Treachery, unpatriotic hesitation, self-distrust, irresolution, and political weakness seizing on a nation are not local, superficial, and passing irritations. They are the eruptions of an inward disorder which has been latent until the constitution must fling it to the surface or sink into its insidious mine. There are evidences, then, in the national condition, in the state of public sentiment, in the atmosphere of Congress, in the paralysis of government, in the madness of States, in the attitude of parties, in the dead-lock of affairs, of something terribly wrong somewhere, evidences of some great, accumulated offence against the Divine conditions of peace and prosperity, evidences of some impending interposition or retribution; as when the strong man drops beneath some unseen stroke and physicians know not what has occasioned it, but know certainly that "the curse causeless does not come;" that *something* serious and organic has befallen the interior structure of the patient!

My brethren, a nation, like an individual, has a soul which it may lose, an intellect which it may sophisticate, a conscience it may fritter away, an honor with which it may palter, a self-respect it may forfeit, a life which it may take with its own suicidal hand. And it is with nations as it is with persons. The process of deterioration may go on so slowly and decorously that character and reputation ooze away without public reproach or acute remorse, until some unexpected blow reveals the weakness and hollowness which have become complete. We may have been selling our national birthright for a mess of pottage, in the eagerness of our young appetite as a people. We may have been, for the sake of immediate quietness, trying to persuade ourselves, and succeeding only too well, by successive and infinitesimal steps, that wrong was right, and evil good. We may have been so much intoxicated with our material prosperity, the fatness of our broad, deep soil, the growth of our world-wide commerce, the ease and luxury within our reach, as to forget that man does not live by bread alone, much less by the wine from the reeking press of our heated life of trade. We may have unconsciously forgotten that our nation was born in a manger; that it began in poverty and principle; in the fear of God and the contempt of riches; in the love of man and the hatred only of oppressors; that conscience drove our fathers and founders from the ease and prosperity which by the surrender of principle they could have enjoyed at home, and that not national spread and power, not successful trade and smooth times, were the objects that brought them to the wilderness, but the love of liberty and the fear of God. If it be so, if with unconscious descent, we have slid down all the interval which separates a God-fearing, conscience-animated, right-minded, and sound-hearted people, who count honor, justice, truth, virtue, piety, for the principal things, into a covetous, luxurious, worldly, selfish, and demoralized people, who practically say, "let us eat and drink, for to-morrow we die; let us make money, though we make shipwreck of our souls; let us have good times, though we purchase them with smothered consciences, blinded intellects, and drugged sensibilities;" then we need not wonder that the national soul begins to show signs of moral dissolution, that its whole heart is sick, and its whole body sore.

There is nothing that indicates national demoralization more than *panic*, commercial or political. The sensitiveness of a stock market is the quavering, feeble, or fevered pulse of a diseased cupidity. A nation subject to commercial panics is too money-loving for happiness, virtue, or patriotism. Only an excessive haste and rivalry to be rich can produce that over-trading, over-crediting, over-importing, over-risking style of business, which disables men from any command of their resources, and keeps them at the continual mercy of the breeze of rumor. The pecuniary agues that have shaken our national trade at such shortening intervals during the last twenty years, are evidences of serious demoralization in the heart of the people. They have lost the true perspective of things. They put the last first, and the first last. I hear the most frightful heresies from the lips of men deemed wise and prudent, touching the very aim of government, as if its first, last, and total object was the protection of property, not of life, liberty, righteousness, and morality. And I know that thousands, perhaps millions, would welcome an Emperor of France or of Russia if they could only be assured that property would be less liable to fluctuation and ruin. Only a gross demoralization of the national soul could account for such monarchical speculations, or for the distrust of the democratic principles on which our institutions rest. If our gold has cankered into the heart of our national faith, we need not wonder that God's testimonies now are witnessing against us, in our inability to arouse a patriotism, and call forth a moral or a spiritual power adequate to meet our difficulties and solve our despair. Where are our great men? Has cupidity fettered the brain of the country that revolution itself unlocks no capacious intellect to answer our pressing questions? Has prosperity dragged the ark of God itself in its ox-cart, and made the ministers of religion everywhere the mere echoes of those that hire them, instead of God's witnesses over the madness of the people? Must a sectional hatred and jealousy, represented by acrimonious presses and legislatures, flinging insults at each other across the boundaries of States, take the place of patriotic pride and devotion, and moral candor and religious forbearance, and wise and efficient counsel? I fear that we have nothing better to hope than to be left to the fruits of our own doings—the consequences of long neglect of our political duties, the corruption of our party politics, the elevation of the worst men to power, the pulverizing of patriotism in the furnace of universal cupidity.

How far the whole corruption of our national mind and conscience is due to the original sin which has been to our constitution and history what Adam's fall was to the race—the original toleration of slavery in the very charter of liberty—I might not have your entire sympathy in expressing. But I am inclined to believe that the dissolution of this Union was provided for in its very formation; that the serpent crept into the garden at its first planting, and that the fruit of all our woe was sowed in that first disobedience to the will of God, and even to the monitions of conscience in the founders themselves. I am afraid that neither I nor you, nor anybody in this generation, knows the full extent of the wrong done to God's fixed will in the legalization and perpetuation of slavery, nor all the terrible retribution that awaits its aiders and abettors. There is nothing indeed more sad to me, than the total silence concerning the wrong itself, the seeming indifference to the existence of this moral evil, which the political policy of the present crisis has naturally enough enforced. We all hasten to say, we have no intention of interfering with it in the States—which is both true and important to be said—but we somehow suppress, at least for the time, what ought to be our ever-growing sense of the hideousness of its existence there, and our affectionate but solemn entreaties and warnings to those who are invoking the vengeance of a just God, by every hour of its perpetuation, and by every new effort for its spread. Consent on our part to its extension, in any form of compromise or concession involving the principle of no more slave soil, I hold to be a sin against the Holy Ghost, which cannot be pardoned in this world and hardly in the world to come. Nothing but demoralization of the national soul, deadness of the national conscience and heart, could account for any doubt on this point in the free States. Nevertheless, I expect concession and compromise; I fear the strength of temptation, brought to bear upon our national representatives—the corrupting influence of power just within the grasp of a new party. May God give us understanding that we may know His testimonies, and see that all our national disgraces, political deterioration, and general untoning as a people, have proceeded from our tampering with this wrong—from our past compromises and patches—and that nothing but worse evils can proceed from any new one. We must have done with all further complicity with this iniquity, if it costs us separation and disunion. Better, a thousand times better, absolute and final division, than any change in our constitution favorable to the existence and strengthening of slavery. Indeed, I do not know that peaceful separation is not absolutely essential to the preservation of whatever remains there are of self-respect, conscience, and reason in the North. Let us leave, if we must and they will it, our deluded brethren to their own obstinate hugging of the common chain that strangles them and the poor slave in one remorseless bite. We would gladly aid them to unbind the burden; but we have not been pure enough to make them believe in our charity, and so they despise, for our punishment, our proffered entreaties and aid. In God's name, then, what remains but to say, "Ephraim is joined to his idols, let him alone." Alas! popular instincts and passions will probably prove too potent even for this policy! I tremble when I think of the imminent collision of Western with Southern impetuosity and pride. Are we then reduced to the melancholy alternative, either side of which is almost equally repulsive: a further compromise with what we know and feel to be an organized treason against God and humanity; or a civil war, in which sister States shall be seen like enraged tigresses devouring each other in their common den?

If there be not some higher note struck than any that yet vibrates through the murky air of Congress, or sounds from pulpit or press, I shall feel that judicial blindness has visited the nation; that North and South we have sinned away our inheritance, that our prayer, "Give me understanding that I may know Thy testimonies," is not felt to be sincere and heart-wrung enough to be answered in mercy, and that only universal calamity, and sword, and fire, can heal the breaches in God's holy law, and restore our national soul from its prodigality and ruin.

THE BIBLE VIEW OF SLAVERY.

A Sermon delivered in the Greene Street Hebrew Synagogue, New York City, January 4, 1861,

BY REV. DR. M. J. RAPHALL, RABBI.

"The people of Nineveh believed in God, proclaimed a fast and put on sackcloth, from the greatest of them even to the least of them. For the matter reached the King of Nineveh, and he arose from his throne, laid aside his robe, covered himself with sackcloth and seated himself in ashes. And he caused it to be proclaimed and published through Nineveh by decree of the King and his magnates, saying, Let neither man nor beast, herd nor flock, taste any thing, let them not feed nor drink any water. But let man and beast be covered with sackcloth, and cry with all their strength unto God; and let them turn every individual from his evil way and from the violence that is in their hands. Who knoweth but God may turn and relent; yea turn away from his fierce anger that we perish not? And God saw their works that they turned from their evil way; and God relented of the evil which he had said that he would inflict upon them; and he did it not.—*Jonah* iii. 5-10."

1. MY FRIENDS—We meet here this day under circumstances not unlike those described in my text. Not many weeks ago, on the invitation of the Governor of this State, we joined in thanksgiving for the manifold mercies the Lord had vouchsafed to bestow upon us during the past year. But "coming events cast their shadows before," and our thanks were tinctured by the foreboding of danger impending over our country. The evil we then dreaded has now come home to us. As the cry of the Prophet, "Yet forty days and Nineveh shall be overthrown," alarmed that people, so the proclamation, "the Union is dissolved," has startled the inhabitants of the United States. The President, the chief officer placed at the helm to guide the vessel of the Commonwealth on its course, stands aghast at the signs of the times. He sees the black clouds gathering overhead; he hears the fierce howl of the tornado, and the hoarse roar of the breakers all around him. An aged man, his great experience has taught him that "man's extremity is God's opportunity," and, conscious of his own inability to weather the storm without help from on high, he calls upon every individual "to feel a personal responsibility towards God," even as the King of Nineveh desired all persons "to cry unto God with all their strength;" and it is in compliance with this call of the Chief Magistrate of these United States that we, like the many millions of our fellow-citizens, devote this day to public prayer and humiliation. The President more polished, though less plain-spoken than the King of Nineveh, does not in direct terms require every one to turn from his "evil way and from the violence that is in their hands." But to me these two expressions seem in a most signal manner to describe our difficulty and to apply to the actual condition of things, both North and South. The "violence in their hands," is the great reproach we must address to the sturdy fire-eater who, in the hearing of an indignant world, proclaims "Cotton is King." King, indeed, and a most righteous and merciful one, no doubt, in his own conceit, since he only tars and feathers the wretches who fall in his power, and whom he suspects of not being sufficiently loyal and obedient to his sovereignty. And the "evil of his ways" is the reproach we must address to the sleek rhetorician, who in the hearing of a God-fearing world, declares "Thought is King." King, indeed, and a most mighty and magnanimous one, no doubt, in his own conceit; all powerful to foment and augment the strife, though powerless to allay it. Of all the fallacies coined in the North the arrogant assertion that "Thought is King" is the very last with

which, at this present crisis, the patience of a reflecting people should have been abused. For in fact, the material greatness of the United States seems to have completely outgrown the grasp of our most gifted minds; so that, urgent as is our need, pressing as is the occasion, no man or set of men have yet come forward capable of rising above the narrow horizon of sectional influence and prejudice, and with views enlightened, just and beneficent, to embrace the entirety of the Union, and to secure its prosperity and preservation. No, my friends, "Cotton" is not King, and "Human Thought" is not King. *Adonai Meleck.* The Lord alone it King! *Umalkootho bakol mashala,* and His royalty reigneth over all. This very day of humiliation and of prayer, what is it but the recognition of His supremacy, the confession of His power and of our own weakness, the supplications which our distress addresses to His mercy? But in order that these supplications may be graciously received, that His supreme protection may be vouchsafed unto our country, it is necessary that we should begin as the people of Nineveh did; we must "believe in God." And when I say "WE," I do not mean merely us handful of peaceable Union-loving Hebrews, but I mean the whole of the people throughout the United States, the President and his Cabinet, the President-elect and his advisers, the leaders of public opinion North and South. If they truly and honestly desire to save our country, let them believe in God and in His Holy Word; and then, when the authority of the Constitution is to be set aside for a higher Law, they will be able to appeal to the highest Law of all, the revealed Law and Word of God, which affords its supreme sanction to the Constitution. There can be no doubt, my friends, that however much of personal ambition, selfishness, pride, and obstinacy there may enter into the present unhappy quarrel between the two great sections of the Commonwealth—I say it is certain that the origin of the quarrel itself is the difference of opinion respecting slaveholding, which the one section denounces as sinful, aye, as the most heinous of sins, while the other section upholds it as perfectly lawful. It is the province of statesmen to examine the circumstances under which the Constitution of the United States recognizes the legality of slaveholding, and under what circumstances, if any, it becomes a crime against the law of the land. But the question whether slaveholding is a sin before God is one that belongs to the theologian. I have been requested by prominent citizens of other denominations that I should on this day examine the Bible view of slavery, as the religious mind of the country requires to be enlightened on the subject. In compliance with that request, and after humbly praying that the Father of truth and of mercy may enlighten my mind and direct my words for good, I am about to solicit your earnest attention, my friends, to this serious subject. My discourse will, I fear, take up more of your time than I am in the habit of exacting from you; but this is a day of penitence, and the having to listen to a long and sober discourse must be accounted as a penitential infliction.

The subject of my investigation falls into three parts:—

1. How far back can we trace the existence of slavery?
2. Is slaveholding condemned as a sin in sacred Scripture?
3. What was the condition of the slave in biblical times, and among the Hebrews; and saying, with our Father Jacob, "for Thy help, I hope, O Lord!" I proceed to examine the question, how far back can we trace the existence of slavery?

1. It is generally admitted that slavery had its origin in war, public or private. The victor, having it in his power to take the life of his vanquished enemy, prefers to let him live, and reduces him to bondage. The life he has spared, the body he might have mutilated or destroyed, become his absolute property. He may dispose of it in any way he pleases. Such was, and through a great part of the world still is, the brutal law of force. When this state of things first began it is next to impossible to decide. If we consult sacred Scripture, the oldest and most truthful collection of records now or at any time in existence, we find the word *Ngebed,* slave, which the English version renders "servant," first used by Noah, who, in Genesis ix. 25, curses the descendants of his son Ham, by saying they should be *Ngebed Ngabadim,* "the meanest of slaves," or as the English version has it, "servant of servants." The question naturally arises, how came Noah to use the expression? How came he to know any thing of slavery? There existed not at that time any human being on earth, except Noah

and his family of three sons, apparently by one mother, born free and equal, with their wives and children. Noah had no slaves; from the time he had quitted the ark he could have none. It therefore becomes evident that Noah's acquaintance with the word slave and the nature of slavery must date from before the flood, and existed in his memory only, until the crime of Ham called it forth. You and I may regret that in his anger Noah should from beneath the waters of wrath again have fished up the idea and practice of slavery; but that he did so is a fact which rests on the authority of Scripture. I am therefore justified when, tracing slavery as far back as it can be traced, I arrive at the conclusion that next to the domestic relations of husband and wife, parents and children, the oldest relation of society with which we are acquainted is that of master and slave.

Let us for an instant stop at this curse by Noah with which slavery, after the flood, is recalled into existence. Among the many prophecies contained in the Bible and having reference to particular times, persons, and events, there are three singular predictions, referring to three distinct races or peoples, which seem to be intended for all times, and accordingly remain in full force to this day. The first of these is the doom of Ham's descendants, the African race, pronounced upwards of four thousand years ago. The second is the character of the descendants of Ishmael, the Arabs, pronounced nearly four thousand years ago, and the third and last is the promise of continued and indestructible nationality promised to us Israelites full two thousand five hundred years ago. It has been said that the knowledge that a particular prophecy exists helps to work out its fulfilment. And I am quite willing to allow that with us Israelites such is the fact. The knowledge we have of God's gracious promises renders us imperishable, even though the greatest and most powerful nations of the olden time have utterly perished. It may be doubted whether the fanatic Arab of the desert ever heard of the prophecy that he is to be a "wild man, his hand against every man, and every man's hand against him." (Gen. xvi. 12.) But you and I, and all men of ordinary education, know that this prediction, at all times, has been, and is now literally fulfilled, and that it has never been interrupted. Not even when the followers of Mahomet rushed forth to spread his doctrines, the Koran in one hand and the sword in the other, and when Arab conquest rendered the fairest portion of the Old World subject to the empire of their Caliph, did the descendants of Ishmael renounce their characteristics. Even the boasted civilization of the present century, and frequent intercourse with Western travellers, still leave the Arab a wild man, "his hand against every body, and every man's hand against him," a most convincing and durable proof that the Word of God is true, and that the prophecies of the Bible were dictated by the Spirit of the Most High. But though, in the case of the Arab, it is barely possible that he may be acquainted with the prediction made to Hagar, yet we may be sure that the fetish-serving benighted African has no knowledge of Noah's prediction; which, however, is nowhere more fully or more atrociously carried out than in the native home of the African. Witness the horrid fact, that the King of Dahomey is, at this very time, filling a large and deep trench with human blood, sufficient to float a good-sized boat; that the victims are innocent men, murdered to satisfy some freak of what he calls his religion; and that this monstrous and most fiendish act has met with no opposition, either from the pious indignation of Great Britain, or from the zealous humanity of our country.

Now I am well aware that the Biblical critics called Rationalists, who deny the possibility of prophecy, have taken upon themselves to assert, that the prediction of which I have spoken was never uttered by Noah, but was made up many centuries after him, by the Hebrew writer of the Bible, in order to smooth over the extermination of the Canaanites, whose land was conquered by the Israelites. With superhuman knowledge like that of the Rationalists, who claim to sit in judgment on the Word of God, I do not think it worth while to argue. But I would ask you how is it that a prediction, manufactured for a purpose—a fraud in short, and that a most base and unholy one, should nevertheless continue in force, and be carried out during four, or three, or even two thousand years; for a thousand years more or less can here make no difference. Noah, on the occasion in question, bestows on his son Shem a spiritual blessing: "Blessed be the Lord, the God of Shem,' and to this day it remains a fact which cannot be denied, that whatever knowledge of God and of religious truth is possessed by the human race, has been promulgated by the descendants of Shem. Noah bestows on his son Japheth a blessing, chiefly temporal, but partaking also of spiritual good. "May God enlarge Japheth, and may he dwell in the tents of Shem," and to this day it remains a fact which cannot be denied, that the descendants of Japheth (Europeans and their offspring) have been enlarged so that they possess dominion in every part of the earth; while, at the same time, they share in that knowledge of religious truth which the descendants of Shem were the first to promulgate. Noah did not bestow any blessing on his son Ham, but uttered a bitter curse against his descendants, and to this day it remains a fact which cannot be gainsaid that in his own native home, and generally throughout the world, the unfortunate negro is indeed the meanest of slaves. Much has been said respecting the inferiority of his intellectual powers, and that no man of his race has ever inscribed his name on the Pantheon of human excellence, either mental or moral. But this is a subject I will not discuss. I do not attempt to build up a theory, nor yet to defend the moral government of Providence. I state facts; and having done so, I remind you that our own fathers were slaves in Egypt, and afflicted four hundred years; and then I bid you reflect on the words of inspired Isaiah, (lv. 8,) "My thoughts are not your thoughts, neither are your ways my ways, saith the Lord."

II. Having thus, on the authority of the sacred Scripture, traced slavery back to the remotest period, I next request your attention to the question, "Is slaveholding condemned as a sin in sacred Scripture?" How this question can at all arise in the mind of any man that has received a religious education, and is acquainted with the history of the Bible, is a phenomenon I cannot explain to myself, and which fifty years ago no man dreamed of. But we live in times when we must not be surprised at any thing. Last Sunday an eminent preacher is reported to have declared from the pulpit, "That the Old Testament requirements served their purpose during the physical and social development of mankind, and were rendered no longer necessary now when we were to be guided by the superior doctrines of the New in the moral instruction of the race." I had always thought that in the "moral instruction of the race," the requirements of Jewish Scriptures and Christian Scriptures were identically the same; that to abstain from murder, theft, adultery, that "to do justice, to love mercy, and to walk humbly with God," were "requirements" equally imperative in the one course of instruction as in the other. But it appears I was mistaken. "We have altered all that now," says this eminent divine, in happy imitation of Moliere's physician, whose new theory removed the heart from the left side of the human body to the right. But when I remember that the "now" refers to a period of which you all, though no very aged men, witnessed the rise; when, moreover, I remember that the "we" the reverend preacher speaks of, is limited to a few impulsive declaimers, gifted with great zeal, but little knowledge; more eloquent than learned; better able to excite our passions than to satisfy our reason; and when, lastly, I remember the scorn with which sacred Scripture (Deut. xxxii. 18) speaks of "new-fangled notions, lately sprung up, which your fathers esteemed not;" when I consider all this, I think you and I had rather continue to take our "requirements for moral instruction" from Moses and the Prophets than from the eloquent preacher of Brooklyn. But as that reverend gentleman takes a lead among those who most loudly and most vehemently denounce slaveholding as a sin, I wished to convince myself whether he had any Scripture warranty for so doing; and whether such denunciation was one of those "requirements for moral instruction" advanced by the New Testament. I have accordingly examined the various books of Christian Scripture, and find that they afford the reverend gentleman and his compeers no authority whatever for his and their declamations. The New Testament nowhere, directly or indirectly, condemns slaveholding, which, indeed, is proved by the universal practice of all Christian nations during many centuries. Receiving slavery as one of the conditions of society, the New Testament nowhere interferes with or contradicts the slave code of Moses; it even preserves a letter written by one of the most eminent Christian teachers to a slave-owner on sending back to him his runaway slave. And when we next refer to the history and "requirements" of our own sacred Scriptures, we find that on the most solemn occasion therein recorded, when

PULPIT 2

God gave the Ten Commandments on Mount Sinai—

> There where His finger scorched, the tablet shone:
> There where His shadow on his people shone,
> His glory, shrouded in its garb of fire,
> Himself no eye might see and not expire.

Even on that most solemn and most holy occasion, slaveholding is not only recognized and sanctioned as an integral part of the social structure, when it is commanded that the Sabbath of the Lord is to bring rest to *Ngabdeena ee Amathecha*—"thy male slave and thy female slave." (Exod. xx. 10; Deut. v. 14.) But the property in slaves is placed under the same protection as any other species of lawful property, when it is said, "thou shalt not covet thy neighbor's house, or his field, or his male slave, or his female slave, or his ox, or his ass, or aught that belongeth to thy neighbor." (Ibid. xx. 17; v. 21.) That the male slave and female slave here spoken of do not designate the Hebrew bondman, but the heathen slave, I shall presently show you. That the Ten Commandments are the Word of God, and as such of the very highest authority, is acknowledged by Christians as well as by Jews. I would therefore ask the reverend gentleman of Brooklyn and his compeers—How dare you, in the face of the sanction and protection afforded to slave property in the Ten Commandments—how dare you denounce slaveholding as a sin? When you remember that Abraham, Isaac, Jacob, Job—the men with whom the Almighty conversed, with whose names He emphatically connects His own most holy name, and to whom He vouchsafed to give the character of "perfect, upright, fearing God and eschewing evil" (Job i. 8)—that all these men were slaveholders, does it not strike you that you are guilty of something very little short of blasphemy? And if you answer me, "Oh, in their time slaveholding was lawful, but now it has become a sin," I, in my turn, ask you, 'when and by what authority you draw the line?' Tell us the precise time when slaveholding ceased to be permitted and became sinful? When we remember the mischief which this inventing a new sin not known to the Bible is causing, how it has exasperated the feelings of the South and alarmed the conscience of the North, to a degree that men who should be brothers are on the point of imbruing their hands in each other's blood, are we not entitled to ask the reverend preacher of Brooklyn, "What right have you to insult and exasperate thousands of God-fearing, law-abiding citizens, whose moral worth and patriotism, whose purity of conscience and of life, are fully equal to your own? What right have you to place yonder gray-headed philanthropist on a level with a murderer, or yonder virtuous mother of a family on a line with an adulteress, or yonder honorable and honest man in one rank with a thief, and all this solely because they exercise a right which your own fathers and progenitors during many generations held and exercised without reproach or compunction." You profess to frame your "moral instruction of the race," according to the "requirements" of the New Testament—but tell us where and by whom it was said, "Whosoever shall say to his neighbor, Raca (worthless sinner), shall be in danger of the council: but whosoever shall say, thou fool, shall be in danger of the judgment." My friends, I find, and I am sorry to find, that I am delivering a pro-slavery discourse. I am no friend to slavery in the abstract, and still less friendly to the practical working of slavery. But I stand here as a teacher in Israel; not to place before you my own feelings and opinions, but to propound to you the Word of God, the Bible view of slavery. With a due sense of my responsibility, I must state to you the truth and nothing but the truth, however unpalatable or unpopular that truth may be.

III. It remains for me now to examine what was the condition of the slave in Biblical times and among the Hebrews. And here at once we must distinguish between the Hebrew bondman and the heathen slave. The former could only be reduced to bondage from two causes. If he had committed theft and had not wherewithal to make full restitution, he was "sold for his theft." (Exod. xxii. 3.) Or if he became so miserably poor that he could not sustain life except by begging, he had permission to "sell" or bind himself in servitude. (Levit. xxv. 39, *et seq.*) But in either case his servitude was limited in duration and character. "Six years shall he serve, and in the seventh he shall go out free for nothing." (Exod. xxi. 2.) And if even the bondman preferred bondage to freedom, he could not, under any circumstances, be held to servitude longer than the jubilee then next coming. At that period the estate which had originally belonged to his father or remoter ancestor reverted to his possession, so that he went forth at once a freeman and a landed proprietor. As his privilege of Hebrew citizen was thus only suspended, and the law, in permitting him to be sold, contemplated his restoration to his full rights, it took care that during his servitude his mind should not be crushed to the abject and cringing condition of a slave. "Ye shall not rule over one another with rigor," is the provision of the law. (Lev. xxv. 46.) Thus he is fenced round with protection against any abuse of power on the part of his employer; and tradition so strictly interpreted the letter of the law in his favor, that it was a common saying of Biblical times and homes, which Maimonides has preserved to us, that "he who buys an Hebrew bondman gets himself a master." Though in servitude, this Hebrew was in no wise exempt from his religious duties. Therefore, it is not for him or his that the Ten Commandments stipulated for rest on the Sabbath of the Lord, for his employer could not compel him to work on that day, and if he did work of his own accord, he became guilty of death, like any other Sabbath-breaker. Neither does the prohibition, "thou shalt not covet the property of thy neighbor," apply to him, for he was not the property of his employer. In fact, between the Hebrew bondman and the Southern slave, there is no point of resemblance. There were, however, slaves among the Hebrews, whose general condition was analogous to that of their Southern fellow-sufferers. That was the heathen slave, who was to be bought "from the heathens that were round about the land of Israel, or from the heathen strangers that sojourned in the land; they should be a possession to be bequeathed as an inheritance to the owner's children after his death forever." (Levit. xxv. 44–46.) Over these heathen slaves the owner's property was absolute; he could put them to hard labor, to the utmost extent of their physical strength; he could inflict on them any degree of chastisement, short of injury to life and limb. If his heathen slave ran away or strayed from home, every Israelite was bound to bring or send him back, as he would have to do with any other portion of his neighbor's property, that had been lost or strayed. (Deut. xxii. 3.) Now you may, perhaps, ask me how I can reconcile this statement with the text of Scripture so frequently quoted against the Fugitive Slave Law, "Thou shalt not surrender unto his master the slave who is escaped from his master unto thee." (Deut. xxiii. 16.) I answer you that according to all legists this text applies to a heathen slave, who from any foreign country escapes from his master, even though that master be an Hebrew, residing out of the land of Israel. Such a slave—but such a slave only—is to find a permanent asylum in any part of the country he may choose. This interpretation is fully borne out by the word of the precept. The pronoun "thou" is not here used in the same sense as in the Ten Commandments. There it designates every soul in Israel individually; since every one has it in his power, and is in duty bound, to obey the Commandments. But as the security and protection to be bestowed on the runaway slaves are beyond the power of any individual, and require the consent and concurrence of the whole community, the pronoun "thou," here means the whole of the people, and not one portion in opposition to any other portion of the people. And as the expression remains the same throughout the precept, "With thee he shall dwell, even among ye in the place he shall choose in one of thy gates, where it liketh him best," it plainly shows that the whole of the land was open to him, and the whole of the people were to protect the fugitive, which could not have been carried out if it had applied to the slave who escaped from one tribe into the territory of another. Had the precept been expounded in any other than its strictly literal sense, it would have caused great confusion, since it would have nullified two other precepts of God's law: that which directs that "slaves, like lands and houses, were to be inherited forever," and that which commands "property, lost or strayed, to be restored to the owner." Any other interpretation would, moreover, have caused heart-burning and strife between the tribes, for men were as tenacious of their rights and property in those days as they are now. But no second opinion was ever entertained; the slave who ran away from Dan to Beersheba had to be given up, even as the runaway from South Carolina has to be given up by Massachusetts; whilst the runaway from Edom or from Syria found an asylum in the land of Israel, as the runaway slave from Cuba or Brazil would find in New York. Accordingly Shimei reclaimed and recovered his runaway slaves from Achish, King of Gath, at that time a vassal of Israel. (Kings ii. 39, 40.) And Saul of Tarsus sent back the runaway slave Onesimus unto his owner Philemon. But to surrender to a ruthless, lawless heathen the wretched slave who had escaped from his cruelty, would have been to give up the fugitive to certain death, or at least to tortures repugnant to the spirit of God's law, the tender care of which protected the bird in its nest, the beast at the plough, and the slave in his degradation. Accordingly the extradition was not permitted in Palestine any more than it is in Canada. While thus the owner possessed full right over, and security for, his property, the exercise of that power was confined within certain limits which he could not outstep. His female slave was not to be the tool or castaway toy of his sensuality, nor could he sell her, but was bound to "let her go free," because "he had humbled her." (Deut. xxi. 14.) His male slave was protected against excessive punishment; for if the master in any way mutilated the slave, even to knock a single tooth out of his head, the slave became free. (Exod. xxi. 26, 27.) And while thus two of the worst passions of human nature, lust and cruelty, were kept under due restraint, the third bad passion, cupidity, was not permitted free scope; for the law of God secured to the slave his Sabbaths and days of rest; while public opinion, which in a country so densely peopled as Palestine must have been, all-powerful, would not allow any slave-owner to impose heavier tasks on his slaves, or to feed them worse than his neighbors did. This, indeed, is the great distinction which the Bible view of slavery derives from its divine source. The slave is a *person* in whom the dignity of human nature is to be respected; *he has rights.* Whereas, the heathen view of slavery which prevailed at Rome, and which, I am sorry to say, is adopted in the South, reduces the slave to a *thing*, and a thing can have no rights. The result to which the Bible view of slavery leads us is: 1st. That slavery has existed since the earliest time. 2d. That slaveholding is no sin, and that slave property is expressly placed under the protection of the Ten Commandments. 3d. That the slave is a person, and has rights not conflicting with the lawful exercise of the rights of his owner. If our Northern fellow-citizens, content with following the Word of God, would not insist on being "righteous overmuch," or denouncing "sin" which the Bible knows not, but which is plainly taught by the precepts of men, they would entertain more equity and less ill-feeling towards their Southern brethren. And if our Southern fellow-citizens would adopt the Bible view of slavery, and discard that heathen slave code which permits a few bad men to indulge in an abuse of power that throws a stigma and disgrace on the whole body of slaveholders—if both North and South would do what is right, then "God would see their works, and that they turned from the evil of their ways;" and in their case, as in that of the people of Nineveh, would mercifully avert the impending evil, for with Him alone is the power to do so. Therefore, let us pray:

Almighty and merciful God, we approach Thee this day, our hearts heavy with the weight of our sins, our looks downcast under the sense of our ingratitude, national and individual. Thou, Father all-bounteous, hast in Thine abundant goodness plentifully bestowed upon us every good and every blessing, spiritual, mental, temporal, that in the present state of the world men can desire. But we have perverted and abused Thy gifts; in our arrogance and selfishness we have contrived to extract poison from Thy most precious boons; the spiritual have degenerated into unloving self-righteousness; the mental have rendered us vain-glorious and conceited; and the temporal have degraded us into Mammon-worshipping slaves of avarice. Intoxicated with our prosperity, we have forgotten Thee; drunken with pride, we reel on towards the precipice of disunion and ruin. What hand can stay us if it be not Thine, O God! Thou who art long-suffering as Thou art almighty, to Thee we turn in the hour of our utmost need. Hear us, Father, for on Thee our hopes are fixed. Help us, Father, for Thou alone canst do it. Punish us not according to our arrogance; afflict us not according to our deserts. Remove from our breasts the heart of stone, and from our minds the obstinacy of self-willed pride. Extend Thy grace unto us, that we may acknowledge our own transgressions. Open our eyes that we may behold and renounce the wrong we inflict on our neighbors. God of justice and of mercy, suffer not despots to rejoice at our dissensions, nor tyrants to triumph over our fall. Let them not point at us the finger of scorn, or say, "Look there at the fruits of freedom and self-government—of equal rights and popular sovereignty—strife without any real cause—destruction without any sufficient motive."

Oh, let not them who trust in Thee be put to shame, or those who seek Thee be disgraced. Almighty God, extend thy gracious protection to the United States. Pour out over the citizens thereof, and those whom they have elected to be their rulers, the spirit of grace and of supplication, the spirit of wisdom and brotherly love, so that henceforth, even as hitherto, they may know that union is strength, and that it is good and pleasant for brethren to dwell together in unity. And above all things, Lord merciful and gracious, avert the calamity of civil war from our midst. If in Thy supreme wisdom Thou hast decreed that this vast commonwealth, which has risen under Thy protection, and prospered under Thy blessing, shall now be separated, then we beseech Thee let that separation be peaceful; that no human blood may be shed, but that the canopy of Thy peace may still remain spread over all the land. May we address our prayers to Thee, O Lord, at an acceptable time ; mayest Thou, O God, in Thy abundant mercy, answer us with the truth of Thy salvation. Amen.

SERMON,

Delivered in St. George's Church, New York, on the day of the National Fast, September 26, 1861.

BY STEPHEN H. TYNG, D. D.

"And the Lord said unto Moses, Wherefore criest thou unto me? Speak unto the children of Israel, that they go forward."—EXODUS xiv. 15.

THERE is an instinct in man, which compels him, in an hour of difficulty, to call upon God. It presses its urgency of appeal, both in his individual and in his social dangers. It speaks in him personally, and it speaks in the community and nations of men, when a crisis arrives in human concerns, which manifestly appears beyond the control of mere human wisdom and power. It is the voice of God in the soul of man, the divinely established witness in human consciousness of the being and authority of God. It is that inward impulse which leads to prayer, and which becomes the instrument of the Divine Spirit, in bringing man to faith and true calling upon God. It is that which forms the basis of the sanctifying power of afflictions, and opens the way, in seasons of human distress, for the cultivation of a religious dependence and submission in the heart of man.

Such a crisis led Moses to call upon God, on the borders of the Red Sea. He knew the power of Divine protection, and the privilege of humble prayer for the Divine aid. And therefore, when an hour arrived in his government of Israel of peculiar darkness and intricacy, he privately but earnestly sought for the direction which God alone could give. It was his own secret prayer for aid. We read of no offering here of united or national supplication. The murmuring people cried unto Moses. But the believing Moses cried unto God. And the Divine answer to his prayer we have before us, "Wherefore criest thou unto me? Speak unto the children of Israel, that they go forward."

It is not forbidding the prayer of faith, but the cry of doubt and fear. It is not repressing the soul's reference, in the hour of danger, to an Infinite Protector; but reminding the fearful soul of a previous command and promise. God had already commanded them, "Ye shall encamp by the sea." He had warned them that "Pharaoh would follow after them." But he had promised them that he would be "honored upon Pharaoh and upon all his host, that the Egyptians might know that he was the Lord." When, therefore, the crisis came, of which they had been forewarned, their duty to trust and obey God, who had thus commanded and promised, was settled and clear. It was a just occasion for the utterance of the confiding prayer of faith, which would sanctify and strengthen the performance of duty, but not for the lifting up of the cry of despair or doubt, which, in its very origin, was a rejection of the promise, and a refusal of the command.

The performance of duty sanctified by prayer, is the Christian's privilege and right. The withholding of conscious duty in the mere cowardly cry for help, is sinful and unbelieving. To the former, the reply justly is, Pray, but work; calmly trust, but actively go on. To the latter, the answer must be, Go on in the fulfilment of known obligation, and cease the mere outcry of indolence or fear.

It is a national crisis which has called us together to pray. The authoritative proclamation which has assembled us, wears a singularly religious aspect, as creditable as it is in such messages unusual. Let us listen to it.

It bids us acknowledge the government of God, to remember that national judgments are his chastisements, to confess and deplore our own sins as having deserved them. It recites our present national condition as a divine judgment, and calls for united confession of the faults and crimes as a nation, which have called for it; and then urges us to the offering of fervent supplications to Almighty God for our deliverance. Its whole aspect is that of sincerity in conviction of truth prompting the appeal. And if we go forward in the path of duty, calling upon God, adding earnest prayer to earnest effort and labor, and do not rest ourselves in a mere formal or fearful cry for help, abstracted from conscious duty, and withholding manifest duty in the refusal of its performance, the occasion, the appeal, and the observance may be made a blessing to our land, and to the cause of truth and righteousness therein.

THE CRISIS.

We may consider, therefore, the CRISIS, and the DUTY which it involves and demands.

The crisis is the severe and now tremendous conflict in which our National Government is engaged with the combined armies of those who would overthrow and destroy it. Is it a crisis which justifies prayer? Is it a cause and an occasion in which we may reverently and acceptably call upon God? This is the first occasion since this outbreak of violence occurred, on which I have spoken upon this subject to you. My own opinions and views upon the conflict itself I have withheld from the pulpit, in the desire rather to edify and sustain your hearts in the trials which it brings, than to discuss the elements of the conflict itself. On this occasion, I shall calmly but distinctly speak what I think upon the whole subject.

A year ago, we were a nation, in great earthly prosperity, and at rest. Our relative position among the nations was lofty and commanding. Our domestic relations were unaffected by the entire freedom of public discussion and argument, in speaking and through the press, which had always marked our history as a people. In every election of rulers, as in every decision of principles of legislation, the weaker party in number, however disappointed, had quietly yielded to the authority and will of the greater number. Most of our political questions were at rest. One only important, all-pervading subject of discussion remained. This one subject was the maintenance and perpetuation of African slavery. To that portion of the nation who still maintained and defended the system of service, and from which the one great party in the present conflict has been gathered, the control of the Government had been intrusted for the greater part, and the latter part of its existence. The laws which they required had been adopted, and no single law or act injuriously affecting their claims upon this subject had been or could have been perfected. Its existence in their States could not be molested. Its open entrance into any or all of the Territories had never been by any national act prevented or resisted. Yet for the avowed defence and protection of this one institution, in the midst of universal peace, with the National Government in their own hands, they seized the property, the arms, and the fortifications of the nation, and arrayed themselves in preparation for a sectional warfare—a determined sectional independence—and a complete overthrow of the Government, which they had failed to manage adequately to their own advantage. Waiting for no constitutional consideration of their demands; submitting to no umpire for decision of their affected wrongs; having no real injury of which to complain, and no single act of oppression from the nation, or from the Government controlled by themselves, to allege, they rushed into an unrelenting and impetuous warfare upon our Constitution, our nation, and our people. They pressed forward with unsparing eagerness of determination, to destroy the national capital; to overturn the Government of the country; to banish or put to death the justly elected rulers of the nation; to revolutionize by violence the States in which their wicked rebellion had been inaugurated; to oppress, rob, banish, or murder peaceful citizens dwelling among them, for refusing to co-operate in their crimes; to commission pirates under the promise of reward to capture and destroy the commerce and the seamen of the nation on the sea; to organize professed revolutionary governments in the States which they had violently seized, and a confederated government of all these States, by the same violence of purpose and action; and to gather armies with the avowed design of overrunning the other States and cities of the Union, to establish over all a Constitution, the fundamental law and principle of which was the absolute perpetuation throughout the whole land of African slavery, as the determined and desirable shape of human society forever.

This made the crisis. This threw upon a Government and people wholly unprepared for such a contingency, and without real anticipation of the actual consummating of the violent threats which had been heard, the simple but absolute necessity of defending and protecting the immense interests intrusted to their charge. The national capital was to be defended. The existing and established authority of a peaceful nation was to be maintained. The public property of the nation was to be protected. The lives and welfare of peaceful citizens were to be guarded. The established institutions of peaceful States were to be preserved. Persecuted families and communities, under the tyranny of this violent insurgence, were to be sheltered. The inherited freedom, religion, education, and laws of a whole nation were to be supported. The great interests of human liberty were to be perpetuated. The hopes of human advancement, prosperity, and honor; the open refuge for the victims of oppression from all lands; the one great human shelter for the poor, the downcast, the banished ones of this groaning earth; the inheritance purchased by our fathers' blood and sacrifice; the simplest, grandest, and most fundamental rights of free, civilized, and Christianized man, were all at stake, and all committed to the one question, Will this Government and nation basely yield these precious trusts committed by Divine Providence to their care, or honorably and righteously maintain them, at whatever cost of toil and treasure?

IMPORTANCE OF THE CRISIS.

In such a crisis, the struggle, fearful as it is, is for our national life, for our very being, for our homes, our children, and every object which a merciful God has made justly dear to us on earth. We must either preserve our country, and maintain our legal Government, or we must consent to be scattered, sacrificed, and destroyed, with all the incalculable interests which have been intrusted to us. It is a struggle forced upon us, not by the South, but by the factious demagogues of the South; not by all the slaveholders of the South, but by that violent portion of them whose spirits are desperate, whose ambition has been disappointed, and whose only hope of personal exaltation and advancement appeared to themselves to consist in the successful inauguration of a reign of universal violence, terror, and blood. Not to maintain our country and Government in such a struggle, is simply to yield to this incursion of violence every thing which is worth defending on earth, and every thing which, in our varied responsibilities, we are solemnly bound to defend. To yield in this conflict, is to acknowledge the unrighteous demands of the most inexcusable rebellion, and of the most unjustifiable rebels.

The alternative of the struggle is either to consent to submit to their imposed authority in our universal subjection to their will, or to concede the right of the public robbers of our national territory and property to depart in the secured possession of all that they have been able to seize. The one alternative is to establish human slavery throughout our whole nation; to turn every city on our peaceful and free soil into an acknowledged mart for the sale and purchase of slaves; to break up forever the hope of human freedom here, and the prospect of freedom for the rest of mankind; to yield the right of speech, of choice, even of thought, to a terrific despotism; to place ourselves and our children under a shocking and violent tyranny; to sacrifice every object for which past generations have contended and suffered in the warfare for the liberty of man; to yield the vast majority of free and independent citizens in these Northern and Western States—freemen, and the children of freemen—to the will of a conspiracy more unprincipled and unscrupulous probably than was ever before seen; literally to become, by our own act and consent, the most contemptible and debased of slaves; and to doom our innocent and helpless posterity, as the prey of our cowardice, to a similar inheritance; and to maintain a future peace in our land only by maintaining a perpetual speechless subjection to the tyranny whose foot we have invoked upon our neck.

The other alternative is to dismember our territory in an impossible division; to shut up far from the ocean, and from all foreign relations, the great majority of our nation; to put into the hands of aliens and enemies the very mouths of our rivers and the keys of our territory; to incarcerate under a horde of buccaneers, who could live upon the pillage, the whole commerce of the land; to perpetuate a system of border warfare never to be silenced; to destroy by our own act the whole future influence of our nation for the welfare of the world; to exhaust the whole strength of our people in constant internecine quarrels; to yield into the hands of unrighteous and violent robbers the property they have stolen, because they have stolen it; to perpetuate the wretched slavery and the wicked slave-trade of the Africans among untold generations; to give over into the hands of a violent, armed faction in the very States of the South, a whole population of free and oppressed citizens, who have been dragged into this rebellious separation without their own consent, who are now groaning beneath its load with vainly suppressed complaints, or flying from its grasp in hopeless poverty, leaving every thing they have owned to ruin,—to be punished and persecuted by these unpitying tyrants, without one remaining hope of protection or recovery. Now, then, is this a crisis in which we may righteously contend, justly defend ourselves, and reverently and successfully pray for the blessing of God upon us? I ask, Who can doubt it? Was there ever a national crisis which involved higher and deeper, more vital and important principles of truth and duty? Take all the word of the living God—all its principles, promises, and commands—can there be a moment's doubt on which side they are arrayed, or by the success of which side they are to be maintained and propagated? Not more certainly was Israel in the path of duty when Moses cried at the sea, than is our nation in the struggle in which we are engaged. Not more appropriate was the prayer of faith sanctifying duty in their case, than in ours; not more wrong the unbelieving, trembling cry of despair or doubt, when uttered then by them, than if uttered by us now. "Why criest thou unto me? Speak unto the children of Israel, that they go forward." If they go forward in prayer, victory will crown their nation. If they stand still to cry, or vainly court a sinful peace with crime because they are afraid to resist it, they may invoke the pardon of Pharaoh, they may yield to his slave-bearing authority, but they will find no peace in subjection to his will.

DUTY IN THE CRISIS.

What, then, is our duty in this crisis? "Go FORWARD. Speak unto them that they go forward."

The Government must go forward. The people must insist upon it, that they do go forward. Forward in the prosecution of this actual struggle, until, cost what it may, it has been triumphantly and finally settled in the full reëstablishment of our Government, our Country, our Laws, our Liberty, and our Territory, over every foot of soil which violent insurgence has pretended to claim. To stop anywhere short of this, is to do nothing permanently, and to have done and suffered every thing in vain. To yield at any point within this, makes the whole contest past a mere insanity, and every life and every dollar a useless sacrifice. We had better have left off the contention before it were meddled with, and have allowed the robber peaceably to depart, after he had spoiled our goods, before our resistance had resulted in the murder of our children, and the wounding of ourselves. The great principles at stake are only to be secured by final victory. If they are to be yielded in a time-serving and cowardly peace, at any point of the contest, the responsibility of prolonging it to that point is just so much the greater; and the oppression of the tyranny to which we yield is to be just so much the more violent, for the suffering and loss which by our resistance we have caused it. We cannot afford to rest at any point, as a nation keeping the truth, till, by the blessing of God, we have made that truth triumphant. To doubt whether we may as a rightful nation do this, is to deny the whole authority and purpose of human government. We habitually pray in our Liturgy, that God would "so direct and dispose the hearts of all Christian rulers, that they may truly and impartially administer justice, to the punishment of wickedness and vice, and to the maintenance of his true religion and virtue." It is as much the righteous duty of a government to punish vice, as to maintain true religion and virtue. And what state or aspect of vice more destructive, more inexcusable, more an outrage upon men, could have ever been imagined by man, than the widespread and slaughtering rebellion with which our country is now struggling? The duty of the Government is to go forward, and the duty of the people is to speak unto them that they go forward, with increasing vigor and determination, at whatever cost of wealth, and with whatever employment of arms or men.

PRINCIPLES OF THE CRISIS TO BE MAINTAINED.

But they must go forward in the principle and purpose of the contest, as well as in the power of its maintenance. The one great outward purpose and end of this contest, the external form of the result which we are to secure, is the complete reëstablishment of our Constitution and Union. Under its control and wise direction, we have prospered and grown through the years and generations past. It has been esteemed by the wisest of statesmen and scholars a model for the peaceful, righteous government of men. It is the outward form and model of our nation as a nation. And we cannot sacrifice it to the claims of anarchy, or allow it to be overthrown by the arm of violence. Its administration has, beyond all question, elucidated in it defects which must be remedied, and provisions which require it to be altered. But these alterations must be accomplished by the regular appointed, peaceful, considerate method which the Constitution provides. Any other method would be but the very subversion of the Constitution by the arm of force—itself the hostility and violence on the part of others against which we are now contending. Yet we cannot but see, and we are compelled to consider, national difficulties and national crimes perpetuated and maintained under this Constitution—however, without the design, and with the intense, declared abhorrence of the great and venerable men who formed it—to the complete abolition of which we are forced to look, and the intertwining of which with all our present troubles we cannot hide or deny.

The demanded supremacy and universal acknowledgment of established slaveholding was the one real occasion of this struggle. This was the demand, pressed in every variety of shape, and by every class of public appeal. In Congress, in the courts, in public addresses, in convention resolutions, they have said to the resisting people: Acknowledge it; cease to contend with it; allow its establishment; submit to its dominion; it is the right, and the only right, relation of the black man to the white, or of labor to capital; it is scriptural; it is benevolent; it is humane; it is refining; it is exalting; no other system of social dependence and services is equally so; allow its universal sway and law, and we will consent to be at peace. This was the constant cry in the time of peace. This was the varied cry for war. This was the unceasing demand of those who have made the war. A vast portion and a final majority of the people have calmly but earnestly resisted the extension of this oppression in every shape. They would earnestly have desired, in a peaceful colonization, in a liberal purchase at any cost, in any system of progressive and gradual emancipation, to have removed the evil, unitedly and peacefully. Every offer, every suggestion, was refused and reviled; and now it has been forced into the issue of war. And the Government must go forward, and the rising people must speak unto them that they go forward, and make the final issue of the war the settling of this all-corroding question. It has now come before the tribunal, without our seeking it. Let us take care that the cause be so righteously adjusted, that there be no further appeal to the vindicating and chastening providence of God, in future contests for its sake. Its merits are now in contest in our mature generation. Let us not in timorous hesitation throw it forward to our children or their children, to adjudicate in further loss of blood, and peace, and treasure, to them, as an issue which our time-serving policy weakly dreaded to meet. Let it cost us what it may, our interest, and the welfare of our posterity, demand that we should not again throw forward the load upon others. We hesitated at the demand of righteousness and mercy in the complete overthrow of this system of bondage, when, a quarter of a century since, 2,000,000 were the clients for our justice. Is it an easier task now that they have increased to 4,000,000? Will the case be more readily adjudicated in the future doublings of the numbers involved? Why shall we require our sons to bear a yoke which neither we nor our fathers have been able to bear? As long as it remains unsettled, we are not only at war among ourselves, we are at war with Providence, with justice, with God. Well did Mr. Jefferson say, when this people were in their infancy, of little more than half a million: "I tremble for my country, when I remember that God is just." Had the men of his day removed the load forever, how peaceful, and free from fear and contest would have been our dispensation and appointed life. Every motive of interest, of justice, of duty to our country, and duty to our posterity, requires that we should determine on the absolute extinction of this burden now. Others have the responsibility of bringing up this subject to view in a shape and relation which we should never have desired. Let us not lose the occasion of putting it, in a final extinction of slavery in our land, beyond the reach of further poisoning our inheritance, and embittering all the relations of our life. To do this now, or solemnly to purpose to do this, wisely, quietly, but with an unshrinking determination, is, in this great relation, "to do justly, to love mercy, and to walk humbly with our God." It is the absolute call of righteousness in the nation, of public acknowledgment of national injustice, of justice to an innocent people oppressed and trodden upon because they have been weak, and of due and honorable regard to the sense of public justice and national duty, in the concurrent judgment of mankind.

AN INEVITABLE ALTERNATIVE.

More than this. Here are one million of enslaved Africans in the midst of this contest, in the vigor of adult years. They cannot be made, and they will not be kept, neutral in the contest. They understand its operation. They have, perhaps, very exaggerated expectations of its results. If our nation and Government do not in some way declare and establish, or enter upon the determined plan for their emancipation, we cannot doubt that sooner than the insurgents will consent to submission, they will array, with the promise of freedom, this whole immense host against us. It seems indubitable to my anticipation, that we have but the choice whether they shall be on our side or against us; whether by an act of gracious justice, we shall place them on the standing of freemen, and take them out of the warfare so far as we can; or whether we shall consent to see them thrust into a relation in which we really have no alternative left but their utter extermination, or our own untold losses and sufferings from their unreasoning and brutal warfare. That such a choice and alternative alone remain to us, I confess I have no doubt. Justice and mercy to this people, so long delayed, involve far more and greater difficulties than if they had been timely ministered in their healing power to bless and save them.

I fully appreciate all the difficulties of dealing with this subject successfully according to our Constitution. But I also appreciate the fact that the Constitution itself is at stake in this contest, and will, I believe, never be brought out of this contest if this question be left unsettled. I have hoped that the great principle laid down by Mr. Adams, that, in a time of civil war, this great internal question was taken out of the process of civil law and put under the control of military necessity, might be considered established. Then a proclamation from the highest military authorities might adjudicate and settle it; and define and decree the terms and conditions of emancipation; both in limited localities and applications like the cases already occurring, and in the general and universal relations of the whole subject to the successful prosecution of this struggle for the nation's life. I do not ask for any violent action. The result of sanguinary insurrection and brutal warfare is the very thing which I deeply dread. But I do ask for a solemn, united purpose, on the part of the Government and people: We will not leave this question unsettled; nor again construct a Union with perpetuated slavery therein; nor throw forward, in a mere temporary healing of the difficulty, the whole grievous burden on other generations, provoking their hatred, the abhorrence of mankind, and the just anger of a holy God.

CONCLUDING VIEW.

At any rate, this is my view of the necessity, freely and calmly expressed. I would call the wisdom of the Administration to the consideration of the question, for the method of its final adjustment. And then I would say to the Executive power: "Go forward. Proclaim liberty throughout the land." And to the waiting, rising people, in the majesty of their sovereignty and strength: "Speak unto them that they go forward." Sound it from every hill-top on the continent. Echo it from every valley. Let the inhabitants of the cities take it up. Let high and low, rich and poor, one with another, solemnly, unitedly resolve, "We will break every yoke, we will let the op pressed go free." Such a stand, assumed and carried out in this crisis, would command the homage of the world, as it displayed the uprising wisdom and justice of a great people; would bring down the blessing of God, as it exhibited a people determined to do right, and to be the protectors of the feeble and the oppressed; would open through the sea a path to certain triumph, because it would make the contest, in all its aspects, righteous, lofty, and just; and would insure a permanent dominion of peace, because it would leave no festering sore in the body, or gall-bearing root in the ground. For such a cause, and in such a crisis, thus to be settled on principles of righteousness and truth forever, we may surely lift up the prayer of faith, and reverently and acceptably ask the blessing of a just and holy God, confessing our crime as a nation in this prolonged injustice, and imploring His mercy, "that our arms may be blessed and made effectual for the reëstablishment of law, order, and peace throughout our country," and that God Himself may be our God, as our fathers' God, for evermore.

SERMON

Preached in the Hall of the House of Representatives, at Washington, D. C., Sunday, April 28, 1861.

BY BYRON SUNDERLAND, D.D.

But he that shall endure unto the end, the same shall be saved.—*Matt.* xxiv. 13.

TIME, ever big with momentous events, fulfils the prophecy of Jesus. Amid the mighty convulsions predicted by Him, there was one to take place in a distant age and country that should stir the foundations of a great Government, and fire the hearts of its people across the breadth of a continent. In the full presence of that commotion, we are standing here to-night.

Heart and tongue seem alike to fail under the pressure and the power of this heart-throb of the nation. And yet we must rise up to the magnitude of the events which are breaking upon us.

No language can express the emotions with which I stand in this assembly, on this sacred Sabbath—signatory of our divine religion—heraldic of our hopes of Heaven—in the Capitol of the Confederacy, before the representatives of our collected armies—stand here, an humble minister of Jesus, to speak to you, my fellow-men, my fellow-countrymen, soldiers of the Republic, for God and our country.

Because I come to announce the doctrine of patriarchs and prophets, of apostles and confessors—the great doctrine of believers in all ages, that God can be just and yet save man—that great doctrine which creates purity in the midst of corruption; which kindles hope in the midst of despair; which gives light in darkness; which produces joy out of the heart of sorrow, and lifts a shout of triumph over the most terrible siege.

Let me say to you, first of all, then, my commission is to bring you these tidings—salvation by Christ to every man of us who will believe in Him with an abiding faith; the soul's salvation, now, finally, and forever; salvation from sin, and at length from suffering; courage now, glory hereafter; and to say also, that if the salvation is perfect, the terms are also plain —"He that endureth unto the end shall be saved." It implies that circumstances may arise to shake a man's faith, to turn him aside from duty, to overpower him, and cut him off from reaching the end.

Yet, next to salvation itself, the mode of its attainment is most important. What is needed in this, as in any other warfare, is fortitude, perseverance, and determination. The soldier of Christ must expect to endure hardness, must follow his Captain, must obey His orders, must smite down temptation on every hand, and reach the object of the campaign at every cost. Discipline is the life of the hero. Through this, and only this, he marches to victory. The life to which God calls us is a time-long conflict, from which there is no discharge and no retreat, and from which we may thank God there is none. The true soldier wants none, else he would be willing to turn back from the conquest and the final rewards of triumph.

The salvation which calls us to endure unto the end, is the salvation of a great spiritual kingdom; the salvation of righteousness, and peace, and joy in the Holy Ghost; the salvation which stays the heart of man, by faith, upon the eternal strength of God, and in the unshaken hope of a glorious immortality—so that the soul so stayed and girded shall look out of the windows of her earthly habitation and laugh to scorn the enemies of her peace, the assailants of her security. All physical evils, all temporal dangers and distresses, are nothing to a spirit thus kindled with God's great virtue, and beating with the pulses of that infinite life, which flows from the heart of Christ into the soul of his follower.

Then look to it, my brethren. See that, first of all, your soul is right with God; "all the fitness He requires is to feel our need of Him." Go to Him, cast yourself upon Him, take the oath of fealty to Him, receive from Him your spiritual weapons which "are mighty through God to the pulling down of strongholds." And this is your panoply in the warfare, "For we wrestle not against flesh and blood," alone, "but against principalities, against powers, against the rulers of the darkness of this world, against spiritual wickedness in high places. Wherefore, take unto you the whole armor of God, that ye may be able to withstand in the evil day, and having done all, to stand. Stand, therefore, having your loins girt about with truth, and having on the breastplate of righteousness, and your feet shod with the preparation of the Gospel of peace; above all, taking the shield of faith, wherewith ye shall be able to quench all the fiery darts of the wicked; and take the helmet of salvation, and the sword of the Spirit, which is the Word of God; praying always with all prayer and supplication, and watching thereunto with all perseverance." Thus will you fight the good fight, and keep the faith, and be enabled at last to say, "I have endured unto the end; I have finished my course with joy; Oh, grave, where is thy victory? Oh, death, where is thy sting! Henceforth, there is laid up for me a crown of righteousness, which the Lord, the righteous Judge, shall give me at that day."

These are the prospects which support a man in stern and trying times; in days that test the soul; in hours which rise surcharged with wrath and blackness; when the swift spirit of God's judgment travels in the invisible air; when all earthly things are to be given up; when men no longer lingering amid pleasant dalliances, or in the peaceful walks of home life and customary engagements, are suddenly summoned to meet a stern and terrible emergency, and to act their part in solemn and eventful times. Such a period has come to us and to our beloved country.

It is for this cause, that you with all your brethren in arms are gathering to the Capital of the Nation. It is a spectacle, which in my day I never thought to see. But who can tell what are to be the developments of the morrow; and who but the man that is resolved on enduring to the end, and on seeing the great promised salvation, is thoroughly prepared to meet so grave and momentous a crisis. Next to the service of our God is the service we owe our country. The one implies the other. Christianity fosters patriotism. Spiritual religion and free government are both ordained of God. He that is right with his Maker is most likely to be true to the interests of his country in her hour of danger; and therefore, there is a political, yea even a militant, as well as a religious sense, in which the declaration is true, "Whosoever shall endure unto the end, the same shall be saved."

For a long time a certain subtle poison of dissatisfaction and disloyalty to the General Government has been diffusing itself among a portion of the people of our country. The cloud of insubordination has been rising and spreading itself on our political horizon, and the muttering of the thunder of dissolution has been heard—till at length a settled plan and purpose to break up this great political structure has been undertaken, and its progress has been fearfully rapid. Forbearance and conciliation have been wrested and perverted to stimulate and encourage this proceeding; and for months it has been permitted to go on, aggravated by circumstances which it does not become me here to detail, but which must cause the heart of every honest man to ache, and his cheek to tingle with the blush of shame. By such means the Government was brought to the brink of ruin, and the first feeble endeavor to exercise its rights was met by a resistance as determined as it was unrighteous. But at length the batteries which opened upon Sumter have opened the eyes of this nation to the impending destruction. In this fearful crisis we have no doubt that the President of the United States and those gentlemen who are acting with him in his Cabinet, and all the thousands of our fellow-citizens who have responded to the appeal which has gone forth—and responded so promptly, so nobly, without distinction of party or diversity of sentiment—in their efforts and sacrifices to uphold and maintain the government made by our fathers, the government under which we were born and have lived and expect to die, the government which has been the beneficent instrument, under Providence, of so many and so great blessings, for so long a time, the government under which such a boundless prospect for future usefulness and happiness spreads out before us—are, one and all, engaged in a cause as righteous as ever men undertook to defend and maintain.

We hold that nothing but prompt measures —such measures as Christianity and patriotism may now suggest—measures conceived not in the violence of passion or the spirit of prejudice, but in the temper of firmness, of coolness, of humanity, of faith in God, and under a full sense of responsibility to Him, and of all the momentous interests involved, can retrieve the errors of the past or avert the dangers threatened in the future. We cordially approve of the earnest efforts now being made by the President, aided as he is by our war-worn General —the venerable Chieftain of the American people—to preserve the Government and to maintain the Constitution and the laws; and we feel that he has "an oath solemnly recorded in Heaven" to use his best endeavors to this end. We discountenance all efforts from every quarter to interfere with this object. We disapprove of all appeals made to him, from whatever motive, to embarrass or cripple him in his work. This is emphatically his work; and therefore to entreat him to desist from it, is to undertake to seduce or to solicit him to perjury. The principle and spirit of my text applies to him and his work, as well as to you and to me and to our work. Our only salvation lies in "enduring to the end." If this Government is permitted, through his unfaithfulness, to crumble in pieces on his hands, it will be a crime against God and nature, against earth and heaven, and the curse and ruin of anarchy will surely succeed.

It is not the man who is President, or the party that raised him to his high place, that we have rallied to sustain; but it is the Government which he, for the time being, administers. It is that flag—the only symbol of national supremacy we know—which has been despised, insulted, dragged down, and trailed in the dust. Amid repeated provocations, crowned by the last and most melancholy outbreak of all, on the very spot where our national song was composed, in the Monumental city, upon brethren, soldiers from a sister State hastening from the home of Webster, to stand by us in our peril, by a ruthless mob. Oh, could not the memories of other days have restrained their fury! Oh, to prevent such disgrace, could not the spirit of our army, in the war of 1812, have again animated the breasts of those, who dwell on the spot where the writer of the Star-Spangled Banner composed his imperishable hymn, graven in every heart; and which now, with no less enthusiasm, we repeat, thankful to God for the occasion which called it forth, and the victory upon the soil and in the waters of our sister State that inspired it:

Oh, say, can you see, by the dawn's early light,
What so proudly we hailed at the twilight's last gleaming;
Whose broad stripes and bright stars, through the perilous fight,
O'er the ramparts we watched while so gallantly streaming?
 And the rockets' red glare,
 The bombs bursting in air,
 Gave proof through the night
 That our flag was still there;
The Star-Spangled Banner, Oh long may it wave,
O'er the land of the free and the home of the brave!

Oh thus be it ever, when freemen shall stand
Between their loved homes and the war's desolation;
Blest with victory and peace, may the Heaven-rescued land
Praise the power that hath made and preserved us a nation.
 Then conquer we must,
 For our cause it is just,
 Let this be our motto,
 " In God is our trust;"
And the Star-Spangled Banner in triumph shall wave,
O'er the land of the free and the home of the brave.

But, brethren, we know why you have gathered around us at this time; why the mustering thousands of the loyal States have been moved as by the spirit of one man to hasten hitherwards. You have come as friends and as brothers, not as enemies or as aliens. We understand the purpose of your coming, and we applaud it. New England's heart has been touched to the core; and the same shaft of anguish has pierced the great soul of New York, and of Pennsylvania, and of the whole broad Northwestern States; yea, and the soul of every patriot throughout the land. It was the cry of the genius of Liberty, as she saw the stars and stripes go down before the unnatural wrath of a once sister State. Oh, would that the same anguish could have rent the heart of the Southern States, showing still, despite all partisan strife and all sectional interest, that the body is yet one, and thrills to the living pulse of an unbroken nationality through every fibre and limb! But the North have felt the shock, and have come not as an army of invaders; not as the Scandinavian hordes that issued from the realms of Thor, rolling like a sea over the plains of Italy; not like the legions of Napoleon, in later times, resurging from the South to the walls of the Kremlin, to perish in northern snows; but like themselves alone, Americans and patriots, the sons of the sires of the Revolution, lovers of their country and ready with their lives. What indeed, in such a time as this, are wealth, and riches, and friends, and pleasures, and case, and recreation; what are cities and marts, and proud thoroughfares of trade and travel, and argosies of commerce, and all the pomp and treasure of an ever-advancing civilization; what are dangers and self-denials, and personal hardships; nay, what is life itself, if the glorious visions of American Liberty and Independence, of American institutions and ideas and principles, can only be preserved!

God only knows the issue of this great business. I confess to you, it looks to me sometimes grim and terrible; and the baptism through which we are called to pass seems awful to our mortal nature, even as that more terrific and unspeakable mystery of Christ our Saviour, in which He was baptized. Yet, I cannot but hope and believe, that as His death proved the life, and light, and hope of the world, so our suffering and toil, if we are true and faithful, will produce a harvest of fruits at last, of which none of us shall ever need to be ashamed!

Above all, let us remember whose we are, and the mighty God whom we serve; let us put our trust in that "Name which is above every name, and shall endure forever." All we can do for our country will finally prove but the just tribute of our age and our generation to that mightier kingdom which Jesus Christ has set up, and over which He will reign perpetually. When life's work is finished, and the consummation of all things is come, may it then be found of each of us, that we have "endured unto the end," and have inherited salvation.

Oh, soldiers of Christ, if indeed you are such, what a life is before you! what a victory and reward await you! I see the last enemy approaching! There lies between you and yonder welcome, but one more conflict. Earth is receding! Heaven begins to open.

It shall be when life is over and the battle ended; it shall be after you have worn the harness of this warfare, and having worn it well, shall unbind the corselet and lay aside the weapons of the fight; it shall be when the earthly evolutions are all spent; when the crisis is decided; when the tents are struck, and the camp-fires wasted; it shall be after that long sleep of the grave, in the muster-morning of the Resurrection, when the trumpet of the Archangel shall breathe its living blast through "every soldier's sepulchre," and Heaven shall open, upon the sight of the rising myriads, its long-expected glories. Oh, fellowmen, if indeed you belong to Christ,

"I see you on your winding way"

from these distant regions of the grave to that resplendent and august Metropolis in yonder skies. The night—that last long night of death—which put an end to the combat and forever, is past; the dawn of that day eternal opens to your vision the full realness and magnitude of the battle you have fought and won; and the morning drum-beat of the mustering angel calls you up from the damp sod where the night found you fighting.

Oh, what a victory and welcome! There, under the triumphal arch, before the Celestial City, greeting the glad eye of the victor, there is your beautiful crown, ready for the soldier's temples, the gift of Him whose cause you served, winning that peace which is now your eternal fruition. There too, is the array, more gorgeous and magnificent than army ever made in a home-return from conflict, an array that you will join, in your upward march, at the clarion sound of seraphic heralds, amid the plaudits of unnumbered angel voices, bidding you welcome in the name of Him, for whom that night of earthly battle found you fighting to the last!

Once again, therefore, let me point you to the religion of the Cross; to that only solace which can assuage our sorrows; to that refuge and support which alone is adequate to life's solemn undertakings. There may you learn how the soul overcomes in every changing fortune of the strife; and there may you furnish the spirit expectant, for the dawn of the eternal morrow—when away from the conflict and the bivouac of mortal warfare, your vestments shall glisten in a purer light, and your tents be pitched under a fairer sky. Amen.

LOYALTY AND RELIGION.

A Discourse for the Times: Delivered in the Church of the Messiah, St. Louis, Mo., Aug. 18th, 1861.

BY REV. W. G. ELIOT, D.D.

Render therefore unto Cæsar the things that are Cæsar's, and unto God the things that are God's.—*Matt.* xxii. 21.

This passage is often interpreted as if it created a conflict between our duties to God and those to human government. The precise contrary was intended. Many of the Jews wished to avoid their civil obligations under the plea of zeal for religion. The answer brings the two classes of obligation under one rule. *A part of our duty to* God is our duty to the State. To separate the two is injurious to both. Undoubtedly the supreme allegiance is to God, whose we are, and whom we are bound continually to serve. Under no pretence, not even to preserve life itself, are we justified in doing violence to the plain dictates of conscience, by violation of the Divine law. But they who set up this rule as justification for rebellion or resistance against the Government under which they live, must make a clear case of urgent necessity, or the plea cannot be allowed. RELIGION and LOYALTY, religious and civil duties, obedience to the laws of God, and to the ordained laws of man, commonly lead us in the same path of quietness, good order, and peace. *Submission to law*— words lately brought into strange contempt, just as belief in Christ was the subject of scorn in the French Revolution—is among the prime duties of religion, and the "Supreme Law of the Land" partakes of the sacredness of the Supreme Law of God.

So would I teach, and so have I always taught in this place. The subject may not need to be frequently or directly introduced into the pulpit, but there should be no ambiguity on this point. The minister of Christ and the Church of Christ (whether connected by law with the State or not) should, as a general rule, be the steady, uniform supporters of the established Government, that is to say, of the Constitution, the National Union, and the laws.

Exceptions may exist. The right of revolution (*not secession*) is inherent under every form of government and to every people, nor has it ever been denied, except by tyrants and their sycophants. We certainly do not deny it. But it can be exercised only under three conditions, neither of which can be pleaded for revolution now:

1st. When a government becomes, by wrongs done and grievances committed, no longer endurable.

2d. When all other practicable methods of relief have first been tried.

3d. When there is reasonable assurance of success, by honorable and honest means.

Revolution, even when successful, is a terrible means of redress. Nothing can justify it, except the sternest and most urgent necessity. It involves, in its progress, all manner of evil, whatever its final result. Temporarily at least, and probably for months and years, it stops all good influences upon which the welfare of society depends, and sets in active operation all the elements of evil to do the work of devastation, of social ruin, of anarchy and crime. Therefore, whoever leads or abets in revolution, under whatever circumstances, assumes a fearful responsibility, and ought to be very sure of his ground. If he expects to do his work peacefully, without bloodshed, without civil war and all its horrors, he must be equally ignorant of the principles of civil government and of the whole teaching of history. The beginning of revolution is nothing but rebellion, and is sure to be so treated. The attempt to overthrow an established government is the plainest treason, and nothing but complete success can save, or ever has saved, its promoters from the punishment and brand of traitors. Samuel Adams and John Hancock, if they had failed, would have died upon the scaffold, and they knew that this was the alternative. The work of revolution cannot be done peaceably and amicably, under whatever ingenious name introduced, and they who unfurl its banner *are openly declaring war.* The readiness with which men sometimes enter upon it, almost without thought, has therefore been to me a matter of astonishment. For if necessity is required to justify it, and success to save its promoters from the traitor's name and fate, and if, in its progress, civil war and social ruin are the steps to triumph, then it surely follows that those who rashly and with insufficient cause, undertake to overthrow an established government, are guilty by the laws of God and man of the gravest of all crimes, the most heinous of all human offences. In all countries, by all codes of law, treason is reckoned as the extreme offence, including all other criminality, because it opens the door to all other crime.

I am speaking, as you observe, in general terms, without direct application to passing events, and if the same words had been spoken twelve months ago, they would have passed as the mere "commonplaces," or axioms, without which civil government could not at all exist. If recent events give to the words some harshness, it is the fault of the events, not mine. They will serve to show the seriousness of my subject, in its moral and religious bearings, and to declare the general principles on which my present argument will rest.

Religion and law are the great conservative influences of society. The teachers of religion, like the administrators of law, are naturally and properly upon the conservative side. They are bound to the advocacy of peace and good order. They are the natural opponents of violence and revolutionary change. Only under the plainest arguments of necessity, can they properly become agitators and disturbers of established rule.

But the same reasons which should make the minister of Christ conservative, and which have generally led me to exclude from the pulpit the excitements of political discussion, seem to me to require plain and earnest speech, at a time like this. Whether you call the action of the Southern States rebellion or revolution, it has for its avowed object the dismemberment of the Commonwealth, by a division into two or more confederacies, and this upon principles which, if admitted, would deprive the remaining "Union" of all unity and national strength. For if the doctrine of peaceable secession, whenever a State has, or supposes itself to have, cause of complaint, be once admitted, all *national* existence would be destroyed, and an indefinite work of subdivision begun, which would undoubtedly end in almost as many nations as there are States. We would avoid all questions of detail. We do not assume to decide whether the controversy might not have been settled without war, in some honorable and statesmanlike manner. In the beginning of the trouble, six or eight months ago, I thought that it could; but subsequent developments, showing the extent and deliberateness of the conspiracy, and the matured plans of those who had resolved, not upon redress of wrongs and guarantees of protection in their rights, but upon a revolution and division of the Government, have materially modified my opinion. Open war might have been delayed a few weeks or months, but it was sure to come, and perhaps under circumstances to work still greater ruin. At all events, we may say that if the General Government had consented to the dismemberment of the nation and its own virtual destruction, without an effort made or blow struck, it would have been a thing without parallel in history, which those making the attack had no right to expect, and which it is evident by their preparations for war, they did not expect. And now, not only is this general revolution in progress, and the whole country converted into a camp, but our own State has been made one of the principal seats of war, with the view of compelling it to revolt against the General Government, and renounce its allegiance to the United States. By a large popular vote, the people of Missouri determined to remain loyal, and their decision was declared by a Convention called and instructed for the purpose. But the attempt to coerce the State out of the Union was made by those who deny the right of coercing her to remain in it, and the expressed will of her citizens, and the loyal action of her Convention, are now set at defiance. We desire to speak dispassionately, and I know that as to the different steps in this progress of events, diversity of opinion exists. But this general statement of the question at issue may be made, in the fairness of which all will concur: First, that the whole country is in the condition of civil war, the object of which is, on the one side, to accomplish a revolution by separating a part of the States from the Government of the United States; and on the other, to resist, and if possible prevent, such a result. And secondly, in our own State, it is a struggle to determine whether we shall remain in the Union or go out of it. For whatever may be the incidental questions involved, no one can doubt that if the Confederate troops with the late Governor succeed, the secession or revolt of the State is a foregone conclusion. If the United States forces and the loyal citizens prevail, the death-blow of secession in Missouri is struck.

Now I assume that, in such a case, no one who loves his country, or has any interest in its welfare, can or ought to be silent. No one who at all comprehends the magnitude of the interests involved, can hold his peace, or affect neutrality without partaking in the wrong of failure and losing the merit of success. To be indifferent is impossible, and I should be unable to plead any good reason for inaction, except that sort of conservatism which always finds itself upon the stronger side.

I know that some of you differ from me as to the propriety of introducing the subject in this place. It is urged that offence will be given, that it is impolitic and unwise. But it is not a matter of policy nor choice with me, not of mere conventional propriety and taste, not of praise or blame. It is a matter of positive obligation. I may do no good, but I must try. No man can answer to his country, to his conscience, to his God, who does not do his best, however little that may be. My convictions are too strong to be repressed. From the abundance of the heart the mouth will speak, and is very like to speak plainly.

May I not also add that I have earned a right to speak plainly, at whatever risk of giving offence. My many years of service here, my long citizenship, in which no one has worked harder for the welfare of St. Louis, or more completely identified himself with its interests, entitle me, both as your pastor and fellow-citizen, to claim a patient and respectful hearing. We have yet to learn that the highest praise of the pulpit is to please everybody and offend none. I am persuaded that as you require me to be faithful, you will permit me to be honest and frank.

The radical defect in the existing state of the public mind, is slowness to perceive the magnitude and importance of the present controversy. The subject is often treated in conversation and in the public prints as if it were one of local, party, or temporary concern, like a municipal or Presidential election—as if it were merely to determine whether we are for or against the present Administration, in favor of Mr. Lincoln or opposed to him. "Side issues" are made; mistakes in policy and management pointed out; and diversions of thought from the central question of Union or disunion are thus encouraged. Every technical violation of law—every street outrage—every local annoyance—is seized upon and made the most of, and not unfrequently becomes the ground of treasonable talk and angry conduct, as if the subject discussed were one of temporary loss and gain. Every instance of peculation and fraud on the part of those who make a trade of patriotism, and whose chief object is to put money in their own purse, is alleged as a proof of radical corruption in the General Government, instead of being charged to the sordid avarice of those who commit the crime.

For some of the things complained of there may be no excuse, and I offer none. But they are evils incident upon the tremendous conflict in which the country is engaged, and ought not to be treated as the prominent facts, by which our allegiance or revolt is to be determined. We admit the evils and lament them, but when sensible men make such things the turning points of loyalty or rebellion, it proves that their love of country is very weak, and their loyalty not much better than a name.

Again, there are others whose temperature of patriotism is measured by the defeats and successes of the day. The battle and defeat at Manassas Gap developed wonderful zeal for secession, and the love of many waxed cold. At this moment there are hundreds anxiously waiting for the next news from Southern Missouri and Virginia, to decide them whether they will be for or against their country, friends of the Union or its foes. What wretched logic is this! What miserable and craven fidelity which depends upon sunshine and prosperity! Of course there will be occasional defeats and reverses, and although I have myself no doubt of the ultimate and complete success of the Union cause, in this State and elsewhere, yet I admit the possibility of its failure. Perhaps utter defeat awaits it. What then? If we are brave and true defenders, if we stand upon principle in our defence, we shall not falter while a single hope remains. Then, if the worst comes, we shall at least have the manly satisfaction of having done our best, even if destroyed with the sacred cause which we have no longer the power to defend. It is the part of brave men to *increase*, not lessen, their zeal in time of adversity.

And what is our cause? It is the existary.

or non-existence of our country. The permanence or dismemberment of a great nation. "Republican institutions are on their trial, and according to the result will the verdict of the world be given." The plain question is, shall we be one strong, united people, or scattered into, no one can tell how many, communities, republics, or monarchies, at strife among ourselves, the scorn and contempt of the nations.

Look back to twelve months ago, and what were we then? These United States of America!

It is true that we were not free from party conflicts and strifes. We had reason to complain, or thought we had, of rights infringed, of wrongs unadjusted, of bad laws in force, of good laws unexecuted. There were criminations and recriminations, mobs and violence, threats and denunciations. Fanatics at the North declared that every slave State was a pandemonium; fanatics at the South rejoined that Eden itself would be an imperfect abode without the peculiar institution. We were not a perfect nation, but with stains enough upon our escutcheon, with weaknesses and sins enough; extravagant in boasting, deficient in self-respect. Yet with all our defects we were the foremost nation of the world. With a Constitution securing popular rights, freedom of speech, of conscience, and of the press, we were safe in person and in property, both at home and abroad, with none to molest or make us afraid. As a nation, we were going on from strength to strength, with such gigantic strides towards greatness, that the monarchs of the old world looked on with amazement and prophetic fears. It was the poor man's paradise, the refuge of the oppressed, the sanctuary of the exile, the hope of liberty, the living proof of a Republic. How grandly did the old flag, God bless it, planted at Washington and by WASHINGTON, stretch its broad folds over the earth, everywhere protecting every man who could say "I am an American citizen." Do you remember the thrill of pride, when the adopted citizen KOZTA was claimed and protected from Austrian power by INGRAHAM, on the Turkish waters? The same INGRAHAM who has been since betrayed, by mistaken sense of duty, to become an enemy of the flag under which he had gained so many honors. Our commerce upon every sea was sufficiently protected by the name of the great Republic. Our cities were disputing with London the control of the world's trade. Our great extent of territory already surpassed in magnitude that of the old Roman Empire, insomuch that WENSTER (or EVERETT) in his famous Austrian letter declared that the whole Austrian Empire, with all its dependencies, in comparison with the American States was but a "patch" upon the earth's surface.

Like the great tree, of which we read in the Book of Daniel, "which stood in the midst of the earth, and the height thereof was great; and the tree grew and was strong, and the height thereof reached unto heaven, and the sight thereof to the end of all the earth; the leaves thereof were fair and the fruit thereof much, and in it was meat for all; the beasts of the field had shadow under it, and the fowls of heaven dwelt in the boughs thereof and all flesh was fed of it!" Must the parallel be continued? Are we destined to hear the terrible sentence which the King of Babylon heard? "Hew down the tree, and cut off his branches, shake off his leaves, and scatter his fruits; till seven years have passed over him."

What elements of national greatness did we want? What means of prosperity? What assurance of success? Like the rich man in the parable, we were beginning to pull down our barns and build greater, "where to bestow our goods," to invest our increasing wealth. Already we were preparing to stretch the highway of commerce across the plains, from one ocean to the other, and new visions of glory filled our thoughts. But we had forgotten "to be rich towards God," and the startling threat of Rebellion disturbed our dreams. "This night shall thy soul be required of thee. Then whose shall those things be?" For the soul of our country is THE UNION; this alone is our national existence. A confederation will not do. It was tried and failed, long ago, and now its hope of succeeding would be a hundred times less. Under the secession doctrine no nation could exist. Not by thirty-four State sovereignties, nor by two or three State confederacies, could any of the distinctive advantages of the national union be secured. Instead of them, separate weakness, internecine warfare, ruinous competitions, local insurrections, servile wars, subdivisions of States, oligarchies, and military despotisms would be our fate. And all, to satisfy the ambition and party hatred of a few desperate politicians, who would march over the ruin of their country to the accomplishment of their own schemes. By what dishonesty and long-laid plans of treason they have thus far done their work, let history record.! Well may the monarchies and absolute governments of the world rejoice at the prospect of our disintegration and overthrow; for the one great fear of Absolutism, and the one great hope of Freedom, will have been at once destroyed. The "house of the strong man, divided against itself," will have fallen. The prediction will have been fulfilled:

> "To us was left, in deathless trust,
> A realm redeemed, a glorious name,
> The ashes of the brave and just,
> Fair freedom and immortal fame;
> And should our pride be e'er o'erthrown,
> 'Twill be by native swords alone."

Taking these views of the momentous issues at stake, not only for the present but for coming generations, not only for ourselves, but for the world at large, we are prepared to say, knowing the full meaning and extent of the words, that in comparison with the evils resulting from disunion, the calamities of civil war itself might well be patiently endured. We do not know that this was the best or only means of preventing such a result, and perhaps some better method may presently be found, by peaceable adjustment and mutual forbearance, for the permanent settlement of the national controversy. For, very soon, this war will have proved that our interests are in common, that we are members one of the other, and that in fighting against each other *we are destroying ourselves.* God grant that such a way may be found, and that patriotism, overcoming party spirit, may be ready to adopt it when it appears! For we do not underrate the evils of war. They come next to those of national ruin. We shudder when we think of the terrors and fears by which we are this day surrounded. It sometimes seems an incredible thing, so awful it is, that we, Americans, of the same ancestry, brothers, with the same blood flowing in our veins, the same in language, in social interests, in religion, looking to the same Saviour for redemption, worshipping the same God, are enlisted in opposing armies, imbruing our hands in each other's blood, rejoicing over each other's downfall!

It is a thought of terror which haunts us by night and oppresses us by day. It spoils our daily comfort, and takes from life its best enjoyment. And this is the "beginning of sorrows," for if so fierce a flame is kindled in the green tree, what shall it be in the dry. The passions are yet scarcely unloosed, the hand is yet unskilled in warfare, and pity is not yet dead. May God save us from that continuance of fratricidal warfare which will change all love to hatred, all pity to revenge; which is already beginning to proclaim "no quarter" to the enemy, and may soon result in worse than savage atrocities. It is and will be a fearful conflict—may God grant that it may be a short one!

I am a lover of peace; I am now, and always have been, its advocate. In social, religious, and civil affairs I have always been ready to plead for it. Among the benedictions, no one do I covet more than that upon the peace-makers. While, therefore, I do not assume to decide whether or not the present civil war was unavoidable, I am thankful that the responsibility did not and does not rest upon me. I did all I could to prevent it, and would do any thing in my power to bring it to a just and righteous close. So much I feel bound to say, for I cannot appear as the general advocate of war, even when the progress of events compels me reluctantly to accept it, as the last appeal.

Nevertheless, leaving the responsibility of the beginning and continuance of this conflict to those upon whom it must rest, I feel equally bound to say, that beyond all the evils of the present war, with all its calamities, losses, sufferings, and sins, would be the loss of national existence, the permanent severance of the American Union. A nation may well suffer in the maintenance of the principles on which it was founded. Individual suffering and loss, social and commercial embarrassment or bankruptcy, the prostration of credit, the impoverishment of cities, the loss of life; bad as they are, are yet not to be considered in comparison with the great and enduring evils of national ruin. Whether the present war continues one year or ten, it is not so bad as the continued series of wars and internal strifes that would certainly succeed the disruption of the Union. There would be witnessed here the same tragedies which kept the German States so many generations in almost unending conflict, the effects of which have not yet passed away. Nay, our case would be far worse than theirs, for servile war would be added to all other evils.

The question now before us is not to determine upon war or peace. This has already been determined, with or without our intervention, and beyond all present control. It is manifest, regret it as we may, that the war, the trial of strength, if you please to call it so, must go on until one of two things happens—either, the "seceding States," having sufficiently proved the folly of rebellion and the strength of the Government, will return to the Union, *not as subjugated, but as equal States*, as they were before; or, both parties becoming weary of the contest, a treaty of peace, with some sort of re-adjustment of interests, will be declared. In the former case, a new era of happiness and national glory will begin. In the latter, a temporary truce, with renewals of war and divisions—a condition of things little better than anarchy, for an indefinite period, is the best to be expected. But to attain either result, the active prosecution of the present war for a time, how long no one can say, is now understood to be an unavoidable condition. The only thing left for individuals to do is to choose on which side they will stand. We speak with sadness, and the stern reality of passing events is yet more sad. For weeks, for months, perhaps for years, this fearful civil war is destined to go on. But if it results, at last, as God grant it may, in the full re-establishment of the United States Government in its integrity and pristine vigor, the sacrifice will have been well endured, the suffering will not have been in vain.

Nor do I speak as one who has himself nothing to lose. Few persons, perhaps, have more or greater interests at stake than I. Whatever I possess—not much, but all that I desire, enough for my perfect contentment and that of my family—is in exactly such a position, that either the "secession" of the State, or a long continuance of war, would make it absolutely worthless. But that is comparatively a small matter. My interest in the general prosperity goes much deeper than this. My life, my happiness, my hopes, whether of usefulness of enjoyment, are so intertwined with the prosperity of St. Louis, that I have no thoughts beyond. To meet with failure here, is to have failed in the work of life. This Church, in which a whole generation has grown up under my care, and which is to me my home, my family, friends and kindred, at once the place of working and the haven of rest, for which I am willing to spend and be spent, and in which I have found, through so many years of trial, so many friends and helpers, faithful as brothers and true as steel; the charities of the church, by which hundreds of children are rescued from vice, and hundreds of families shielded from hunger and cold; the various charitable and benevolent institutions of the city, in all of which we have labored to do our proper and more than our proportionate share; the educational enterprises, large in design and successful in their prosecution, already established, as we had fondly hoped, beyond the possibility of failure; these things, together with whatever else belongs to the associations and labors of twenty-seven years of severe yet happy experience, the fruits of a life not idly spent—do they not stand as "hostages given to fortune," binding me to labor for the welfare of this community, for the city in which we live? During the last ten years, this congregation of the Church of the Messiah has contributed, in various works of benevolence and charity, not less than the sum of $50,000 annually, and we had our hopes and plans to do as much in every year to come. These are interests not lightly to be sacrificed, and to any one who knows how to value the uses of life, they stand higher than considerations of personal advantage or gain. But so far as I have, or may hereafter have, to do with them, I would cheerfully see them scattered to the four winds, to begin over again the work of my life, here or elsewhere, under all the disadvantages of impaired health and advancing years, with this one hope to sustain me, that the sacrifice would, in some small degree, contribute to the maintenance of unimpaired national existence, the restoration of the American Union to its former strength.

Do you call this sentimental patriotism? It is not so. It is but the just and reasonable love of country, which every honest man should cherish, and without which honesty is seldom long maintained. The love of country, loyalty, patriotism, is the foundation of all social virtues, the corner stone on which society is built. It lies deeper than filial duty or parental love; it is more sacred than the domestic tie. He who loves father or mother, wife or children, so much as to become a traitor to his country, is a weak and miserable man. A poet has truly said, "he who loves not his country cannot love any thing." It is the virtue which last forsakes the heart of the bad man, and that which adds crowning excellence to the character of the good. It knows no limit and makes no conditions of service, but pledges "life and fortune and sacred honor" to the country's cause. "Pleasant and honorable it is for one's country to die." It has been called an enlarged selfishness, but so much enlarged that it becomes self-sacrifice and heroism. It stands next to religion; and the man who betrays his country can hardly be true to his God. I do not ask the man who has lost his patriotism to be my friend, for I should not know how to trust him who lacks this foundation of trustworthiness. I would not live in a community whose patriotism is dead, for it would not be worth working for, nor capable of improvement. That element of vitality gone, anarchy and misrule would soon prevail. That virtue lost, and soon no other virtue would be retained. We can forgive a great deal to the man who is faithful to his country in her times of danger and trial, and overlook many faults for that one virtue's sake. We look with suspicion upon him who is betrayed by passion, or self-interest, or fear, or by any other cause, to curse his native land, and enroll himself against the flag under whose protection he was born. This war is a fearful retribution, almost too heavy to be endured, and we are justly appalled by its calamities; but if it awakens in the American bosom the half-slumbering virtue of Patriotism, if it teaches us through suffering and loss, how much our country is worthy to be loved, it will not be without its compensations. We had been too greatly blessed, and as the prosperous man forgets Him from whom his wealth proceeds, so were we becoming forgetful of our glorious Father-land, from which we have received so much, and for which we have yet done so little. "Land where our Fathers died!" if we can learn to love her as we ought and to serve her with perfect loyalty, we shall have gained that which, to a nation, is worth a lifetime of suffering. "If I forget thee, O Jerusalem," exclaimed the Psalmist, when his country was overrun with enemies and her children captive in a foreign land, "let my right hand forget its cunning! If I do not remember thee, let my tongue cleave to the roof of my mouth; if I prefer not Jerusalem above my chief joy." The Divine Redeemer, though sent for the salvation of the whole world, came first to "the lost sheep of the house of Israel;" and when, at the close of his ministry and ready to be offered up, "he beheld the city," foreseeing its calamities, "he wept over it," grieving more for its impending destruction than for the near approach of his own agony or the suffering on the cross. "He left us an example, that we may follow in his steps."

Do you say that the time is past for such arguments as these? That the Government is already broken to pieces, the Union already and forever destroyed? Perhaps so; but I, for one, am not yet ready to believe it. I cannot so easily lay aside all my hopes, my American sympathies which include all the States, my prayers which are for the whole country, my allegiance which is, *and always will be*, to the American Union. The words of ANDREW JACKSON, that "brave old Roman," whom I was educated to hate, but whom, with advancing years, I have learned to honor more and more, words not only of courage but of prophecy, will not fail. THE UNION; IT MUST BE PRESERVED. It will be preserved, restored, renewed, strengthened to endure for generations to come. How soon, and with what amount of hardships to be first suffered, or by what intermediate steps, whether as the direct result of successful war, or as its indirect result, through subsequent negotiations, readjusting conflicting interests; whether at the close of one year's madness or of ten, I do not know or guess.

But the time will come when the community of interest will be again acknowledged, and we shall be yet again ONE NATION. "There's a Divinity that shapes our ends," and this great experiment of Republican Institutions, now on trial, will yet succeed. It is our manifest destiny. The geography of the continent, and all natural causes require it. The political necessities of the world and the general balance of power require it. The cause of humanity, of the masses, of political freedom, requires it. As surely as there is a God, whose providence is manifest in history, He will accomplish it. For myself, I would rather be in error, hoping for this result, than a true prophet of evil against it. When that worst comes, of final, hopeless disunion, it will be time enough to believe it. Then, with our own hopes, the hopes of the people throughout the civilized world will be buried too. I have no thought of "subjugated States, held as conquered provinces," by main strength. The thought is absurd, as the fact would be, by the instruction of all human experience, impossible. But I have hope, that through the severe discipline of war, in which both sides will suffer, perhaps almost equally, and through the developed necessities of the whole world's commerce and civilization, the sober second thought of the people themselves will find some way to accomplish that which rebellion would prevent, and military force alone cannot secure.

Meanwhile, for, with whatever sadness, we must return to the facts of our actual condition; meanwhile, the conflict, the civil war, which revolution always involves, must go on. This is a matter, let me once more say, which neither you nor I, as individuals or as a community, have the power or delegated right to determine. It is sure to go on, until the limitations of strength on both sides are more clearly understood and defined than they can now be.

The practical point which we can determine, is our own duty, the conjoined duty of loyalty and religion. What part are we, individually, and as a community, to take, so as "to keep a good conscience, both towards God and towards man." This is a legitimate question for the pulpit, and one which we can answer. Your answer may be different from mine, but I feel no hesitation or doubt upon the subject. "Judge ye what I say." Our duty as Americans, as Missourians, as citizens of this community, as Christians, is very plain.

We say, first, and it simplifies the whole subject so as to bring it within the range of easy treatment, that our present duties to the General Government and to the State as now organized, are coincident. In the States farther South, as things now are, we can understand that there may be a conflict of allegiance, which does not exist here. We can also understand, that if the impracticable position of "armed neutrality," or of neutrality in any sense, had been asserted and could have been honestly maintained, we might individually have claimed the right of doing nothing whatever. We might have stood, looking on with affected indifference, waiting to join the stronger side. Not a dignified position, we grant, and we are not surprised that our late Governor and General Assembly were dissatisfied with it. In fact, it was already evident, that between the two allegiances, we were, commercially and politically, falling to the ground. Like the animal, patient and doubting, the symbol of the tribe of Issachar, between two bundles of hay, (each of them too distant to be reached,) we should have starved to death. It was an untenable position, though the love of peace and natural sympathy with the Southern States, led many of us, and for a short time, myself among the number, to desire it. Neutrality in such a case is impossible. The conflict is not between foreign powers, but between the States, of which Missouri is one. On one side or the other we must stand at the end of the conflict, and common manliness, not less than logical necessity, requires us to declare on which side it shall be.

In logic, there is a mode of argument called the "excluded middle," by which it is shown that one or the other of two positions must be taken, but that there is no standing place between. So it is in all cases of rebellion or revolution. You might as well attempt (as many do) to serve God and Mammon, equally and at the same time. "Either he will hate one and love the other, or else he will hold to the one and despise the other." *That has been verified* by every individual case of those who, under this controversy, have endeavored to stand on neither side, or on both sides at once. In one of Byron's dramatic poems, "Lucifer" requires of Cain to fall down and worship him; but he answered, "I never, as yet, have bowed to my father's God." "Hast thou never worshipped Him?" said the fallen angel. "He who bows not to Him has bowed to me." "But," said Cain, "I will bow to neither." "Nevertheless," said Lucifer, "thou art my worshipper. Not worshipping Him, makes thee mine the same."

But the question of neutrality has been long since determined in Missouri. Through causes, for which each party blames the other, but which need not here be mooted, it has come to pass, not only that Missouri is compelled to take part in the war, but she is placed in the fore-front of the battle. By an undesirable fate she belongs now to a military district under both contestants. Is it not a singular fact that the two States most deeply interested to keep the peace, and having the least to gain by the present conflict, Virginia and Missouri, should have been made by the folly of their own rulers, the battle-ground of the contending armies, to suffer all the worst horrors of civil war? It was a shrewd thing in the South to manage it so, but not so wise in ourselves to permit it.

At present, the great battle for the Union is here. If Missouri were permanently lost to the Union, it would be an irreparable blow, and the strength of the Government would be effectually broken. Commanding, as she does, the mouth of the Ohio and of the Illinois, the Upper Mississippi and the whole of the Missouri River, lying on the highway to Kansas, the gold regions, and the Pacific Ocean, and possessed of inestimable mineral resources, Missouri is a military, commercial, and political necessity to the United States Government. At the same time, lying north of the latitude considered most favorable to slave labor, it is far less essential to the South, even if a permanent Southern Confederacy should be established. We may take it for granted, therefore, that the most terrible struggle will take place, even to the devastation of the whole State, before its secession or its conquest by the South will be conceded. We hold that, let the general issue of the war be what it may, the "status" of Missouri will be in the Union. Nothing but the complete prostration of the United States Government would lead to any other permanent result. This has been generally understood, and accordingly, eight months ago, the people of this State, from mingled feelings of loyalty and self-interest, determined by a large majority to remain as they were, and although, under the influence of designing politicians, and through the effect of local irritations and party strifes, some change in popular feeling may have taken place, (of which I cannot say,) you can scarcely find an intelligent man of whatever shade of politics, who anticipates a different result from that now indicated. Even if we put away all considerations of loyalty and patriotism, which are to me the most important of all, we are bound by our local interests and to save our State and city from utter ruin, to stand firm; to maintain our present allegiance, and summarily to condemn all attempts to change it.

What then shall we do? How manifest allegiance, and resist revolution? There is but one answer, which equally applies to all: We should give our whole, undivided influence, by word and deed, to sustain the cause of the United States, *by holding our own State in the Union.* That is our proper and sufficient work at the present time, which will task all our energies to accomplish. We are not called upon to engage in any work of subjugating the South, or of attacking the Southern States. They are attacking us, and ours is a work of self-defence, the salvation of our State from being laid waste and our cities from being left without inhabitant. Let this be first done, before we talk of any thing else. Let there be no evasion of this first, *home* duty; no dodging, no hesitation; no hiding one's self behind generalities and fault-findings. We shall have opportunity enough for criticisms by and by. There will many things be done which we do not like, and many things omitted that we think, if we were only in such or such a place, we would do. But who can please all? Or, in a time like this, with enemies from without, and disaffection and treason whispering and plotting within, who can expect that every thing will take place with the decorum of profound peace and quietness? Those who began and are continuing this civil commotion are responsible for the troubles incident to putting it down.

In what particular way and by what agencies each one should do his part, depends upon the changing circumstances of the hour, by which more or less immediate action may be required. It also depends upon each one's special abilities, and adaptations, and the position in the community which he occupies. The good will is the main thing. Whoever wishes to help or hinder a cause can always find a way. Only let there be a little less policy and timeserving, with a little more courage and patriotism, and every thing else will take care of itself.

The course pursued by STEPHEN A. DOUGLAS is that, as I think, which every lover of his country should take. It was bold, unequivocal, disinterested, self-sacrificing. No one was under less obligation to defend or apologize for the present Administration than he, for its success was his own defeat, and in almost every point of policy, previous to the actual beginning of the war, he differed from the course pursued. In a great many respects, I think, he was right, as events have proved. But what then? He saw that it was no time to magnify, or even to consider, minor differences. Parties and party lines were all annihilated and forgotten as they should be when our country is in danger. He gave the whole influence of his remaining life, and left the sacred influence of a patriot's death, by which "being dead he yet speaketh," to us not less than to his own children, exhorting us "to be faithful to the Union, and to stand by the flag of our country."

May I not also strengthen my appeal by another example, equally illustrious, of one yet living, who did his utmost to avert the calamities of the day, and who up to the present hour has labored, with a young man's energy and an old man's experience, for his country's good, and to maintain the loyalty of his State; I mean JOHN J. CRITTENDEN. How far superior do such men rise above the hackneyed politicians and office-seekers, the neutrals, the workers upon both sides, who have but one consistent rule of service, which is always to work for themselves!

With regard to the special duties devolving upon us, *as citizens of a disturbed community*, in this time of division and distress, a great deal might be profitably said, but not now. One word of counsel, however, must not be omitted, the necessity of which your own daily observations will confirm: To maintain quietness and good order among ourselves, to keep the peace, to preserve good neighborhood, to govern our tempers, and, so far as good sense requires it, to hold our tongues. Indiscreet speech, bitter and angry words, denunciations, vindictive threats, imprecations of evil—how much harm have these abuses of the "little member, which no man can tame," been doing among us! Men seem to forget that talking, when it goes to a certain extent, *is acting*, and that, while we rightly claim liberty of speech, the abuse of this liberty becomes a crime. *Women* forget this, too,—the more is the pity—and one of the most painful features of the present conflict is found in this: that so many ladies forget the gentleness belonging to their sex, and indulge themselves—strange that it should be an indulgence—in severity of language which a gentleman would hesitate to use. A great part of the rancorous feeling, *on both sides*, now prevalent in this city, is attributable to this cause; and those who have most to fear from civil discord and strife, have done the most to promote it. It cannot proceed from the badness of their hearts. Does it proceed from weakness of the head, or from the normal "untamableness of the tongue"? If I thought that I were addressing any who sin in this way, I might say more, but, under present circumstances, have said enough. How much better does it become her, whose proper office is to refine and purify and harmonize society, to assuage the fierceness of war and pour the oil of kindness upon the troubled waters! Let her "study to be quiet," and fill her own home with the blessedness of peace! Let her seek out the poor and suffering, and strive to lessen the evils she cannot prevent or cure! Thus will she be doing the work of patriotism and Christian love at once.

Let not these words fall to the ground unheeded! We are in danger in this city, and in every neighborhood of it, of becoming so embittered against each other, that neither friendship, nor the ties of kindred, nor domestic love, will endure the test. "A man shall be set against his father, and the daughter against her mother, and the daughter-in-law against her mother-in-law; and a man's foes shall be they of his own household." Let us do what we can to prevent this. Let not the happiness of our homes be destroyed.

Finally, and including all, we have duties as Christians. War is not a Christian work, and the time will come for its abolition, as for that of all other social wrongs and evils. But it has not come yet, and under an existing state of war our Christian duties remain not less than in time of peace. John the Baptist gave rules of conduct to the soldiers who came to him, and the Saviour, and his apostles after him, received the Roman Centurions among their disciples. I hold it to be a Christian duty to defend our country from invasion and rebellion, peaceably if we can, forcibly if we must. Otherwise society would be completely in the hands of the wicked, and social progress would be impossible. There is also a difference in the conduct of warfare, and we may make it a war of barbarism, or of comparative humanity and civilization. There is danger, particularly in this State, where such personal, vindictive feelings have been aroused, that all humanity will be forgotten and savage warfare take its place. Let us do our part to keep Christian principles alive. Remember that among our opponents, for every one designing and scheming man, there are many sincere and many hundred deceived and mistaken. Do not forget that we are fighting against our countrymen, and we shall then stand ready for the first moment of fair and just settlement which may come. It is one thing to be decided, energetic, resolute; quite another to be vindictive, overbearing, blood-thirsty. There are no circumstances in life, under which a Christian may not do his whole duty. Our duty as patriots and our duty as Christians must be done, if at all, at one and the same time. "Render therefore unto Cæsar the things that are Cæsar's, and unto God the things that are God's." The seeming conflict of duties will end in the noblest service that can be rendered by man.

INCENTIVES TO PRAYER AND HOPE.

A Discourse, delivered in the First Baptist Church, before the Baptist Churches of the City of New York, on the occasion of the National Fast, Sept. 26, 1861,

BY HENRY G. WESTON.

"The Lord our God be with us, as He was with our fathers: let Him not leave us nor forsake us."—1 Kings viii. 57.

WE can ask nothing more for our country than is included in this petition. Under God's watchful care and blessing, our history has been marked by signal deliverances in the day of trouble, by exemption from ills which have been the burden of other nations, by prosperity, not only unexampled, but rich in all respects beyond the wildest dream of our fathers, by a national life vigorous, by national liberty complete, by homes peaceful, and altars secure. The warmest patriotism could desire nothing more than that God should be with us as he was with our fathers. And as we can ask nothing more, so we can ask nothing less. Our text is our prayer to-day.

But does God approve this prayer? Is it one which He would have us offer,—one which we cannot without sin fail to offer? We do not come here to-day with a heathen trust in the inherent efficacy of praying, nor with Pharisaic reliance on our righteousness, as a ground of acceptance; our hope is not in fastings and ceremonies, nor in the strength of our desires; we know that "if we ask any thing according to His will, He heareth us." Is the object of our petition, then, so in accordance with God's declared will, that if in other respects we conform to the conditions of effectual prayer, we may expect a favorable answer? The question concerns not our prayers only, for if we are under obligation to pray, we are under equal obligation to make every necessary exertion and sacrifice in accordance with our prayers.

I invite your attention, then, to some considerations which at once make it our duty to offer the prayer in our text, and give us a hope that God will hear us.

1. We pray to-day for the country which God has given us. True patriotism is a sentiment implanted and matured by the Divine Hand. It is not founded on reasoning, nor on the calculations of interest, but it is an original principle of our nature. Some of the early Christians, among whom was Tertullian, misled partly by the arrogant and supercilious character of heathen patriotism, and partly by a wrong idea of the human heart, believed and taught that special love for one's country is inconsistent with that expansive benevolence which should grasp the world. Self-styled philanthropists of later date, and with less excuse, have thought it a mark of large manhood to profess indifference to all divisions of the human race, and have taken as their motto:— "My country is the world, my countrymen are all mankind." The same spirit has fancied that human affections are inconsistent with perfection, and has bid the seeker after spiritual excellence forget all ties of home and kindred. But we know how false and ruinous this philosophy is; we know that he only can love God aright, who loves with special love the mother who bore him, and the whole circle of those to whom God has bound him by peculiar ties. And he only can love the world aright, who loves his own country above all others. True patriotism knows nothing of that heathen spirit, which called all other peoples barbarians; it is not the offspring of vanity or self-conceit; it is not a belief in our country's superiority over all other nations, any more than the warmest filial or parental love implies a belief that our parents or children are more nobly endowed of heaven than others. The most devoted patriot will admire what God has done for other lands, and earnestly desire that his own country may imitate that which is excellent in other nations.

I have said that this affection is implanted

by God as one of the original properties of our constitution, and it is worthy of its position and its author. Peculiarly unselfish, it has always been most deeply felt by the greatest hearts. Next to love to God, it is as noble a feeling as man can know; no other has been so productive of great and heroic deeds, no other so gives strength to the national life, no other so enables a people to maintain a place in the family of nations. Blot it out, bring it down within mean and narrow limits, where it cannot live for want of a nation to be its object—a nation, with a nation's traditions, a nation's successes, a nation's power, and a nation's prospects, and you blast the best hopes which history has inspired, you destroy the noblest possibilities of the race, you dwarf human sympathies, you do the world an unspeakable wrong.

The instinctive veneration of mankind, attests the divine origin of this sentiment. The heart of the schoolboy is stirred by nothing else so much as by the tale of patriot daring and sacrifice; no other words are so welcome to his lips; no other so burn there as the words of patriot heroes; and the greatest hearts and intellects reverence the patriot with a veneration which they deny to every other human being. "Sir," wrote Lord Erskine to Washington, "I have taken the liberty to introduce your august and immortal name in a short sentence which will be found in a book which I send you. I have a large acquaintance among the most valuable and exalted classes of men, but you are the only being for whom I ever felt an awful reverence."

Still further evidence of the place which patriotism holds in God's regard, you may find in the history of His own peculiar people—the Jews. At what pains was this feeling fostered among them. They came out of Egypt banded together by a common suffering and a common deliverance. By their long sojourn in the wilderness, separated from other people, they became homogeneous. Obliged to fight for every foot of their promised land, it became dearer to them, than could be any of which they had taken peaceful possession, which had not been won by common bravery and by common toil. The result of all this training you hear in the inspired wail of the captive in Babylon, "If I forget thee, O Jerusalem, let my right hand forget her cunning. If I do not remember thee, let my tongue cleave to the roof of my mouth, if I prefer not Jerusalem above my chief joy."

If ever a people were called to be patriots, we are that people, called to be so, not more by our glorious memories and promising future, than by the fact that our national edifice is of God. No cunning art or device of man prepared or brought together the stones which constituted its foundations and walls. Said Washington, in his address to Congress in 1789, "No people can be bound to acknowledge and adore the invisible hand which conducts the affairs of men, more than the people of the United States. Every step by which they have advanced to the character of an independent nation, seems to have been distinguished by some tone of providential agency;" and our whole history is an illustration, to use the words of our philosophic historian, of "that mysterious connection of events by which Divine Providence leads to events that human councils had not conceived."

For such a country ought we not to pray? If we should hold our peace while it is in danger of being broken to fragments, would not the very stones cry out: This building of God was the habitation of our fathers, who left it a legacy to their children's children, a holy trust; and shall we look on unaffected, when ruthless hands are raised to despoil it of its fair proportions? How mean and creeping shall we be if any low interest, if any shrinking from sacrifices stifles the cry of patriotism within us, when this edifice of God is rudely assailed, when men mock at its danger, and are ready to scoff at its ruin! The first nation in the world's history, whose foundations were laid by Christian people amid the singing of psalms, and the reading of God's word, and the voice of prayer, is our own; and now, when Samsons, in their blind fury, are striving to grasp the pillars, that they may whelm us in a common ruin, if there is a place on earth to which the lover of his country ought to flee, it is to the altar of God, where he may preface and embolden his petitions with the sacred argument, "We have heard with our ears, O God, our fathers have told us, what work Thou didst in their days, in the times of old."

And our whole country demands our affection. Our body politic is one. By God's providence, by common interests, by the bones, and muscles, and arteries of our national formation, God has made us one. We are not a fortuitous and shapeless mass, capable of dismemberment without injury, but a man-child of God's own making, and when with more than a mother's feeling we cry against this unhappy severance, will not He who is greater than Solomon hear us? If we do not cry, shall we not merit His indignation at once for our impiety and our inhumanity?

2. Our prayers are offered to-day for the preservation of the government God has given us. Governments are ordained of God. Whatever of abstract and philosophic truth there may be in the statement that "all governments derive their just powers from the consent of the governed," the Bible gives no countenance to any interpretation of it which makes government a mere human compact, an invention of necessity, a choice of ills, a refuge from anarchy, an expedient to gain certain benefits, or a common stock of delegated power. Government is God's ordinance founded in man's nature, designed to accomplish certain great ends not only for this world but for the world to come. We can conceive of a constitution like that perhaps under which the angels exist, where God would deal directly with His creatures without any intervention. It has pleased Him to make this world on a different plan, and to accomplish His purposes first through His Son, and then through various human agencies. In accordance with this, He has committed authority over men to various classes ;—in the family to parents, in the State to rulers. The end of this authority is not merely the temporal welfare of those under subjection, but their discipline and instruction, the revelation to them of great truths of God's character, and in various ways their preparation for the service of God here and hereafter. Sometimes the corrective and punitive may be mingled with other ends, and in all probability results are attained which are now not even suspected. If government holds this important part in God's plan, and accomplishes such vast purposes, and is ordained both by positive command and by Divine Providence, it then follows that even if it were possible for society to exist without it, the attempt to abjure and overthrow it, would be rebellion against God. The godless theories which make government a human device, dependent upon human sufferance, which give rulers no higher authority than the popular voice, which make obedience a matter of mere choice, are bearing their bitter fruit to-day, and if this war brings to us no other good than to scatter them forever, it will be worth all it costs. Fit levers are they with which to attempt to destroy our honored political institutions. Few things are more necessary for us as a nation than to have it burned down into the very hearts of both rulers* and ruled that government is God's ordinance, that rulers are God's ministers, that they rule by God's authority, and must give an account of their trust not only to the people, but to Him who appointed their office and placed them; and that, in yielding to them reverence and submission, we are bowing to God's commandment in it. If our Government is to live, it must have this moral restraint and this moral power; it must plant itself upon our moral instincts and be able to summon our moral nature to its support. Otherwise it will go to pieces in the first storm; it will have no strength to resist disaster, it cannot give confidence to the good, it cannot overawe the wicked, it cannot thrust its hand down to the roots of our hearts; it must perish, as all things must perish that have no higher origin than man's contrivance.

It follows necessarily that when I say governments are ordained of God, I do not mean merely government in the abstract. I mean that established governments are, in such sense, ordinances of God, that obedience is due to them as a religious duty. A permanent government is not the work of man, nor of a mo-

* " We are all born in subjection, all born equally, high and low, governors and governed, in subjection to one great, immutable, persistent law, prior to all our devices, and prior to all our contrivances, paramount to all our ideas, and all our sanctions, antecedent to our very existence, by which we are knit and connected in the eternal frame of the universe, out of which we cannot stir.

"This great law does not arise from our conventions and compacts: on the contrary, it gives to our conventions and compacts all the force and sanction they can have ;—it does not arise from our vain institutions. Every good gift is of God ;—and He who has given the power, and from whom alone it originates, will never suffer the exercise of it to be practised upon any less solid foundation than the power itself. If, then, all dominion of man over man is the effect of the divine disposition, it is bound by the eternal laws of Him that gave it, with which no human authority can dispense, neither he that exercises it, nor even those who are subject to it. And if they were mad enough to make an express compact that should release their magistrate from his duty, and should declare their lives, liberties, and properties dependent upon, not rulers and laws, but his mere capricious will, that covenant would be void."—BURKE's *Speech on the Impeachment of Hastings.*

ment. I marvel that sensible men repeat the story that our Government owes "its form and pressure" to the fact that Jefferson was accustomed to attend the monthly meetings of a little Baptist church in his neighborhood, and, pleased with its democratic constitution, made it the model for our Republic. Governments are not so made. They do not spring from the brain of any one man, they are brought into being and moulded by numberless influences, a government and a people being mutually prepared for each other, under the silent and constant direction of God, who does not leave to human caprice a matter of such importance to the human race. Jefferson himself said, "The Revolution received its first impulse not from the actors in that event, but from the first colonists;" and with equal truth he might have gone farther back and said, that our Government is our inheritance from our Saxon and Norsemen fathers. Our political institutions belong to the Gothic races; driven from the land of their birth, they went with our fathers into England, were at Hastings and Runnymede and Marston Moor, were ingrained into the very nature of the Pilgrims, and started by necessity into full life in this country; and now "the old customs brought from the woods of Germany and incorporated into the English common law, are administered by every justice of the peace from Maine to Georgia."

How can government be an ordinance of God, if no particular government is in any sense a divine institution? I could as soon understand that God ordained the family institution, but gave to no child any particular parent, as that he ordained government and gave it divine sanction, but has given to no people any government which may claim obedience by virtue of God's ordinance. This is folly; the Bible and philosophy both teach that when God provides a government for a people, it is His government, and woe to those who undertake to destroy it. That an individual may lawfully withdraw from any country and government, and put himself under allegiance to another, does not affect my argument. I am speaking of the relations of a people and their government, and I say that to destroy or to attempt to destroy an established government, is a crime against the majesty of heaven, one which all nations have agreed in regarding as the highest possible offence, and meriting the severest punishment known to the laws. What can be clearer or more explicit than the declaration of God's word: "The powers that be are ordained of God. Whosoever, therefore, resisteth the power, resisteth the ordinance of God, and they that resist shall receive to themselves damnation. For rulers are not a terror to good works, but to the evil. For he is a minister of God, a revenger to execute wrath upon him that doeth evil. Wherefore ye must needs be subject, not only for wrath, but for conscience sake. For, for this cause, pay ye tribute also: for they are God's ministers, attending continually to this very thing."*

What a commentary upon the doctrine of this passage does history furnish! How clearly has Providence been in favor of existing governments. Could we read the record of all the secret plots, and conspiracies, and machinations for their overthrow, the evidence would be overwhelming that a Being more than human watches over these institutions. Mercifully is this ordered! What horror has the world thereby escaped! What endless insecurity would have been, what destruction of life and property, what waste of the best productions of human labor and genius, had God's providence been otherwise! How few have been the successful attempts radically and suddenly to change any established governments, and how wretched have been the lives, and deaths, and memories of plotters, and traitors, and rebels.† Government being thus an ordinance

---

* Rom. xiii. 1–6.
† Some may shrink from this doctrine, for fear that they can never in any case justify rebellion, or refuse to obey a law which requires them to do wrong, or endeavor to have any unrighteous law modified or repealed. Some may think also that by this reasoning all rulers are made righteous, and the manner in which they gain office has God's approval. We shall all agree that parental authority is not derived from children, but from God; that it is enforced by most solemn sanctions. Cases may arise in which a child is justified in refusing to recognize parental authority; but these exceptional cases do not weaken the statement that parental authority is from God. There are few of God's commands which may not in some conceivable case be disregarded; but he is a sorry Christian who says the extreme case shows that we are not to declare that God's commandments must be obeyed on pain of His displeasure. A child may bow with implicit obedience to a parent, and yet seek to have some command changed or withdrawn. A ruler may be harsh and oppressive, may have become a ruler by unrighteous means, and a parent may be cruel and tyrannical, but in neither case does this destroy the fact that the relation is one of divine origin, and one which has divine sanction; who can tell what results may flow from the very evils of the ruler, or for what wise reason, having its

of God, when my brother man leaves wife, children, home, to fight for the maintenance of the Government, he does not leave an institution of God to fight for a mere human device; he goes forth to do battle for God, and as a minister of God I may urge him to go, may bless him as he goes, and bid him God speed in his work. "I will give," said a wealthy manufacturer, "I will give my last dollar, my last child, myself, if necessary, to prevent the overthrow of this Government." Every heart cries Amen; he speaks as a man should speak. The obligation to uphold our Government, other things being equal, is paramount to any duty we owe to an individual, so that if need be we must forsake father, and mother, and wife, and children, yea and our own life also, for its sake. Of what worth would any of these be if we had no government, or none more stable than the summer breeze?

The sin of those who have rebelled against the Government of the United States, is aggravated by the fact that God has made it blossom with blessings. Who, of all the millions under its care, ever had cause to say aught against it? It has surrounded us at home with its invisible protection, keeping watch with sleepless vigilance over our persons and property, making the walls of our habitation a sure protection, and so laying its hand upon every thing about us that we have slept securely with only the frailest defences. Under the protection of its flag our sons and our brothers have been safe in every port and upon every ocean, and whether sailor, or merchant, or traveller, have all felt alike secure. The shield of our country has been a surer defence than that of Rome, and the boast, "I am an American citizen," has been of more worth than the like claim of a Roman in Rome's palmiest days. If any of us should become poor and friendless, we have the assurance of food, shelter, clothing, needful attendance, and, if we die, a place of burial and rites of sepulture. Our children will be educated, and the gates which lead to the highest places of honor will be open to them. They will be welcomed to the highest post they can win and sustain. All heights are accessible to all, and never did a land promise brighter laurels to the scholar, the inventor, the artisan, and the statesman.

And with all this, while its hand for us has been strong as a giant's, it has been *upon* us gentle as the lightest touch of an infant. Who ever writhed in its grasp, who ever suffered under any burden which it laid upon him? We have had no knowledge of our Government but by its blessings. Nor have they, who with frantic hands have striven to break up its foundations, who addressed themselves with flippant jest to their unholy work, who laughed to see our flagstaff shake, and riddled our banner with balls. Without the shadow of an excuse did they commence and prosecute this unholy work. No voice of an oppressed people, no injuries inflicted too grievous to be borne, summoned them to this task. In a time of profound peace and prosperity when their country had intrusted to them the highest places of power, with oaths of fidelity to the Government fresh on their lips, they entered on their nefarious scheme. Painful as is the fact, and astounding as it is to a correct moral sense, it is nevertheless a fact that the great majority of those foremost in this rebellion have solemnly lifted their right hands to heaven, and called God to witness that they would be faithful to the Constitution of the United States. We know not which to wonder at more, such forgetfulness of God, or such cruelty to man, thus at once to strike at God's institution and bring upon the nation all that it must suffer from this mad attempt to destroy our Government.

We are told that when President Lincoln's first proclamation calling for troops reached Montgomery, the news was received by the Convention then in session with bursts of laughter. It was in fitting accordance with the unprecedented character of every feature in this unnatural and most wicked rebellion, that men who were heedless of the obligations

---

roots in the past, he is appointed. The obedience to government required in the Scriptures is, to use the language of Dr. Pusey, "obedience upon principle, not only when it costs nothing, (as obedience to it ordinarily does, and so can hardly be called the fulfilment of a duty,) but when it costs something."

When it is said that an existing government is an ordinance of God, it is not implied that the means by which the government was established, or the acts of those administering it, have the approval of heaven. Marriage is God's ordinance, but God does not approve of the fraud, or covetousness, or unholy means, by which marriages are often brought about; nor because of such unrighteousness proceeding, may those who have been lawfully united refuse to recognize their obligations to each other; the relation once existing, the duties arising rest upon no less foundation than God's commandment.

of their most sacred oaths, should open their Convention with "fervent prayer," and should hail with such heartless merriment the coming horrors of civil war. If there is on any page of history a parallel to such frivolity, I know not where to look for it.

3. In this contest in which we are engaged, the moral is arrayed against the material.

Every age has its own temptations. The chief one of our time is materialism. Germany shows this in its dead pantheism. Great Britain* shows it by its brutal secularism, so be-

---

* Says the London *Economist* :—" We sympathize with the South, (so far as we sympathize with it at all,) not because we are slaves to our necessity for cotton, or because we fear that emancipation would ultimately cut off the supply,—but, because we think that, politically, the Southern States had a right to leave the Federation without hindrance and without coercion; because their behavior has been more decent and courteous than that of their antagonists; *and because they were desirous to admit our goods at 10 per cent. duty, while their enemies imposed 40 per cent.*"

* * * * * * *

"We admit that we do regard the disruption of the Union as a matter rather of rejoicing than for regret; and we maintain that we do this without laying ourselves open to the just imputation of any mean, narrow, and ungenerous feeling. We avow the sentiment; and we are prepared to justify it as at once natural, statesmanlike, and righteous. * * The great Republic of the West had grown in population, in prosperity, and in power at a rate and in a way which was not well either for her neighbors or herself. * * A boundless territory, an exhaustless soil, a commerce almost unequalled, mineral wealth quite unfathomed and apparently unlimited, a people rapidly increasing in numbers, and endowed with most of those qualities which ensure empire and predominance to their possessors—had fairly, and not unnaturally, turned the heads of the whole nation. * * They were so rough, so encroaching, so overbearing, that all other Governments felt as if some new associate, untrained to the amenities of civilized life, and insensible alike to the demands of justice and courtesy, had forced its way into the areopagus of nations :—yet at the same time they were so reckless and indisputably powerful, that nearly every one was disposed to bear with them, and defer to them, rather than to oppose a democracy so ready to quarrel and so capable of combat."

If this was the spirit of a single newspaper, however influential, it would be unfair to present it as exhibiting the feelings of England. But when the *Times*, the *Post*, the *Globe*, and even the scholarly columns of the *Saturday Review*, are filled with articles of a similar character, there is nothing left for us but to hope for the speedy fulfilment of the days in which this Nebuchadnezzar is doomed to eat grass as oxen.

It is not within the range of human possibilities—it never was—that a great and vigorous nation could be disrupted without passing through such appalling calamities, such strife, such sacrifice, such suffering, as might make angels weep; and when England avows that she rejoices at the prospect of the disruption of this nation,—one which she does not pretend has ever injured her,—a nation nearer to her than any other in race, language, and religion, she manifests so unscrupulous a selfishness that we should be

---

numbing the sensibilities that the nation can look on us now only with the cold eye of mammon, without one manly sympathy, without the capability apparently of mastering the idea of a nation fighting for national existence. We show it by our false philosophies, feeble dilutions of an imported pantheism. Nature is made supreme, but it is nature without the spiritual character which ancient heathenism gave her, it is nature, dead. The preacher echoes this philosophy from the pulpit, reasoning from matter to spirit, as if matter were more real than spirit; from knowledge to faith, as if knowledge were sure and faith uncertain; from the seen to the unseen, as though God's truth depended on our shallow reasonings from so trembling a basis. Shall we never learn that spirit is before matter, greater than matter, more certain than matter?—for God is a spirit. Can we forget that with every human being, however it may be in the teachings of a false philosophy, faith comes before knowledge, and that it is only by faith that knowledge is ever acquired?

But specially are our tendencies shown by the prize which absorbs attention to the exclusion of almost all else,—the accumulation of wealth,—by our pride in the means which are furnished in this country for amassing riches, by the deference which we pay to men of wealth, however mean they are, and by the standard to which every thing is brought. Prosperity with us means little unless it be material prosperity. Nothing is valuable which does not contribute to this end. Science, and art, and literature are of no worth, except as they can be coined into gold, and basest of all, we judge *men* by this ignoble standard; we apply to a man—a free man—a man, made in the image of God,—a man of godlike capabil-

amazed, did we not wonder more at the shameless insensibility with which she parades her selfishness before the world, and still more at that unaccountable stupidity which leads her continually to tell us that we have become by our greatness a terror to her, and that in her fear of what we may do, she is overjoyed at the probability of the downfall of our nation. But suppose no disruption takes place,— suppose we come out of this struggle a nation not only, but a nation flushed with the success of quelling this gigantic rebellion, with military tastes, with military habits, with military experience, with vast armies and ample equipments, with our pursuits all adjusted to war—how wise and far-seeing will then appear the policy of Britain in at once arousing a feeling of bitter and intense hostility to her, and informing us of the fear in which she stands of us as a dreaded and powerful rival.

ities—we apply to him the language we apply to a horse or a house, and ask, How much is he worth? always rating his worth by his money.

Here is the terrible temptation of our times. With constantly increasing rapidity have we been drifting down towards the Dead Sea of materialism. Its deadly vapors have stripped man in our eyes of almost all value except that of a money-maker, we have become unable to see the glorious world around us only through the turbid atmosphere of a low and contracted utility, and now the noxious blast is opening the seams of our good old noble ship of State, and having shorn us of almost all else, men would now persuade us that the State has no higher character than that of a money partnership. Oh! leave us the State, let us have this as God made it; leave us something on this earth, which shall be an object of reverence and a source of inspiration; leave us the State with its own distinctive life, animated by the spirit God gave it, the embodiment of principle, doing its work among the nations, adding its part to the common heritage of the world; let not the State forget to drink of the "primal springs of empire," and sink into a commercial house, to scramble for wealth, and to fatten, and to rot.

For the first time in the history of the world an attempt is made to found a nation on this principle. Commercial conventions are called to prepare for its birth by a display of commercial statistics; the disruption of the Republic and the formation of a Confederacy are urged on the alone ground of profit; the institutions of the nation are defended by the argument of profit; its hopes of existence rest upon the belief that material considerations are omnipotent among Christian nations; that cabinets and people will not hesitate to forget every profession, every principle, every habit, which comes in competition with material prosperity; on their banner they have but one motto, COTTON IS KING. Oh! mean and degrading idolatry! Sad evidence of the peril of our time, that a people can unblushingly fling such a banner to the breeze, can extol the omnipotence of such an idol, can proclaim his protection sufficient, and threaten all who will not worship him with his vengeance.

Can a nation come into being on so base a call as this? Can it live with no higher spring of empire? Can it draw strength from the remembrance of its origin, and give character to a people on such a foundation? Have we come to the time when God's word may be reversed by this false god, when man may live by bread alone? Let who may try this experiment, God forbid we should. Men there have been here at the North, I blush to acknowledge it, who have calculated the pecuniary value of our Union, and have said, "Let the South go, our gains will be greater without them;" and with an effrontery greater than that of the woman before Solomon, have shouted, "Let the sword fall; divide the child; I can make more money out of the portion of the quivering carcass that falleth to me, than out of the living babe;" but I thank God, those arguments have found no echo in the Northern heart, and I think that those who have used them must have blushed for their ignoble thoughts.

Why, sirs, if we tamely give up in this contest, if the state of which we form a component part and which shapes our character and that of our children is to bear no spiritual character, if it is to lay hold of no unseen springs in our nature, if it is to have no great organic life, if upon its bosom we can never be folded, feeling the quickening pulsations of its great heart, if it is to be nothing but a factory or a plantation, and we all are to be mere money gatherers, worshipping our muck-rates, let us lie down and die, for we are meaner than the brutes.

But our opponents boast of this difference between themselves and us, and build great hopes upon it: "You," say they, "are fighting for a sentiment, "and will soon tire of the contest." And across the waters, there comes the expostulation:—"Oh men of the North, gather not armies in such a cause: treasure and blood are too precious to be spilt, when you can be rich and prosperous without the South." It is our boast that we are fighting for a sentiment. The armies whose thunder-tread now shakes this continent are not gathering from material considerations. We have forgotten all these. They come to answer the question, SHALL THIS NATION LIVE?—the grandest question ever submitted to a people's decision. When the roll of the nations is called, shall one name dear to us, dear to the hoping hearts of thousands in other lands, be omitted? Shall this nation in its manly strength, and with its intense vitality, die, because the fingers of perjury and treason have clutched at its throat? Shall this nation with all that it is, and all that it may be to us and to our children, with its high trusts and responsibilities, sluggishly sink with the garnered hopes of the world into its grave without a hand being raised in its behalf? Shall there be on this continent a free Christian nation with a heart and a conscience able to deal with the great matters of its duty and destiny? In one word, we gather our armies to strike for God, for ourselves, for our children, for the world, for a government of the people, for liberty and for law.

Is there power in this sentiment to nerve us for labor and sacrifice? Let that uprising of our people, unparalleled on the pages of history, answer; let our vast armies, hastening with eager emulation to the scene of strife, answer; let our merchants, pouring out their gold as freely as water, answer; let our political parties, forgetting the strifes and predilection of years, and mingling in one common onset against the foe, answer; let our Christian people, gathering to observe this day as no such day was ever before observed in America, answer; let every age, and sex, and condition, let city and hamlet, let mountain and valley answer; there is but one voice, and that comes from depths never before stirred in the history of this nation. Thank God for the unseen! Thank God that we have not been so debauched by years of prosperity that nothing but the material can move us. Thank God that the great heart of the nation beats to a mightier measure than mere mammon-worshippers would have it. The cry of our national sentiment has power to move the nation, and before that mighty uprising we bow with reverence and gratitude. But I anticipate my last remark.

4. The present dealings of God with us give hopefulness to our prayers.

This war shows that God has not left us. He is chastising us, but the very chastisement gives us hope that He has not left us to perish. We are a sinful nation. To-day God is bringing our sins to remembrance, and alas for us, if we do not humble ourselves and repent of them and seek forgiveness.

But may we not err by restricting God's present providences within too narrow limits, and by giving too exclusively a punitive character to His dealings? It is one thing clearly to apprehend our condition and duty as sinners; it is another to fathom the reasons and designs of God's doings. Is there not a style of speech among us which not only points out our sins, but names the very iniquities for which God has sent this war upon us, and makes punishment the exclusive end of God's dealing. The oldest book in God's word should teach us caution on this subject. In no ordinary case have we any right to stand by a sufferer and say God is punishing him for this or for that sin. In no ordinary case are we justified in saying to a bereaved family, For such and such sins, God has taken away your father or your mother. What right has another nation to point the finger at us and say, See, God could no longer forbear, and so He has come out to punish that nation for its Sabbath breaking, its godlessness, its arrogance, its slavery. Which of all the nations of the earth can say this?

Ah! if God were done with us,—if this were the last of us and of the world, then I would be willing to hear only the word, punishment; but while we humble ourselves under God's mighty hand, let us see to it that we adopt no view which makes us sink under that hand, which weakens our hope in God, or our trust for the future. Joseph may be taken away by cruel hands, but before you stand by the side of the poor old father, and lacerate his heart with the cry, Behold the fruit of your parental partiality, God has justly punished you by Joseph's death for your sinful indulgence; be sure that your gaze reaches into Egypt, and that you recognize that ruler of all Egypt with his father and his brethren around him; nay, be sure you look down coming years far enough to discern that triumphant host on the banks of the Red Sea and that your ear catches that glorious song that comes rolling over the waters.

The idea that "the greater the suffering in this life, the greater the sinner," will not do for those who honor the word or study the providence of God. This life is not man's period of retribution, and suffering here is frequently monitory, disciplinary.

It is said that nations, as such, will not be judged hereafter, but must be judged and punished here. I doubt the soundness of this argument. Nations are made up of individuals, and individuals will be judged hereafter, in view of all their conduct, whether as rulers or subjects. No relations of life will be overlooked. The final judgment will comprehend every sphere of moral action and weigh the conduct of every man in every station. Personal, domestic, social, and civil duties will all be considered. Governors will be judged as such, and so, virtually, governments. If nations, as such, will not be judged hereafter, neither will families, nor towns, nor corporations, nor societies of any kind. History forbids us to say that all these now prosper or suffer in proportion to their moral worth. Besides, a great part of human action is in and by these organizations, and if their sins are punished here, retribution is pretty effectually accomplished in this world.

Extraordinary national calamities do not prove extraordinary national sins. Were the aborigines of this country sinners above all other men that they should so rapidly perish? Were the Poles? The Negroes? What enormous crimes have they perpetrated as a people, that they should be singled out for special judgments?

National calamities may have a prospective bearing; they may be wholesome discipline to correct evils not yet incurable, or to develope virtues needing a hard soil for their growth. Some of these evils and virtues may perhaps be discerned by an honest observer. But the value of providential discipline does not always depend on a clear perception of its designs. When a nation has in it no considerable body of Christians, and no peculiarities specially needed for the race, God often destroys it. When a people hold a part of the earth which can be better occupied by another people, God often destroys or removes it. When a nation has virtue and power enough to be improved and made useful to the world, as useful as any other which would take its place, it is chastened, disciplined, spared. Sometimes the best people will profit most by severe trial; if so it will be sent upon them in due time. And while it is not always rash to inquire after the particular sins or evils which are the reasons for God's judgments or disciplinary inflictions, it seems to me very difficult in most cases to determine the exact or special sins for which God visits a people with the rod. Perhaps the ultimate bearing of the discipline, as determined by the light of history, may sometimes point out those sins.

It becomes us on these great subjects, while distinctly recognizing the fact that all suffering is a consequence of sin, to take such views of God's dealings as are worthy of Him and becoming our own ignorance; such views as will not by their manifest impropriety, weaken our hold upon the public conscience; such views as would constitute a proper basis for an appeal to repentance addressed to an individual as well as to a nation; such views as commend themselves to our own hearts and consciences. Let us refrain from any language which implies that our national sinfulness is no deeper than these outward and manifest transgressions that are so readily designated.

By the exclusive presentation of the punitive character of our present condition, there is danger that the public mind will be impressed with the idea that war is necessarily a token of God's displeasure, and peace as necessarily an evidence of His approbation. Our effeminate philosophies and religions had so debauched us that we were fast becoming incapable of appreciating the sterner and more rugged virtues; we were losing the power of feeling indignation against iniquity; the sharp ring of some of the Psalms made us languidly wonder whether they ought to be in the Bible; we could discern no blessing save in the hot glare of prosperity, baking us hard and dry. I know that war has its evils—its terrible evils, but peace has its evils also, evils that do not so start out before us in their ghastliness, but are on that very account the more to be dreaded; evils that "vex less and mortify more, that suck the blood, though they do not shed it, and ossify the heart, though they do not torture it." Was our Revolutionary war a token of God's displeasure? For how many years of soft prosperity would you exchange its record? For how much money would you sell its memories, its inspirations, its influences? For how many years of thrift would you give up Bunker Hill, Yorktown, Lexington, Saratoga? For how many merchant princes the names of Washington, and Hancock, and Adams?

What has this war already done for us—awakening patriotism, quelling party spirit, binding men together, stirring up the better feelings of our nature, proving that we are men and not mere imitations with sordid and cowardly hearts, that there is something dearer to us than silver and gold. Who has not, since that memorable uprising last April, walked the streets of New York with a manlier spirit and a firmer step, with more reverence for his countrymen, with more pride in his citizenship? Whose spirit has not been stirred to quick pulsations, as at morn, or at noon, or at midnight, he has unexpectedly caught sight of our flag streaming in the breeze—our flag, which had been seen all our lives long without awakening any peculiar emotion;—never beheld now without the lips whispering, "Dear old flag, God's blessing on it now and forever."

Yes, there is hope for our country now, and many a patriot heart which one year ago looked sadly forward, beats high with expectation to-day. Now is the time to hope—the time to pray—to pray with confidence. The sweetest songs of the Old Testament prophets were sung in the darkest times, and we owe the most inspiriting descriptions of coming glory, the brightest paintings on the sacred page, not to the days of Jewish splendor and outward prosperity, but to those seasons when the nation felt in every nerve God's chastening stroke.*

Yes, let us hope now, pray and hope now. God loves faith and hope in time of trial, loves those who do not faint under His chastisement, loves those who even under the rod, fly to His heart and ask for blessings. Under the dark cloud do we see God's bow, and now as never before will we pray and hope. What though calamities may yet be in store for us, what though disaster may befall our armies, we will not bate one jot of heart or hope, for this will only be evidence that God has great lessons which He intends we shall learn—lessons that cannot be taught by a sham war, lessons of such importance to us and the world, that the teacher needs time and the learner patience. We believe that the ends God has in view are too great to be secured by our soldiers dancing into Virginia, singing "I wish I was in Dixie," only to walk over a deserted field and to achieve a bloodless victory. To-day the digger amid the ruins of Nineveh brings to the light a brick on which stand out clearly the sharp outlines traced ages ago by cunning steel in the hands of the graver. Once that brick was clay, and the knife easily drew those outlines; it was put into the fire, and it came out with that hardness that to-day it bears, centuries after the fire has died out and the hand that kindled it has perished. And if as a nation we are to be any thing or to do any thing for coming ages, God's finger must not only pass over us in the soft days of prosperity, but His voice must cry "To the furnace;" and if we are God's own, that furnace will be heated in the sight of the nations seven times hotter than before, but the Son of God will be there, and when the nation has come out of those flames without the smell of fire upon it, then shall God be exalted as never before.

And so to-day, my hearers, we pray with humble but joyous confidence, because God is so dealing with us. It is a privilege to live at such a time as this, to labor and pray, to hope and have faith in God and in His love for our country now. So far as my country is concerned, I would rather live now than at any previous period of her history—never more need we envy those who bore their part in earlier scenes of toil and daring. Girding ourselves up with the memories of the past and with the hopes of the future, let us with Christian manliness give ourselves to our work, to whatever labor or sacrifice God may demand of us, rejoicing that we are "come to the kingdom for such a time as this."

* "It is in periods of apparent disaster, during the sufferings of whole generations, that the greatest improvements on human character have been effected, and a foundation laid for those changes which ultimately prove most beneficial to the species. The wars of the Heptarchy, the Norman Conquest, the Contest of the Roses, the Great Rebellion, are apparently the most disastrous periods of our annals; those in which civil discord was most furious, and the public suffering most universal. Yet these are precisely the periods in which its peculiar temper was given to the English character, and the greatest addition made to the causes of English prosperity; in which courage arose out of the extremity of misfortune, national union out of oppression, public emancipation out of aristocratic dissension, general freedom out of regal ambition. The national character which we now possess, the public benefits we now enjoy, the freedom by which we have been distinguished, the energy by which we are sustained, are, in a great measure, owing to the renovating storms which have in former ages passed over our country."—*Alison.*

THANKSGIVING SERMON,

Preached in Christ's Church, New Orleans, on Thanksgiving Day.

BY REV. DR. W. T. LEACOCK.

A DAY of Thanksgiving—one day of every year set apart for the expression of a nation's thanks to the God and Father of our spirits, grows out of the nature of God's blessings to men. Some of his blessings are individual blessings, and for them individuals should be thankful every day. Others are national blessings, and for them the nation should, at one and the same time, lift up its heart and voice to God in praise. That time is this—we of this State are, on this day, called upon to bless God for all his benefits.

But even our individual blessings require a fixed period of time for praise, because they are not understood or felt to be blessings at the time they are given. God's dispensations are not always self-evident mercies. We know they are mercies. For God has nothing now but mercies for his creatures—his very chastisements are mercies—mercies in disguise—but they are not understood by our hearts at first, and therefore they seem hard; and, seeming hard, the language of our hearts is the language of rebellion, not of praise. But time develops the mercy in the dispensation. What once appeared hard is now seen to be merciful in the good in which it issues, and then our hearts, penetrated by a deep sense of repentance for our rebellion, overflow with gratitude to God, and praise is extorted from our lips.

Now, this fact, the fact that the mercy is not seen in the dispensation as soon as it occurs, is a reason for one day in the course of the year to be set apart for the purpose of thanksgiving.

Every day should be a day of thanksgiving and praise, because every day is itself a blessing and brings blessings with it; but the events of every day are not understood; they require time to be developed; the dispensation which seems hard to-day, may, in the process of a few months, be felt to be a great mercy. Every touch of the artist has its value, but the value of the touch can not well be discovered till the picture is completed; and every event of God's providence has its mercy—but the mercy may not be discovered till the event is developed—and this development requires time.

Now, the Christian, and the Christian heart alone, knows every event of God's providence to be a mercy, and he is willing to praise God in advance for the mercy, knowing that if he does not see it then, he will see it soon; but every heart is not a Christian heart—every heart, though a believing heart, does not possess this faith—and, therefore, in the course of each year a day is wisely set apart for reviewing the dispensations of God in our being, that we may see the benefits they are calculated to bring, and assure our weak hearts that we are not in a fatherless world, but in a world in which nothing can occur without its use, and that use our good.

The child thinks his father's discipline hard, and the lessons which he is required to learn useless; but when that child becomes a man, he then sees that the discipline and lessons were both strong evidences of love in his parent.

And thus it is with our hearts and God. Dispensations which seem hard in January, may prove themselves in December to have been nothing but mercies to our souls, mercies, too, which deserved a lifetime of praise.

We have met, then, to-day, to open the Book of Providence and read there the events which have occurred, and in which we have had a share, during the period that has elapsed since our last similar meeting, that in solemn assembly we might lift up our hearts and voices to the Lord our God in thanksgiving and praise. Some of the events may not yet have developed themselves, but others have; and those that have should teach us that there is mercy in those that have not, only we know it not yet, and therefore that we should number them among our blessings. Let us then pause, look back, and consider.

And we shall soon take up the language of the Psalms and say: "Bless the Lord, O my soul! and forget not all his benefits; who forgiveth all thine iniquities, who healeth all thy diseases, who redeemeth thy life from destruction, who crowneth thee with loving kindness and tender mercies, who satisfyeth thy mouth with good things."

Let us take these benefits as they are enumerated. Who has not cause to praise God for the forgiveness of his iniquities? Take this forgiveness in the lowest and most limited sense—in the sense of simply averting from us the temporal consequences of our errors—who has not cause to praise God in this?

Who would not have lowered himself in the estimation of others—who would not have marred his own prospects and diminished his own happiness—if the consequences of every unadvised word and act had been visited upon him? Who has not cause to praise God for disease escaped, or for sickness healed, during the past year? Who can tell how near he has been, even in the broad blaze of noon, to that destruction from which the providence of God has rescued him? Which of us, even among those who have endured the heaviest sorrows, and shed the bitterest tears, cannot discover, on comparing what we have experienced with what we have deserved, or even with what we might have expected, will not find a large amount of loving kindnesses and of tender mercies, for which he is a debtor to God? And if the mouth be not literally satisfied with good things, how can we tell that the things which we most desired were *really good?* Who can tell that the love of the creature, which he is seeking, and with which he is yet unsatisfied, may not deceive him, as it has deceived others? Who can tell that the affluence which he had accumulated, but which has been snatched from his grasp, might not have destroyed his soul if it had been retained? Who can tell that the object of his secret aim, whatever it might have been, that was irrespective of God, and from which he now seems farther off than he was twelve months ago—that this might not have been the rock upon which, if he had struck, he might have made shipwreck at once and forever of faith and of a good conscience? All real blessings, all blessings that will bear to be tested by the result, are subjects of praise, though some may have approached us under the lowering aspect of sorrow, and others under the forbidding frown of disappointment; for who will not testify—who, at least, that knows himself and examines the past—will not testify that the most untoward events have often proved most beneficial in the result—thus adding another testimony to this glorious truth: that all things, at all times, are working together for good to them that love God.

But this is a national day, and we must speak of national as well as individual mercies; and we have them, blessed be God, we have them to lift up our hearts to God in prayer.

We have been greatly blessed as a people. We know nothing of those evils which commonly fall to the lot of nations, and, therefore, we feel not, as we should, the blessings which surround us. War, pestilence, and famine have been removed from our borders; abundance has crowned our fields; prosperity has attended our commerce; and peace has united us with the nations abroad. And should we not be thankful? But there is a rising cloud in our hemisphere—a cloud as on a summer's eve—of which we cannot tell, until it bursts, whether it will bring the desolating tempest, or the cool, refreshing shower. But there is a hand that directs the storm; and there is a hand in that very cloud, which has long forewarned us of its coming, and prepared us with a refuge. The agitation of the slavery question, once thought an evil, God has made a blessing to us.

You and I remember, when the slavery question was first mooted in our national councils, we dreaded the consequences and trembled at the bare mention of the subject, we stood aghast before our adversaries; and why? Because we were not as well-informed on the subject of slavery as we are now; many of us doubted whether we could religiously hold our servant; there was no bond of union between us and them but the bond of property, and as all property is timid, negro property, under the circumstances of our ignorance, was cowardly, and therefore the moment this property was invaded in discussion it made us cowards, and as a band of cowards we were for imploring silence from our adversaries, and thus our cowardice only gave them courage to make their attacks more frequent, and more and more severe. But the question has been sifted to its very foundation, and we now feel ourselves safe, we now feel that as Christians we can hold them, and this feeling has dissipated our cowardice and given us an advantage over our adversaries; we shun them not now, we fear them not now, we are willing to meet them not only on Constitutional grounds, but on reason, on religion, on expediency, and dare them to their face to dislodge us from our position.

But how have we been placed in this position? Have we always occupied it? No—there was a time when we saw no mercy in God's permitting the subject of slavery to be brought before the public mind for examination, but it has been examined, and we now see the mercy—mercy in having our own minds fortified—mercy in calming down the opposition of the wise and virtuous. And should we not be thankful for this mercy? Should we not on this day give thanks to God for the termination he has given to a subject which at first seemed fraught with nothing but calamity to our very souls? Surely, surely, then, the agitation once thought an evil is now discovered to have been a blessing.

But this is not all—this is not the only blessing for which we should feel thankful. While the truth-seeking, truth-loving portion of our community are convinced that our position is of a character which cannot be changed, and therefore should not be tampered with, there are others who, regarding not the truth, and following nothing but their own prejudices and interest, have invaded our rights—invaded them by deceiving an ignorant but honest portion of our countrymen to unite themselves for the support of a band of robbers and assassins to murder and to rob.

They have murdered our people—they have robbed them—they are yet robbing us—but what is the result of their combined action? This: the slaves themselves have been so deceived by them as to fear them, and are now, many of them, unwilling to trust them; and the masters, seeing the facility with which the slaves can escape, have so endeared themselves to their slaves as to make them unwilling to leave their service, which they know, for a condition which they know not. I speak of the border States, and all who live there know what I say to be true.

Now, what more alarming than to have a body of thieves let loose among us, pensioned by some, assisted by others, and encouraged by their own mistaken views of religion and philanthropy, to commit such depredations upon us? Yet what have they done? Great injury, to be sure, but great good also. And while we should deplore the evil, should we not also be thankful for the good?

But we have another cause for thankfulness. You and I thought, a few months ago, that the Abolitionists were few compared with the population of the North; and whenever we expressed any fears for our condition, we were answered—" Oh, the Abolitionists are comparatively few, and by their very numbers and insignificance utterly powerless;" we allowed ourselves to be lulled into slumber under this assurance, forgetting that we were slumbering on the very crater of a volcano. But this election has shown their force—has shown not only their numbers, but their power. They have come upon us like an avalanche, and the suddenness of their appearance and the number of their body have awakened us to action—awakened us in full time to check their destructive career. And should we not be thankful? Suppose they had not exhibited their strength as they have done; suppose they had gone on increasing, and lulling us all the while by the fancied paucity of their numbers, and then have burst upon us when the whole North had been absorbed by their views, what would have been our condition then? Nothing but inglorious submission. But what is it now? We have been roused to harmonious action by their formidable appearance at a time when yet we have friends in the North, but those friends powerless of themselves, and only waiting action on our part to take position by our side; and is not this a subject of thankfulness to be expressed on this day to our Heavenly Father? But we have yet another cause for thankfulness. When we consider the treatment we have received from the hands of our enemies: our character they have defamed; our feelings they have lacerated; our rights they have invaded; our property they have stolen; our power they have defied; our existence they have threatened; murderers and robbers have been let loose upon us, stimulated by weak, or designing, or infidel preachers, armed by fanatics, and sustained by a band of assassins, both political and civil, out of the very wealth which they have accumulated by their connection with us. Nothing has been left untried which the deepest and blackest malice could invent for our injury or destruction; we have been proscribed as unworthy members of the great American household; we have been banished from their very houses of prayer; we have been ridiculed, and taunted, and flouted as unfit for the society of men, and accursed of God. And has not all this proved a blessing to us? For what has it not done for us? It has awakened us to the truth that there can be no concert of action between our enemies and ourselves, and hastened the period of adopting such measures as are best calculated for our interest. And what shall the measures be? Shall we fold our arms ingloriously, and do nothing but beg like craven cowards that they will not disturb us? I leave this question for your own hearts to answer.

It is not for me to show what should be done. It is only for me to say what I believe to be the hand of God, in what has been done—that the recognition of that hand might add fervor to our thanksgiving and praise.

Then bless the Lord, O my soul, and forget not thou his benefits. But how shall we bless God? We should bless him not only with our lips, but in our lives, by giving ourselves up to his service, by walking before him in holiness and righteousness all our days, by doing our duty in that state of life in which it has pleased him to call us; and there is no state of life, there is no circumstance in which we may not give praise to God—(the tradesman in the conduct of his business—the artisan in the practice of his craft—the parent in the government of his household, or in the instruction of his child—the domestic in the performance of her most menial service—the beggar in receiving a Christian charity—the exhausted and suffering inmate of a hospital in the endurance of a protracted and agonizing disease—all may give themselves up to God's service)—for we do this when we act uprightly, when we labor diligently, when we rule mildly, when we obey cheerfully, when we suffer patiently, when we submit ourselves to the will of God in the afflictions and visitations of life, and are only concerned to glorify him through faith in his Son, Jesus Christ.

Now, in justice to myself, I must be permitted to make a remark before I close. But a few weeks ago, I counselled you, from this place, to avoid all precipitate action; but at the same time to take determined action—such action only as you felt you could take with the conscious support of reason and religion. I give that counsel still. But I am one of you. I feel as a Southerner. Southern honor is my honor. Southern degradation is my degradation. Let no man mistake my meaning or call my words idle. As a Southerner, then, I will speak, and I give it as my firm and unhesitating belief, that nothing is now left us but secession. I do not like the word, but it is the only one to express my meaning. We do not secede—our enemies have seceded. We are on the Constitution—our enemies are not on the Constitution; and our language should be, if you will not go with us, we will not go with you. You may form for yourselves a Constitution; but we will administer among ourselves the Constitution which our fathers have left us. This should be our language and solemn determination. Such action our honor demands; such action will save the Union, if any thing can. We have yet friends left us in the North, but they cannot act for us till we have acted for ourselves; and it would be as pusillanimous in us to desert our friends as to cower before our enemies. To advance is to secure our rights; to recede, is to lay our fortunes, our honor, our liberty, under the feet of our enemies. I know that the consequences of such a course, unless guided by discretion, are perilous. But, peril our fortunes, peril our lives, but come what may, let us never peril our liberty and our honor. I am willing, at the call of my honor and my liberty, to die a freeman; but I'll never, no, never, live a slave; and the alternative now presented by our enemies is secession or slavery. Let it be liberty or death!

OUR NATIONAL SINS.

A Sermon preached in the Presbyterian Church, Columbia, S. C., on the day of the State Fast, Nov. 21, 1860.

BY REV. J. H. THORNWELL, D.D.

And it came to pass, when King Hezekiah heard it, that he rent his clothes, and covered himself with sackcloth, and went into the house of the Lord.—*Isaiah* xxxvii. 1.

I HAVE no design, in the selection of these words, to intimate that there is a parallel between Jerusalem and our own Commonwealth in relation to the Covenant of God. I am far from believing that we alone, of all the people of the earth, are possessed of the true religion, and far from encouraging the narrow and exclusive spirit which, with the ancient hypocrites denounced by the Prophet, can complacently exclaim, The temple of the Lord, the temple of the Lord, are we. Such arrogance and bigotry are utterly inconsistent with the penitential confessions which this day has been set apart to evoke. We are here, not like the Pharisee, to boast of our own righteousness, and to thank God that we are not like other men; but we are here like the poor publican, to smite upon our breasts, and to say, God be merciful to us, sinners. My design, in the choice of these words, is to illustrate the spirit and temper with which a Christian people should deport themselves in times of public calamity and distress. Jerusalem was in great straits. The whole country had been ravaged by a proud and insolent foe. The Sacred City remained as the last hold of the State, and a large army lay encamped before its walls. Ruin seemed to be inevitable. *It was a day of trouble, and of rebuke, and of blasphemy. The children had come to the birth, and there was not strength to bring forth.* In the extremity of the danger, the sovereign betakes himself to God. Renouncing all human confidence, and all human alliances, he rent his clothes, and covered himself with sackcloth, and went into the House of the Lord.

In applying the text to our own circumstances, widely different in many respects from those of Jerusalem at the time referred to, I am oppressed with a difficulty, which you that are acquainted with my views of the nature and functions of the Christian ministry can readily understand. During the twenty-five years in which I have fulfilled my course as a preacher—all of which have been spent in my native State, and nearly all in this city—I have never introduced secular politics into the instructions of the pulpit. It has been a point of conscience with me to know no party in the State. Questions of law and public administration I have left to the tribunals appointed to settle them, and have confined my exhortations to those great matters that pertain immediately to the kingdom of God. I have left it to Cæsar to take care of his own rights, and have insisted only upon the supreme rights of the Almighty. The angry disputes of the forum I have excluded from the house of the Lord. And while all classes have been exhorted to the discharge of their common duties, as men, as citizens, as members of the family—while the sanctions of religion have, without scruple, been applied to all the relations of life, whether public or private, civil or domestic—the grounds of dissension which divide the community into parties, and range its members under different banners, have not been permitted to intrude into the sanctuary. The business of a preacher, as such, is to expound the Word of God. He has no commission to go beyond the teaching of the Scriptures. He has no authority to expound to senators the Constitution of the State, nor to interpret for judges the law of the land. In the civil and political sphere, the dead must bury their dead. It is obvious, however, that religious sanctions cannot be applied to civil and political duties without taking for granted the relations out of which these duties spring. Religion cannot exact submission to the powers that be, without implying that these powers are known and confessed. It cannot enjoin obedience to Cæsar, without taking it for granted that the authority of Cæsar is acknowledged. When the Constitution of the State is fixed and settled, the general reference to it which religion implies, in the inculcation of civil and political duties, may be made without intruding into the functions of the magistrate, or taking sides with any particular party in the Commonwealth. The relations which condition duty are admitted, and the conscience instantly recognizes the grounds on which the minister of the Gospel exhorts to fidelity. The duties belong to the department of religion; the relations out of which they spring belong to the department of political science; and must be determined apart from the Word of God. The concrete cases to which the law of God is to be applied, must always be given; the law itself is all that the preacher can enforce as of Divine authority. As the law, without the facts, however, is a shadow without substance; as the duty is unmeaning which is determined by no definite relations; the preacher cannot inculcate civil obedience, or convict of national sin, without allusions, more or less precise, to the theory and structure of the government. He avoids presumption by having it distinctly understood that the theory which he assumes is not announced as the Word of God, but is to be proved, as any other facts of history and experience. He speaks here only in his own name as a man, and promulgates a matter of opinion, and not an article of faith. If the assumptions which he makes are true, the duties which he enjoins must be accepted as Divine commands. The speculative antecedents being admitted, the practical consequents cannot be avoided. There are cases in which the question relates to a change in the government, in which the question of duty is simply a question of revolution. In such cases the minister has no commission from God to recommend or resist a change, unless some moral principle is immediately involved. He can explain and enforce the spirit and temper in which revolution should be contemplated and carried forward or abandoned. He can expound the doctrine of the Scriptures in relation to the nature, the grounds, the extent and limitations of civil obedience; but it is not for him, as a preacher, to say when evils are intolerable, nor to prescribe the mode and measure of redress. These points he must leave to the State itself. When a revolution has once been achieved, he can enforce the duties which spring from the new condition of affairs.

Thus much I have felt bound to say, as to my views of the duty of a minister in relation to matters of State. As a citizen, a man, a member of the Commonwealth, he has a right to form and express his opinions upon every subject, to whatever department it belongs, which affects the interests of his race. As a man, he is as free as any other man; but the citizen must not be confounded with the preacher, nor private opinions with the oracles of God. Entertaining these sentiments concerning the relations of the sacred office to political affairs, I am oppressed with the apprehension that, in attempting to fulfil the requisitions of the present occasion, I may transgress the limits of propriety, and merge the pulpit into the rostrum. I am anxious to avoid this error, and would, therefore, have it understood in advance, that whatever theory may be assumed of the nature and structure of our Government, is assumed upon the common grounds of historical knowledge, and is assumed mainly as fixing the points from which I would survey the sins of the country. If true—and no man has a right to reject them without being able to disprove them—my conclusions in reference to our national guilt are irrefragably established. If not true, we must either deny that we are sinners, or must seek some other relations in which to ground the consciousness of sin. If that consciousness should be thoroughly grounded, the services of this day will be not in vain. I can truly say that my great aim is not to expound our complex institutions, but to awaken the national conscience to a sense of its responsibility before God. It is not to enlighten your minds, but to touch your hearts; not to plead the cause of States' rights or Federal authority, but to bring you as penitents before the Supreme Judge. This is no common solemnity. The day has been set apart by the constituted authorities of this Commonwealth, by joint resolutions of both branches of the Legislature, and proclaimed by the Chief Magistrate of the State, as a day of fasting, humiliation, and prayer. South Carolina, therefore, as an organized political community, prostrates herself this day before God. It is a time of danger, of blasphemy, and rebuke, and, imitating the example of Hezekiah, she rends her clothes, covers herself with sackcloth, and comes into the House of the Lord. The question is, how she should demean herself under these solemn circumstances. Every minister this day becomes her organ, and he should instruct the people as to the attitude we should all assume in the presence of Jehovah. It is a day of solemn worship, in which the State appears as a penitent, and lays her case before the Judge of all the earth.

The points to which I shall direct your attention, are, first, the spirit in which we should approach God; and second, the errand on which we should go.

I. As the individual, in coming to God, must believe that He is, and that He is the rewarder of them that diligently search for Him; so the State must be impressed with a profound sense of His all-pervading providence, and of its responsibility to Him, as the moral Ruler of the world. The powers that be are ordained of Him. From Him the magistrate receives his commission, and in His fear, he must use the sword as a terror to evil doers and a praise to them that do well. Civil government is an institute of heaven, founded in the character of man as social and moral, and is designed to realize the idea of justice. Take away the notion of mutual rights and the corresponding notions of duty and obligation, and a commonwealth is no more conceivable among men than among brutes. As the State is essentially moral in its idea, it connects itself directly with the government of God. It is, indeed, the organ through which that government is administered in its relations to the highest interests of earth. A State, therefore, which does not recognize its dependence upon God, or which fails to apprehend in its functions and offices a commission from heaven, is false to the law of its own being. The moral finds its source and centre only in God. There can be no rights without responsibility, and responsibility is incomplete until it terminates in a supreme will. The earthly sanctions of the State, its rewards and punishments, are insufficient either for the punishment of vice or the encouragement of virtue, unless they connect themselves with the higher sanctions which religion discloses. If the State had to deal only with natures confessedly mortal; if its subjects were conscious of no other life than that which they bear from the cradle to the grave; if their prospect terminated at death; if they were only brutes of a more finished make, but equally destined to everlasting extinction, who does not see that the law would lose its terror, and obedience be stripped of its dignity. The moral nature of man is inseparably linked with immortality, and immortality as inseparably linked with religion. Among pagan idolaters, the instinct of immortality, though not developed into a doctrine, nor realized as a fact in reflection, is yet the secret power which, in the spontaneous workings of the soul, gives efficacy to punishment, and energy to rewards. Man feels himself immortal, and this feeling, though operating blindly, colors his hopes and his fears. The State, therefore, which should undertake to accomplish the ends of its being, without taking into account the religious element in man, palsies its own arm. Subjects that have no religion are incapable of law. Rules of prudence they may institute; measures of precaution they may adopt; a routine of coercion and constraint they may establish; but laws they cannot have. They may be governed like a lunatic asylum; but where there is no nature which responds to the sentiment of duty, there is no nature which confesses the majesty of law. Every State, therefore, must have a religion, or it must cease to be a government of men. Hence no Commonwealth has ever existed without religious sanctions. "Whether true or false, sublime or ridiculous," says the author of the Consulate and the Empire, "man must have a religion. Everywhere, in all ages, in all countries, in ancient as in modern times, in civilized as well as in barbarian nations, we find him a worshipper at some altar, be it venerable, degraded, or blood-stained."

It is not only necessary that the State should have a religion, it is equally necessary, in order to an adequate fulfilment of its own idea, that it have the true religion. Truth is the only proper food of the soul, and though superstition and error may avail for a time as external restraints, they never generate an inward principle of obedience. They serve as outward motives, but never become an inward life, and when the falsehood comes to be detected, the mind is apt to abandon itself to unrestrained licentiousness. The reaction is violent in proportion to the intensity of the previous delusion. The most formidable convulsions in States are those which have been consequent upon the detection of religious imposture. "When a religion," says McCosh, "waxes old in a country—when the circumstances which at first favored its formation or introduction have changed—when in an age of reason it is tried and found unreasonable—when in an age of learning it is discovered to be the product of the grossest ignorance—when in an age of levity it is felt to be too stern—then the infidel spirit takes courage, and, with a zeal in which there is a strange mixture of scowling revenge and light-hearted wantonness, of deep-set hatred and laughing levity, it proceeds to level all existing temples and altars, and erects no others in their room." The void which is created is soon filled with wantonness and violence. The State cannot be restored to order until it settles down upon some form of religion again. As the subjects of a State must have a religion in order to be truly obedient, and as it is the true religion alone which converts obedience into a living principle, it is obvious that a Commonwealth can no more be organized, which shall recognize all religions, than one which shall recognize none. The sanctions of its laws must have a centre of unity somewhere. To combine in the same government contradictory systems of faith, is as hopelessly impossible as to constitute into one State men of different races and languages. The Christian, the Pagan, Mohammedan, Jews, Infidels, and Turks, cannot coalesce as organic elements in one body politic. The State must take its religious type from the doctrines, the precepts, and the institutions of one or the other of these parties.

When we insist upon the religious character of the State, we are not to be understood as recommending or favoring a Church Establishment. To have a religion is one thing, to have a Church Establishment is another; and perhaps the most effectual way of extinguishing the religious life of a State is to confine the expression of it to the forms and peculiarities of a single sect.

The Church and the State, as visible institutions, are entirely distinct, and neither can usurp the province of the other without injury to both. But religion, as a life, as an inward principle, though specially developed and fostered by the Church, extends its domain beyond the sphere of technical worship, touches all the relations of man, and constitutes the inspiration of every duty. The service of the Commonwealth becomes an act of piety to God. The State realizes its religious character through the religious character of its subjects; and a State is and ought to be Christian, because all its subjects are and ought to be determined by the principles of the Gospel. As every legislator is bound to be a Christian man, he has no right to vote for any laws which are inconsistent with the teachings of the Scriptures. He must carry his Christian conscience into the halls of legislation.

In conformity with these principles, we recognize Christianity to-day as the religion of our Commonwealth. Our standard of right is that eternal law which God proclaimed from Sinai, and which Jesus expounded on the Mount. We recognize our responsibility to Jesus Christ. He is head over all things to the Church, and the nation that will not serve Him is doomed to perish. Before men we are a free and sovereign State; before God we are dependent subjects; and one of the most cheering omens of the times is the heartiness with which this truth has been received. We are a Christian people, and a Christian Commonwealth. As on the one hand we are not Jews, Infidels, or Turks, so on the other we are not Presbyterians, Baptists, Episcopalians, or Methodists. Christianity, without distinction of sects, is the fountain of our national life. We accept the Bible as the great moral charter by which our laws must be measured, and the Incarnate Redeemer as the Judge to whom we are responsible.

In contending that Christianity is the organic life of the State, we of course do not exclude from the privilege of citizens, nor from the protection of the laws, those who do not acknowledge the authority of Jesus. They do not cease to be men, because they are not Christians, and Christian principle exacts that their rights should be sacredly maintained by an institute which is founded in the idea of justice. As, moreover, the religion of the State realizes itself through the religious life of its subjects, it is not to be supported by arbitrary tests or by civil pains or disabilities. Religion is essentially free and spontaneous. It cannot be enacted as a law, nor enforced by authority. When the State protects its outward institutions, such as the sanctity of the Sabbath, it enjoins nothing which does violence to any man's conscience. It is only giving vent to the religious life of the people, without exacting from others what they feel it sinful to perform; and so long as freedom of conscience and the protection of their rights are secured to men, they have no reason to complain that they are not permitted to unsettle the principles upon which all law and order ultimately rest. As long as they are not required to profess what they do not believe, nor to do what their consciences condemn; as long as they are excluded from no privilege and deprived of no right, they cannot complain that the spirit and sanction of the laws are a standing protest against their want of sympathy with the prevailing type of national life. If Christianity be true, they ought certainly to be Christians. The claim of this religion, in contradistinction from every other, or from none at all, is founded only in its truth. If true, it must be authoritative, and the people who accept it as true would be traitors to their faith if they did not mould their institutions in conformity with its spirit. It is only as a sanction, and not as a law, that we plead for its influence; and how a Christian people can have any other than Christian institutions, it surpasses our intelligence to compass. That the State should treat all religions with equal indifference, is to suppose that the subjects of the State can have a double life, flowing in parallel streams, which never approach nor touch—a life as citizens, and a life as men. It is to forget the essential unity of man, and the convergence of all the energies of his being to a religious centre. It is to forget that religion is the perfection of his nature, and that he realizes the idea of humanity in proportion as religion pervades his whole being. A godless State is, in fact, a contradiction in terms; and if we must have some god, or cease to be citizens because we have ceased to be men, who will hesitate between the God of the Bible and the absurd devices of human superstition and depravity?

It is, then, before the Supreme Jehovah that we prostrate ourselves to-day. We come as a Commonwealth ordained by him. We come as His creatures and His subjects. The sword by which we have executed justice, we received from His hands. We believe that He is—that He is our God; that His favor is life, and His loving kindness better than life. We ascribe to His grace the institutions under which we have flourished. We trace to His hands the blessings which have distinguished our lot. Under Him the foundations of the State were laid, and to Him we owe whatsoever is valuable in our laws, healthful in our customs, or precious in our history. We come this day to acknowledge our dependence, swear our allegiance, and confess our responsibility. By Him we exist as a State, and to Him we must answer for the manner in which we have discharged our trust. *God standeth in the congregation of the mighty. He judgeth among the gods.*

II. Having explained the spirit in which we should approach God, let me call your attention, in the next place, to the ERRAND which brings us before Him this day—fasting, humiliation, and prayer. These terms define the worship which we are expected to present. Fasting is the outward sign; penitence and prayer are the inward graces. In fasting, we relinquish for a season the bounties of Providence, in token of our conviction, that we have forfeited all claim to our daily bread. It is a symbolical confession that we deserve to be stripped of every gift, and left to perish in hunger, nakedness, and want. On occasions of solemn moment, and particularly when "manifestations of the Divine anger appear, as pestilence, war, and famine, the salutary custom of all ages has been for pastors to exhort the people to public fasting and extraordinary prayer." Through such a solemnity Nineveh was saved; and if we are equally penitent, who shall say that we may not also be delivered from the judgments which our sins have provoked? Fasting, apart from inward penitence, is an idle mockery. *Is it such a fast as I have chosen? a day for a man to afflict his soul? is it to bow down his head as a bulrush, and to spread sackcloth and ashes under him? wilt thou call this a fast and an acceptable day to the Lord? Is not this the fast that I have chosen? to loose the bands of wickedness, to undo the heavy burdens, and to let the oppressed go free, and that ye break every yoke? Is it not to deal thy bread to the hungry, and that thou bring the poor that are cast out to thy house? when thou seest the naked that thou cover him; and that thou hide not thyself from thine own flesh?* The great thing with us to-day is, to be impressed with a sense of our sins as a people; to confess them humbly before God; to deprecate His judgments, and to supplicate His favor. We are too apt to restrict the notion of sin in its proper sense to the sphere of the individual; to regard it as altogether private and personal, and not capable of being predicated of the mal-administration of the State. But if the State is a moral institute, responsible to God, and existing for moral and spiritual ends, it is certainly a subject capable of sin. It may endure, too, the penalty of sin, either in its organic capacity, by national judgments, by war, pestilence, weakness, and dissolution, or in its individual subjects, whose offences as citizens are as distinctly transgressions as any other forms of iniquity, and enter into the grounds of the Divine dispensations towards them. The State exists under a law which defines its duty. It is a means to an end, which limits its powers and determines its functions. It is the realization of an idea. Like an individual, it may sin by defect in coming short of its duty, and sin by positive contradiction to it. It may fail to comprehend its vocation; it may arrogate too much, or claim too little. It may be wanting in public spirit, or it may give public spirit a wrong direction. It may subordinate the spiritual to the material, and, in encouraging the increase of national wealth, neglect to foster national greatness. In aspiring to be rich and increased in goods, it may forget that the real glory of a nation is to be free, intelligent, and virtuous. The power which it has received as an instrument of good, it may pervert into an engine of tyranny. It may disregard the welfare and prosperity of its subjects, and degenerate into a tool for the selfish purposes of unscrupulous rulers. It may seek to aggrandize factions, instead of promoting the well-being of the people. The State, too, as a moral person, stands in relations to other States, in consequence of which it may be guilty of bad faith, of inordinate ambition, of covetousness, rapacity, and selfishness. The same vices which degrade the individual among his fellows, may degrade a commonwealth among surrounding nations. It may be mean, voracious, insolent, extortionary. It may cringe to the strong, and oppress the weak. It may take unworthy advantages of the necessities of its neighbors, or make unworthy concessions for temporary purposes. The same laws regulate, and the same crimes disfigure, the intercourse of States with one another, which obtain in the case of individuals. The political relations of the one are precisely analogous to the social relations of the other. The same standard of honor, of integrity, and magnanimity which is incumbent upon their subjects, is equally binding upon the States themselves, and character ought to be as sacred among sovereign States as among private individuals.

The true light, therefore, in which national defects and transgressions should be contemplated, is formally that of sin against God. Their injustice to their people is treachery to Him and their failure to comprehend or to seek to fulfil the end of their being, is contempt of the Divine authority. We take too low a view, when we regard their errors simply as impolitic; their real magnitude and enormity we can never apprehend until we see them in the light of sins.

It is to be feared that this notion of sin has not the hold which it should have of the public conscience. We are not accustomed to judge of the State by the same canons of responsibility which we apply to individuals. In some way or other, the notion of sovereignty, which only defines the relation of a State to earthly tribunals, affects our views of its relations to God; and, whilst we charge it with errors, with blunders, with unfaithfulness to its trust, and deplore the calamities which its misconduct brings upon its subjects as public evils, we lose sight of the still more solemn truth, that these aberrations are the actions of a moral agent, and must be answered for at the bar of God. The moral law is one, and the State is bound to do its duty, under the same sanctions which pertain to the individual. When the State fails, or transgresses, its offences are equally abominations in the sight of God. It is clearly idle to talk of national repentance, without the consciousness of national sin. This doctrine, therefore, I would impress upon you in every form of statement, that the misconduct of the State is rebellion against God, and that a nation which comes short of its destination, and is faithless to its trust, is stained with sin of the most malignant dye. God may endure it in patience for a season, but it is loathsome and abominable in His eyes, and the day of reckoning will at last come. Sin must either be pardoned or punished, confessed and forsaken, or it will work death. Sin has been the ruin of every Empire that ever flourished and fell. Assyria, Persia, Greece, and Rome have paid the penalties to the Divine law. The only alternative with States, as with their subjects, is, repent or perish. The first duty, therefore, which, as a Christian people, we should endeavor to discharge this day, is to confess our national sins with humility and penitence. We should endeavor to feel their magnitude and enormity, not as injuries to man, but as offences against the majesty of God. Our language should be that of David: *Against Thee, Thee only, have we sinned, and done this evil in thy sight.*

Another errand which it behooves us equally to prosecute to-day is, to seek Divine guidance and Divine strength for the future. *It is not in man that walketh to direct his steps,* and States are no more competent than individuals to discharge their duties without the grace of God. Let us endeavor to cherish a sense of our dependence, and aspire to the distinction of that happy people whose God is the Lord. It is a great thing to contemplate our civil duties in the light of obedience to Him; and when they are undertaken in the spirit of worship, they are likely to be performed in the spirit of faithfulness. If we are truly penitent, and truly sensible of our dependence upon God; if it is the reigning desire of our hearts to know His will, and our fixed purpose, in reliance on His strength, to do it, He may give us an answer of peace, He may bring light out of darkness, and extract safety from danger.

Having indicated the spirit in which we should approach God, and pointed out the purposes for which we should go, it remains that we apply the truth to our present circumstances, by signalizing the sins which it behooves us to confess, and by designating the blessings which it behooves us to implore. The conscience is never touched by vague generalities; we must come to particulars; thus and thus hast thou done. The State appears as a penitent this day. She has, therefore, sins to confess. There is a burden upon her heart which must needs be relieved. What are these sins? What is this burden? The completeness of our answer to these questions will measure the extent and sincerity of our repentance.

To understand our sins we must look at ourselves in a double light: first, as a member of this Confederacy, as part and parcel of the people of these United States; and, in the next place, as a particular Commonwealth, a perfect State in ourselves. As long as we are members of this Confederacy we cannot detach ourselves from a personal interest in the sins and transgressions of the whole people; and, though there may be offences in which we have had no actual participation, we are not at liberty to indulge in a self-righteous temper, nor to employ the language of recrimination and reproach. The spectacle of sin is always sad. The fall of none should be contemplated with exultation or with triumph. We should look upon the errors of our brethren with pity and with sorrow, and, as Daniel confessed, in humility and contrition, and with deep commiseration for their misery, the sins of his people, so we should endeavor this day to deplore the shortcomings of our common country, as a matter of personal distress to ourselves. When we come before God, we should endeavor to contemplate the moral aspects of the country in the light of His awful holiness. And the more profoundly we are impressed with the malignity of our national guilt, the deeper should be our concern for the transgressors themselves. Sinners cannot triumph over sinners. Those whose only plea is mercy to themselves, ought not to be unmerciful to others. Much more should we be filled with sorrow when the sins we deplore are likely to prove the ruin of a great nation. To behold a vast, imperial republic, like ours, bequeathed to us by a noble ancestry, consecrated by a noble history, the work of illustrious statesmen and patriots, falling a prey to national degeneracy and corruption, is enough to make angels weep, and should wring from our hearts tears of bitterness and blood. The sin must be enormous where the punishment is so fearful. In less than a century we have spoiled the legacy of our fathers. A Christian people, with Christian institutions, the envy and admiration of the world, have not lived to the age of pagan Greece. Surely, God has a controversy with us, and it becomes us to inquire, with all solemnity, into the cause of His fierce anger. The Union, which our fathers designed to be perpetual, is on the verge of dissolution. A name once dear to our hearts has become intolerable to entire States. Once admired, loved, almost adored, as the citadel and safeguard of freedom, it has become, in many minds, synonymous with oppression, with treachery, with falsehood, and with violence. The Government to which we once invited the victims of tyranny from every part of the world, and under whose ample shield we gloried in promising them security and protection —that Government has become hateful in the very regions in which it was once hailed with the greatest loyalty. Brother has risen up against brother, State against State; angry disputes and bitter criminations and recriminations abound, and the country stands upon the very brink of revolution. Surely, it is time to come to ourselves; to look our follies and our wickednesses in the face; time for every patriot to rend his garments, cover himself with sackcloth, and come into the House of the Lord. Let us deal faithfully this day; let us survey the sins of the land, not to accuse one another, but to humble ourselves under the mighty hand of God.

1. To appreciate the sins which attach to us in our unity as a confederated people, we must advert for a moment to the peculiar structure of our Government. When we came out of the Revolution, it is admitted on all hands that we were separate and independent States. Each was sovereign—that is, completely a nation in itself; but our fathers looked around them, and saw that the grounds of unity were as conspicuous as the elements of diversity. The people were of one blood, one language, one religion. They were, in short, one race. They surveyed the continent from north to south, from east to west, and its geography indicated that it ought to be the dwelling-place of a united population. While there were differences in soil, climate, and productions, that would naturally develop different types of industry, and give rise to different forms of interest, there were great connecting bonds in the mighty rivers which traversed the country, that as clearly signified that the diversity was not inconsistent with unity. The problem, accordingly, which the wisdom of our ancestors undertook to solve was, to harmonize this diversity with unity; to make the people, who were already many, at the same time, one. One nation, in the strict and proper sense, they could never become; that would be to absorb the diversity in unity. Many nations, in all the relations of sovereign States, they could not be; that would be to abolish the unity altogether. The problem was solved by a happy application of the federal principle. The diversity existed already in the many States which had just achieved their independence. These many States, in the exercise of their sovereignty, formed an alliance, which cemented them together in one body politic. This alliance was, in its principle, a treaty, and

in its result, a Government. In its principle it was a treaty, because it was a compact among sovereigns. In its result it was a Government, because it created organs of political power which, under certain conditions, acted immediately upon the people of all the States, without the formal ratification of their own Legislatures, and in all foreign relations stood as the representative of their common sovereignty. It is obvious that the ultimate ground of the authority of Federal legislation is the consent of the confederating States. The laws of Congress bind me, only because South Carolina has consented that I should be bound. The rights of Congress are only the concessions of the sovereign States. This will appear from a moment's reflection. It is obvious that the States might have required that no measures of the Federal Government should be of force within their own borders, without the formal sanction of their own Legislatures. In that case, there could have been no dispute as to the ultimate ground of obedience. The difficulties of such an arrangement are too obvious to be enumerated, but how were these difficulties to be avoided? By surrendering the principle on which the authority of Congress depended, or by changing the mode of its application? To have surrendered the principle would have been to abjure their own sovereignty. There was evidently, then, only a change in the mode of its application. That change consisted in defining the conditions under which consent might be presumed beforehand. The Constitution of the United States, in its grants of power to Congress, is only a device by which a general description is given, in advance, of the kind of legislation that each State will allow to be obligatory on its own people. The provisions of the Constitution are really anticipations of the concurrence of the States. They are formal declarations to the Federal Legislature, that within such and such limits, you have our consent to bind our people. In this way our fathers organized a government that united us for all common purposes, and left us in our original diversity to prosecute our separate and local interests. Congress is, therefore, only the creature of the States, and acts only through them. It is their consent, their treaty, which gives to its enactments the validity of law. As the Federal Legislature was clearly designed to realize the unity of the people, its powers are restricted, from the very necessities of the case, to those points in which all the States have a common interest. The creature of a treaty, in which the contracting parties were all equal, it is manifestly the servant, and not the master, of the States. It is an agent, and not a principal.

If this view of the subject be correct, the Federal Government is preëminently a government, whose very existence depends upon a scrupulous adherence to good faith. It requires the sternest integrity to work it. Its very life-blood is honor. Now, there are two respects in which it may fatally err. In the first place, Congress may transcend its powers, and thus be guilty of a breach of trust, and of disloyalty to its own masters. It may presume upon the consent of the States, where no consent has been given. It may forget that it is a servant, and aspire to be lord. It may forget that it is an agent, and arrogate to itself the rights and authority of the principal. When it surveys the extent of its jurisdiction, the amount of its patronage, and the weight of its influence abroad, it may become dazzled with the contemplation of its own greatness, and attribute to itself the light that is reflected upon it. Its one people it may construe into one nation, and, unmindful of its origin, treat the sovereignties which created it as dependent provinces. Treating upon a footing of equality with foreign powers, it may insensibly ascribe to itself the authority of kings and emperors. All this is conceivable; to some extent it is inevitable, unless the most scrupulous integrity should reign in the Federal Councils. But to sin in any of these respects is fraud, and fraud connected with treason. In the next place, the States may break faith with one another. They may refuse to fulfil their engagements. They may pervert the Federal authorities to the accomplishment of selfish and sectional ends. They may undertake to make their common agent the minister of partial advantages, or they may use lawful powers for unlawful purposes. Here, too, in the relation of the States to each other, is wide scope for fraud.

In one, or in both these directions, we may look for instances of national transgression; and on this day, we should solemnly review the history of the Republic, for the purpose of bringing our consciences before the tribunal of God. Perfidy, under all circumstances, is an aggravated sin; but when it brings in its train the destruction of institutions which have been the hope and admiration of the world; when it subverts the foundations of a great empire, scattering the seeds of dissension, bitterness, and strife; when it arms house against house, and State against State, and converts a happy union into a scene of implacable and deadly feuds, language is hardly competent to describe the enormity of the guilt. The fraud which makes our Government a failure, must darken the prospects of liberty throughout the world. No policy can be devised which shall perpetuate freedom among a people that are dead to honor and integrity. Liberty and virtue are twin sisters, and the best fabric in the world, however ingeniously framed, and curiously balanced, can be no security against the corroding influences of bad faith. Perfidy is always weakness; and a government whose basis is the faith of treaties, must inevitably perish before it. The combination of the federal principle with the sovereignty of States, is the only principle which can maintain free institutions upon a broad scale. This combination can secure freedom to a continent; it might even govern the world. The day of small States is passed, and as the federal principle is the only one which can guarantee freedom to extensive territories, the federal principle must constitute the hope of the human race. It was the glory of this country to have first applied it to the formation of an effective Government, and, had we been faithful to our trust, a destiny was before us which it has never been the lot of any people to inherit. It was ours to redeem this continent, to spread freedom, civilization, and religion through the whole length of the land. Geographically placed between Europe and Asia, we were, in some sense, the representatives of the human race. The fortunes of the world were in our hand. We were a city set upon a hill, whose light was intended to shine upon every people and upon every land. To forego this destiny, to forfeit this inheritance, and that through bad faith, is an enormity of treason equalled only by the treachery of a Judas, who betrayed his master with a kiss. Favored as we have been, we can expect to perish by no common death. The judgment lingers not, and the damnation slumbers not, of the reprobates and traitors, who, for the wages of unrighteousness, have sapped the pillars and undermined the foundations of the stateliest temple of liberty the world ever beheld. Rebellion against God, and treason to man, are combined in the perfidy. The innocent may be spared, as Lot was delivered from the destruction of Sodom; but the guilty must perish with an aggravated doom. The first instances of transgression may seem slight and insignificant, but when they strike at the principle of good faith, like a puncture of the heart, they strike at the root of our national life. The Union was conceived in plighted faith, and can only be maintained by a complete redemption of the pledge. The moment faith is broken, the Union is dissolved. Entertaining these views of the radical relations of good faith to the success and stability of our Government, I would impress upon the country the flagrant iniquity of dealing loosely with its covenants. It is here that our dangers are concentrated, and here we should look for the sins that have provoked the judgments of God. Here is the secret of our bitter strifes, our furious contention, our deadly animosities; and, should this Government be destined to fall, the epitaph which may be written on its tomb, is a memorial of broken faith.

The foregoing remarks are general, and designed to bring no railing accusation against any section of the country, but to excite every part of it to a faithful review of its dealings under the Constitution. There is one subject, however, in relation to which the non-slaveholding States have not only broken faith, but have justified their course upon the plea of conscience. We allude to the subject of slavery. They have been reluctant to open the Territories to the introduction of slaves, and have refused to restore fugitives to their masters, and have vindicated themselves from blame by appealing to a higher law than the compacts of men. The doctrine of a higher law, properly interpreted and applied, we are far from repudiating. God is greater than man, and no human covenants can set aside or annul the supreme obligations of His will. But, in the present case, the plea is improperly applied. If it is wrong to countenance slavery by restoring fugitives to their masters, or by permitting it to enter into the Territories, then the true method is to abrogate the contract which requires both. We repent of sin by forsaking it, and the only way to undo a wicked bargain is to cancel it. If the non-slaveholding States cannot in conscience redeem their faith, they are bound in honor to take back their pledges, to withdraw from the Union, and to release their confederates from all the conditions of the contract. No other course can they pursue without sin. To swear to observe the Constitution, when the Constitution binds them to do what they believe to be wicked, is an oath which, whether broken or kept, cannot be taken without dishonor. To keep it, is to violate the conscience in the unlawful article. To break it, is to be guilty of perjury. The only escape from this dilemma is, not to take it at all.

But, in truth, even upon the supposition that slavery is immoral, there is nothing wrong in the oath to observe the Constitution. The responsibility of slavery is not upon the non-slaveholding States. It is not created by their laws, but by the laws of the slaveholding States; and all they do in the case of the fugitive from his master, is to remand him to the jurisdiction of the laws from which he has escaped. They have nothing to do with the justice or injustice of the laws themselves. They are simply required to say that the accident of being on their soil shall not dissolve the relation between a subject and its government. The treaty existing among the States, in reference to this point, is precisely analogous to a treaty among foreign nations, requiring the surrender of criminals that have fled from justice. The country surrendering passes no judgment upon the merits of the case. It leaves the whole of the responsibility to the laws of the country claiming jurisdiction. All that it does is not to interpose and arrest the operation of those laws. Surely, there is nothing unrighteous in this; nothing unrighteous in refusing to screen a man from the authority of the code under which Providence has cast his lot. There is no obligation to do it without a treaty; but there is nothing inherently unlawful in making such a treaty, and in strictly adhering to it when made. The plea of conscience proceeds from a palpable misapprehension of the nature of the case.

The plea is still more flagrantly inadequate when applied to the exclusion of slavery from the Territories. All the States have confessedly an equal right of property in them. They are a joint possession. The citizens of any State may go there and take up their abode, and, without express contract to the contrary among the proprietors, they are at liberty to observe the customs of their own States. It is as if the land were distributed, and each State had a part. In that case, each State would evidently put its part under the jurisdiction of its own laws. The joint possession, to the extent of the partnership, places the Territory in the same relation to the laws of all the States. One has no more right to introduce its peculiarities than another, and without positive contract the peculiarities of none can be excluded. The case is as if a Christian and a Pagan people should acquire a common territory. Would it be competent for the Christian people, in the absence of a positive stipulation, to say to their Pagan neighbors, You shall not bring your idols into this land? You may come yourselves, but you come only on condition that you renounce your worship? If there is any wrong, it is in making the treaty at first; but if Christians and Pagans can enter into treaties at all, there is no crime in observing them. If they can lawfully acquire joint possession of a soil, the Pagan has as much right to introduce his idols as the Christian his purer worship. In respect to the question of slavery, if there is wrong anywhere, it is in the union of slaveholding and non-slaveholding States in one confederacy; but, being confederate, there can be no just scruple as to the fulfilment of their contracts. It is a mistake to suppose that the North sanctions slavery by doing justice to the South. It leaves the whole responsibility of the institution where God has placed it, among the people of the South themselves. We do not ask the North to introduce it upon their own soil; we do not ask them to approve it; we do not ask them to speak a single word in its defence: we only ask them to execute in good faith the contract which has been solemnly ratified betwixt us. We ask them not to interfere with the jurisdiction of our own laws over our own subjects, nor with the free use of our own property upon our own soil. This is the head and front of our pretensions, and when these reasonable demands are met by the plea of conscience and the authority of a higher law, they must pardon our dulness, if we cannot understand that delicate sensibility to honor which makes no scruple of an oath that it does not mean to observe, and holds to the profit, without fulfilling the conditions of the contract. When they ask to be released from their engagements, and, in token of their sincerity, are willing to release us from ours; when they are willing to abandon the Union rather than ensnare their consciences; when they abhor the wages, as sincerely as the deeds, of unrighteousness—then, and not till then, they may expect their plea to be admitted.

2. In the next place, we shall find ample ground of humiliation, if we consider the manner in which the organs of Government have been perverted from their real design, and changed in their essential character. All our institutions are representative. We legislate by parliaments, we judge by courts, and we execute by officers appointed for the purpose. The people in their collective capacity do nothing but choose their representatives. They enact no laws; they conduct no trials; they execute no sentences. Now, what is the genius and spirit of a representative assembly? Is it to give expression to the popular will? Is it to find out and do what the people, if assembled in mass, would do? Is it simply a contrivance to avoid the inconveniences of large convocations, and bound to seek the same results which these convocations would be likely to effect? This doctrine I utterly and absolutely deny. Representatives are appointed, not to ascertain what the will of the people actually is, but what it ought to be. The people are not permitted to legislate *en masse*, because their passions and caprices are likely to prove stronger than reason and truth. Representation is a check upon themselves. Every State is bound to realize the idea of justice. This requires calm deliberation and sober thought. To provide for this deliberation, to protect themselves from their own prejudices and passions, and to cause the voice of reason to be heard, they retire from the scene, and leave the inquiry and decision of their duty to chosen men, in whose wisdom they have confidence. This is the true theory of parliamentary government. Courts are appointed to interpret the law, and officers to execute the decrees of the courts, in order that justice and not passion may rule in every trial. The supremacy of reason and justice is the supremacy of law and order. Contemplated in this light, parliamentary government is the most perfect under heaven. It avoids equally the extremes of the despotism of a single will, which is sure to terminate in tyranny, and of the still more hateful despotism of mobs, which is sure to terminate in anarchy. It gives rise to a free commonwealth. It aims at the true and right, and truth and rectitude are the safeguards of freedom. Such is the genius of our own institutions. But how has the gold become dim, and the fine gold changed! Has the Congress of these United States fulfilled its high idea? Called together to deliberate, to discuss, to inquire after truth; bound to listen to no voice but the voice of wisdom and justice—has it always presented the spectacle of gravity, decorum, and candor, which we expect to behold in the Senate of a free people? What shall we say, when gold has usurped the authority of truth, when votes have been bought and sold, and the interests of a faction allowed to outweigh the rights and interests of a whole people? What shall we say, when blows have taken the place of argument, and our halls of legislation have been converted into an arena for the combats of fierce gladiators? What shall we say, when, instead of the language of calm deliberation, the representatives of the people have vied with each other in vituperation and abuse, and, when they have exhausted the dialect of Billingsgate, have rushed upon each other with the ferocity of tigers, or with the fury of the bulls of Bashan? The offence is rank, and smells to heaven. Such an awful prostitution of high functions cannot take place with impunity. The hall which should have inscribed upon its portals *the scene of wisdom and of high debate*, cannot become a den of robbers, or a rendezvous for bullies and hectors, without provoking the just judgments of God. It is a lamentation, and shall be for a lamentation, that the Federal Legislature, which ought to have been a model of refined, impartial, and courteous debate—a model to which we could always point with an honest pride, has made itself a scandal to a civilized people. The day of reckoning was obliged to come. The country is brought to the brink of dissolution.

The corruption is of the same kind when the tribunals of the law are set aside, and mobs usurp the jurisdiction of the courts. There may be occasions when the established order is unable to check a threatening evil. In such cases, the necessities of self-defence may justify society in falling back upon its primordial rights. But these occasions are rare. But when society assumes, without necessity, the functions of judges and magistrates, it is guilty of an abuse which, if not arrested, must end in anarchy. *There* only is security where the law is supreme; and the worst of all social evils is where the populace is stronger than the law— where the sentence of courts is annulled by the frenzy of mobs, and the officers of justice are insulted and restrained in the execution of their functions.

In these respects, all of which resolve themselves into the abuse of the representative principle, we have national sins to confess. We have poisoned the springs of our Government. We have given to faction what is due to truth. We have dethroned reason and justice, and made our legislation a miserable scramble for the interests of sections and parties. We have deified the people, making their will, as will, and not as reasonable and right, the supreme law; and they, in turn, have deified themselves, by assuming all the attributes of government, and exercising unlimited dominion. They have become at once legislators, judges, juries, and executioners. The last form of evil has been only occasional, but unless checked and repressed, it may strengthen and expand. In proportion as it increases, reverence for law and for the forms of law loses its power. The tendency to sink our institutions into a pure democracy has been steadily growing. We are rapidly losing even the notion of a representative, by merging it into that of a deputy; and it is but the natural product of this error, that Congress should be the battle-ground of conflicting wills, and that its sole inquiry should become: What says the voice of the majority? *Vox populi, vox Dei.*

I have said, I think, enough to show that in our Federal relations, we have reason to be humbled in the presence of God. Our Government is a noble one. Human wisdom could not have devised a better. With all our unfaithfulness it has made us great and prosperous. It has won for us the homage and respect of the world; and had we been faithful to its principles, the blessings it has already conferred upon us would be but the beginning of its triumphs. Could we continue a united people, united in heart as well as in form; could the Government be administered according to the real genius of our Federal and representative institutions, imagination can hardly conceive the scene of prosperity, influence, and glory which would dawn upon our children a hundred years hence. When we contemplate what we might become, and then look at the prospect which is now before us, we have reason to put our hands on our mouths, and our mouths in the dust, and to exclaim: *God be merciful to us sinners!* Let us weep for the country. Let us confess our own sins and the sins of the people. God may hear the cry of the penitent, and say to them, as He said to Moses, when he deplored the sins of his people, *I will make of thee a great nation.*

3. There are other forms of sin which, though not national in the sense that they pertain to the administration of the Government, are national in the sense that they are widely diffused among the people: they enter into the grounds of the Divine controversy with us; and, if not repented of and forsaken, must end in national calamities. Conspicuous among these is the sin of profaneness. The name of God is constantly on our lips, and if the frequency with which it is used were any sign of religion, ours might pass for the most devout people under heaven. We introduce it into every subject, and upon all occasions. A sentence is never complete without it. If we are earnest, it enlivens our discourse; if we are angry, it affords a vent to our passions; if we are merry, it quickens our enjoyments, and if we are sad, it relieves our misery. Like those particles in the Greek tongue, which to the philologist give a delicate turn to the meaning, but which to the common reader might be removed without being missed, the name of God is indispensable in the vulgar dialect of the people, but it takes a practised ear to detect the shade which it gives to the sentence. Many persons would be dumb if they were not allowed to be profane. The only words which, as nimble servitors, are ready to obey their bidding, are the names of God and the awful terms in which He announces the final doom of the guilty. These are their vocabulary. Judging from the discourse which he is likely to hear in the streets, a stranger might infer that the name was all that we had left of God; that we were a nation of atheists, who had at last discovered that He was only a word, and, determined to make reprisals for the terrors

with which superstition had clothed him, we were degrading even the name by the lowest associations. That a puny mortal should thus trifle with the majesty of God, and make a jest of the Divine judgments, is a spectacle which may well astonish the angels, and ought to confound ourselves. Devils hate, but they dare not make light of God. It is only here upon earth, where the patience of God is as infinite as His being, that the name which fills heaven with reverence and hell with terror is an idle word. Profaneness naturally leads to licentiousness, by dissolving the sentiment of reverence.

Closely connected with levity in the use of the Divine name, is the profaneness which treats with contempt the positive institution of the Sabbath. Here the Government is implicated in the sin. It encourages the desecration of the Lord's Day by the companies which carry its mails. The Sabbath, as an external institute, is absolutely essential to the maintenance and propagation of Christianity in the world, and until the Christian religion is disproved, and the supremacy of Christ set aside, no government on earth can annul it with impunity.

It is also characteristic of our people that they are self-sufficient and vainglorious, to a degree that makes them ridiculous. They love to boast, and they love to sacrifice to their own drag and to burn incense to their own net. They feel themselves competent for every enterprise. They can scale heaven, weigh the earth, and measure the sea. Their own arms and their own right hand will get them the victory in every undertaking. Even the style of their conversation is grandiloquent. The hyperbole is their favorite figure, and the superlative their favorite degree of comparison. To hear their self-laudations, you would never dream that they acknowledged a Providence, or depended on any superior power. All this is the grossest atheism. The consequence of this self-sufficiency is a want of reverence for any thing. We honor neither God nor the king. We revile our rulers, and speak evil of dignities, with as little compunction as we profane the ordinances of religion. Nothing is great but ourselves. It is enough to indicate these types of sin, without dwelling upon them. The important thing is to feel that they are sins. They are so common that they cease to impress us, and in some of their aspects they are so grotesque, they provoke a smile more readily than a tear.

4. Having adverted to the sins which belong to us as members of the Confederacy, let us now turn to those which belong to us as a particular Commonwealth. I shall restrict myself to our dealings with the institution which has produced the present convulsions of the country, and brought us to the verge of ruin. That the relation betwixt the slave and his master is not inconsistent with the word of God, we have long since settled. Our consciences are not troubled, and have no reason to be troubled on this score. We do not hold our slaves in bondage from remorseless considerations of interest. If I know the character of our people, I think I can safely say, that if they were persuaded of the essential immorality of slavery, they would not be backward in adopting measures for the ultimate abatement of the evil. We cherish the institution not from avarice, but from principle. We look upon it as an element of strength, and not of weakness, and confidently anticipate the time when the nations that now revile us would gladly change places with us. In its last analysis, slavery is nothing but an organization of labor, and an organization by virtue of which labor and capital are made to coincide. Under this scheme, labor can never be without employment, and the wealth of the country is pledged to feed and clothe it. Where labor is free, and the laborer not a part of the capital of the country, there are two causes constantly at work, which, in the excessive contrasts they produce, must end in agrarian revolutions and intolerable distress. The first is the tendency of capital to accumulate. Where it does not include the laborer as a part, it will employ only that labor which will yield the largest returns. It looks to itself, and not to the interest of the laborer. The other is the tendency of population to outstrip the demands for employment. The multiplication of laborers not only reduces wages to the lowest point, but leaves multitudes wholly unemployed. While the capitalist is accumulating his hoards, rolling in affluence and splendor, thousands that would work if they had the opportunity are doomed to perish of hunger. The most astonishing contrasts of poverty and riches are constantly increasing. Society is divided between princes and beggars. If labor is left free, how

is this condition of things to be obviated? The government must either make provision to support people in idleness, or it must arrest the law of population and keep them from being born, or it must organize labor. Human beings cannot be expected to starve. There is a point at which they will rise in desperation against a social order which dooms them to nakedness and famine whilst their lordly neighbor is clothed in purple and fine linen, and faring sumptuously every day. They will scorn the logic which makes it their duty to perish in the midst of plenty. Bread they must have, and bread they will have, though all the distinctions of property have to be abolished to provide it. The government, therefore, must support them or an agrarian revolution is inevitable. But shall it support them in idleness? Will the poor, who have to work for their living, consent to see others as stout and able as themselves clothed and fed like the lilies of the field, while they toil not, neither do they spin? Will not this be to give a premium to idleness? The government, then, must find them employment; but how shall this be done? On what principle shall labor be organized so as to make it certain that the laborer shall never be without employment, and employment adequate for his support? The only way in which it can be done, as a permanent arrangement, is by converting the laborer into capital; that is, by giving the employer a right of property in the labor employed; in other words, by slavery. The master must always find work for his slave, as well as food and raiment. The capital of the country, under this system, must always feed and clothe the country. There can be no pauperism, and no temptations to agrarianism. That non-slaveholding States will eventually have to organize labor, and to introduce something so like slavery that it will be impossible to discriminate between them, or to suffer from the most violent and disastrous insurrections against the system which creates and perpetuates their misery, seems to be as certain as the tendencies in the laws of capital and population to produce the extremes of poverty and wealth. We do not envy them their social condition. With sanctimonious complacency they may affect to despise us, and to shun our society as they would shun the infection of a plague. They may say to us, *Stand by—we are holier than thou;* but the day of reckoning must come. As long as the demand for labor transcends the supply, all is well: capital and labor are mutual friends, and the country grows in wealth with mushroom rapidity. But when it is no longer capital asking for labor, but labor asking for capital; when it is no longer work seeking men, but men seeking work—then the tables are turned, and unemployed labor and selfish capital stand face to face in deadly hostility. We desire to see no such state of things among ourselves, and we accept as a good and merciful constitution the organization of labor which Providence has given us in slavery. Like every human arrangement, it is liable to abuse; but in its idea, and in its ultimate influence upon the social system, it is wise and beneficent. We see in it a security for the rights of property and a safeguard against pauperism and idleness, which our traducers may yet live to wish had been engrafted upon their own institutions. The idle declamation about degrading men to the condition of chattels, and treating them as cows, oxen, or swine; the idea that they are regarded as tools and instruments, and not as beings possessed of immortal souls, betrays a gross ignorance of the real nature of the relation. Slavery gives one man the right of property in the labor of another. The property of man in man is only the property of man in human toil. The laborer becomes capital, not because he is a thing, but because he is the exponent of a presumed amount of labor. This is the radical notion of the system, and all legislation upon it should be regulated by this fundamental idea.

The question now arises, Have we, as a people and a State, discharged our duty to our slaves? Is there not reason to apprehend that in some cases we have given occasion to the calumnies of our adversaries, by putting the defence of slavery upon grounds which make the slave a different kind of being from his master? Depend upon it, it is no light matter to deny the common brotherhood of humanity. The consequences are much graver than flippant speculators about the diversity of races are aware of. If the African is not of the same blood with ourselves, he has no lot nor part in the Gospel. The redemption of Jesus Christ extends only to those who are partakers of the same flesh and blood with Himself. The ground of his right to redeem is the participation, not of a like, but of a common nature. Had the humanity of Jesus been miraculously created apart from connection with the human race, though it might in all respects have been precisely similar to ours, He could not, according to the Scriptures, have been our Redeemer. He must be able to call us brethren before He can impart to us His saving grace. No Christian man, therefore, can give any countenance to speculations which trace the negro to any other parent but Adam. If he is not descended from Adam, he has not the same flesh and blood with Jesus, and is therefore excluded from the possibility of salvation. Those who defend slavery upon the plea that the African is not of the same stock with ourselves, are aiming a fatal blow at the institution, by bringing it into conflict with the dearest doctrines of the Gospel. To arm the religious sentiment against it, is to destroy it. When the question at stake is, whether a large portion of mankind can be saved, we want something more than deductions from doubtful phenomena. Nothing but the Word of God can justify us in shutting the gates of mercy upon any portion of the race. The science, falsely so-called, which proffers its aid upon such conditions, is such a friend to slavery as Joab to Amasa, who met him with the friendly greeting, *Art thou in health, my brother?* and stabbed him under the fifth rib. I am happy to say that such speculations have not sprung from slavery. They were not invented to justify it. They are the offspring of infidelity, a part of the process by which science has been endeavoring to convict Christianity of falsehood; and it is as idle to charge the responsibility of the doctrine about the diversity of species upon slaveholders, as to load them with the guilt of questioning the geological accuracy of Moses. Both are assaults of infidel science upon the records of our faith, and both have found their warmest advocates among the opponents of slavery. Our offence has been, that in some instances we have accepted and converted into a plea, the conclusions of this vain deceit. Let us see to it that we give our revilers no handle against us; above all, that we make not God our enemy. Let us not repudiate our kindred with the poor brethren whom He has scattered among us and intrusted to our guardianship and care. Let us receive them as bone of our bone, and flesh of our flesh. Let us recognize them as having the same Father, the same Redeemer, and the same everlasting destiny.

Let us inquire, in the next place, whether we have rendered unto our servants that which is just and equal. Is our legislation in all respects in harmony with the idea of slavery? Are our laws such that we can heartily approve them in the presence of God? Have we sufficiently protected the person of the slave? Are our provisions adequate for giving him a fair and impartial trial when prosecuted for offences? Do we guard as we should his family relations? And, above all, have we furnished him with proper means of religious instruction? These and such questions we should endeavor to answer with the utmost solemnity and truth. We have come before the Lord as penitents. The people whom we hold in bondage are the occasion of all our troubles. We have been provoked by bitter and furious assailants to deal harshly with them, and it becomes us this day to review our history, and the history of our legislation, in the light of God's truth, and to abandon with ingenuous sincerity whatever our consciences cannot sanction. Let not the taunts of our revilers shake us from our propriety. Let it be our first care to commend ourselves to God, and if He be for us what does it signify who is against us? Our slaves are a solemn trust, and while we have a right to use and direct their labor, we are bound to feed, clothe, and protect them, to give them the comforts of this life, and to introduce them to the hopes of a blessed immortality. They are moral beings, and it will be found that in the culture of their moral nature we reap the largest reward from their service. The relation itself is moral, and in the tender affections and endearing sympathies it evokes, it gives scope for the exercise of the most attractive graces of human character. Strange as it may sound to those who are not familiar with the system, slavery is a school of virtue, and no class of men have furnished sublimer instances of heroic devotion than slaves in their loyalty and love to their masters. We have seen them rejoice at the cradle of the infant, and weep at the bier of the dead; and there are few amongst us, perhaps, who have not drawn their nourishment from their generous breasts. Where the relations are so kindly, there is every motive of fidelity on our part. Let us apply with unflinching candor the golden rule of our Saviour. Have we rendered to our slaves what, if we were in their circumstances, we should think it right and just in them to render to us. We are not bound to render unto them what they may in fact desire. Such a rule would transmute morality into arbitrary caprice. But we are bound to render unto them what they have a right to desire; that is, we are bound to render unto them that which is just and equal. The Saviour requires us to exchange places in order that we may appreciate what is just and equal, free from the benumbing influences which are likely to pervert the judgment when there is no personal interest in the decision. I need not say that it is our duty as a Commonwealth to develop all the capabilities of good which the relation of slavery contains. They have never yet been fully unfolded. We have had to attend so much to the outer defences that we have not been in a condition to give full play to the energies of the inward life. This is the problem to which Christian statesmen should hereafter direct their efforts.

II. This day is a day of *prayer*, as well as of humiliation and confession. There are blessings which in our present circumstances we urgently need, and we should make them the burden of importunate supplications. The first is the grace of magnanimity, that our moderation may be known unto all men. By moderation I do not mean tameness and servility of spirit; and by magnanimity I do not mean what Aristotle seems to understand by it—a consciousness of worth which feels itself entitled to great rewards. The true notion of it is, a just sense of what is due to the dignity of the State, and an humble reliance upon God to make it equal to every occasion. The mind that feels the responsibility of its spiritual endowments, and aims at the perfection of its nature in the consummation of an end which satisfies the fulness of its being, while it arrogates nothing of merit to itself, but ascribes all its capacities to the unmerited bounties of God; the mind that is conscious of what is due to mind, and intent upon fulfilling its own idea, is truly great; and the more thoroughly it is penetrated with this consciousness, the more deeply it is humbled under the conviction of its manifold shortcomings, and the more earnest in its cries for grace to enable it to win the prize. To know our true place in the universe, to feel that we are possessed of noble powers, and that we are bound to pursue an end that is worthy of them, is not pride, but sobriety of judgment. Pride emerges when we attribute to ourselves the excellence of our gifts; when we cherish a spirit of independence and self-sufficiency, and rob God of the glory which is due to His bounty. Humility is not a confession that mind is intrinsically little; it is only the conviction of its absolute dependence upon God, and of its relative nothingness when compared with Him. A Commonwealth is magnanimous when it comprehends the vocation of a State, when it rises to the dignity of its high functions, and seeks to cherish a spirit in harmony with the great moral purposes it was ordained to execute. A magnanimous State cannot be the victim of petty passions. It is superior to rashness, to revenge, to irritation, and caprice. It has an ideal which it aims to exemplify; cultivates a mind upon a level with its calling, and, turning neither to the right nor to the left, presses with undeviating step to the goal before it. It is calm, collected, self-possessed, resolved. It dares do all that may become a State. It will attempt nothing more; it will be content with nothing less. That we, as a Commonwealth, in the trying circumstances in which we are placed, may be able to exhibit this spectacle of magnanimity to the world; that we may command its admiration by the dignity and self-respect of our bearing, even though we should not secure its assent to the wisdom of our policy; that we may make all men see and feel that we are actuated by principle and not by passion, should be a subject of our fervent supplications this day. Wisdom and courage are the inspiration of God.

In the next place, we should look to Him to raise up for us as guides and leaders in the present emergency, men of counsel and understanding. Statesmen in the State, as Apostles in the Church, are special ministers of God. They arise at His bidding, and execute His behests. Moses and Joshua, Solon and Lycurgus, the Prince of Orange and Washington, were anointed and commissioned of heaven for the work they so happily performed. To construct a government of any kind is a work of no ordinary magnitude; but the government of a free people, with its complicated checks and balances, it is given only to the loftiest minds to be able to conceive, much less to create. If ever there was a time since the adoption of the Federal Constitution when the whole country needed the counsel and guidance of patriotic statesmen, it is now, when, under the lead of demagogues, factions, and politicians, we have corrupted every principle of our polity, and brought the Government to the brink of dissolution. No human arm is equal to the crisis. No human eye can penetrate the future. Our only help is in God; from Him alone cometh our salvation. The highest proof of patriotism in the present conjuncture is in penitence and humility to seek His favor, and if it is His purpose to redeem and save us in answer to our prayers, He will cause the men to stand forth, and the people to honor and accept them whom He has commissioned to conduct us through the wilderness. In the mean time, let us scrupulously resist every influence that is unfriendly to the influence of His Spirit. Let us mortify every thought, and subdue every passion, upon which we cannot sincerely invoke His blessing. If we are to lay the foundations of a new empire, or to readjust the proportions of the old, the only pledge of permanent success is the Divine favor. Happy is that people, and that people alone, whose God is the Lord.

Finally, let us pray that our courage may be equal to every emergency. Even though our cause be just, and our course approved of heaven, our path to victory may be through a baptism of blood. Liberty has its martyrs and confessors as well as religion. The oak is rooted amid wintry storms. Great truths come to us at great cost, and the most impressive teachers of mankind are those who have sealed their lessons with their blood. Our State may suffer; she may suffer grievously; she may suffer long: be it so: we shall love her the more tenderly and the more intensely the more bitterly she suffers. It does not follow, even if she should be destined to fall, that her course was wrong, or her sufferings in vain. Thermopylæ was lost, but the moral power of Thermopylæ will continue as long as valor and freedom have a friend; and reverence for law is one of the noblest elements of the human soul. Let it be our great concern to know God's will. Let *right* and *duty* be our watchword; liberty, regulated by law, our goal; and, leaning upon the arm of everlasting strength, we shall achieve a name, whether we succeed or fall, that posterity will not willingly let die.

THE PENTECOST OF THE NATION:

A Sermon preached in the Church of the Messiah, Broadway, New York, Whit-Sunday morning, May 19, 1861,

BY SAMUEL OSGOOD, D. D.

Comfort ye, comfort ye my people!
Saith your God.
Speak ye comfortably to Jerusalem, and cry unto her,
That her warfare is accomplished,
That her iniquity is pardoned;
For she hath received of the Lord's hand
Double for all her sins. —*Isaiah* xl. 1, 2.

This day beyond all others is the day of the Divine Comforter and it speaks to us now as never before, not merely as to individuals or as a church, but as a nation. As a people we have been and are sorely tried. For many months we have carried the country's burdens as well as our own to our pillows, and our trials take us out of our private isolation and give us fellowship with each other, and with every free and struggling people since time began. In one respect the Bible becomes luminous to us as never before, and from our own experience we can feel the worth of that sacred nationality which is the ruling idea of the Old Testament, and which is exalted instead of being destroyed by the New Testament.

This day of Pentecost or Whit-Sunday which has now once more come, was a great national festival of the Hebrew people, and celebrated the act that made them a nation, the giving of the law by Moses or the adoption of the Hebrew Constitution, fifty days after the Passover —that festival of deliverance from Egyptian bondage. Following our Bible and our Hymn Book, we notice these two occasions, and seven weeks or fifty days have now brought us from one to the other, or from one beautiful Easter, with its festival of children and array of flowers, to this Whit-Sunday. Interpreted by their relation to our own national history, we compare the Passover to our Declaration of Independence, and the pledge by our fathers of their lives, their fortunes, and their sacred honor; and we compare the Day of Pentecost to the adoption of our National Constitution, that great law-giving to our people which we still reverently acknowledge.

The New Testament accepts the historical

facts of the Old, and carries them up into a higher plane. Instead of Moses and the law of the Hebrew nation, it gives us Christ and the Spirit of God with his whole people; and this gospel of the Son and the Spirit, whilst it called men of every tongue and climate into one universal church or fellowship, left them free to form nationalities according to position, blood, or affinity. In fact, instead of destroying national life, it deepened it, by making each true citizen feel that God himself in Christ was his Redeemer, and in his Spirit was his lawgiver. Whether in our religious or civil relations, the idea that belongs to us to-day is this: that all good and true law has the sanction of God's own Spirit, and has not only the witness of the stone table or the statute book, but of the spirit of truth and justice in the heart. The first Christian Pentecost did not destroy the old constitutional law, but gave it inspiration and fire, and the Hebrew company who heard the rushing wind and saw the tongues of fire, did not renounce but deepened and exalted their birthright, and were mightily comforted when the Apostle Peter taught them to regard this new life as a confirmation of the old prophets. In a like temper let us speak now of the Pentecost of our nation, with this rushing wind of enthusiasm that sweeps through the land, and those tongues of fire that flame forth from so many presses and pulpits. Let us hear to-day the voice of the Lord God, our Father in Heaven, comforting us by telling us of the ground of our comfort in being His people, and of the measure of our comfort in the promise of His twofold blessing, from warfare accomplished and iniquity pardoned.

I. Let us be comforted first of all by the phrase by which the prophet is called to address his hearers, *my people*. It shows that they were a people, and a people of God. We take comfort in the same thought, for we are a people, and nothing surely could be baser than for us not to add, in face of all that God has done for us, that we are a people of God. Without a home how desolate a man must be, and absence from home makes a sickness of its own that shows itself among the homesick exiles of all lands. Without a country, home can have little meaning, and the craving for some positive citizenship, some fixed nationality, is as much a trait of our nature as love of the hearth-stone and the altar. If we have slighted our birthright as a people, it is because we have taken it too much as a matter of course, because never disturbed and, like the common bounties of God, the light, water, and air, we have hardly thought of estimating its worth. Now that the blessing is threatened, we see its priceless value and ask God to secure to us our birthright.

A people we certainly are, and if ever in our timidity or our selfishness we doubted the fact, we do not doubt it now. We are a people by our country and our Constitution, made one nation by the external power of our domain, and by the internal power of our essential law. There is comfort in the conviction that we have been virtually a nation for two centuries, or ever since the first colonists began to cherish fellowship with each other for mutual defence, and actually a nation for nearly one century. From the beginning of the settlement of the country, the various communities tended towards mutual alliance, and in 1627 the Dutch of Manhattan sent an envoy to Plymouth. In 1643 Roger Williams, of Rhode Island, performed the part of a peacemaker here; in 1650 the treaty of Hartford took place, and in 1664 the establishment of the English power in New York centralized the elements of our future nationality. Just one hundred years ago James Otis made a speech at Boston, which John Adams, who was then a youth of but 26 years, said "was a flame of fire," and "American Independence was then and there born." Otis was the fiery prophet of our rising empire, and on the 6th of June, 1765, "in single-minded wisdom," as the historian Bancroft styles his forethought, advised the calling of an American Congress, and his advice was followed by the Congress at New York in the following October, when Otis found his most determined supporter in Christopher Gadsden, of Charleston, S. C. Gadsden said at the Congress, "There ought to be no New England man, no New Yorker, known on the continent, but all of us Americans." May some future Gadsden come from the same quarter and take from Carolina the infamy of being first to assail the flag, and threaten the unity of our republic. The July before, Otis had hailed the prospect of "the state of longest duration, greatest glory, and domestic happiness" as about to rise, and seemed to himself to hear the prophetic song of the "sibyls" chanting the spring-time of a "new empire." The vision is verified, for one people we have been, and mean to be, and we are a nation quite as much by our constitutional organization, as by our hereditary domain.

And God has made us so. A people, are we not *His* people, and had any nation ever more decided marks of having the favor of His providence, and His grace? From the beginning of creation this magnificent country has been maturing its growth and hoarding its treasures for us. The coal, iron, lead, copper, silver, and gold of the mines—the rivers, lakes, seas, gulfs, oceans,—prairies, valleys, hills and mountains—the soils of all grades and capacities for this garden, orchard, and granary of the new world—all these were prepared by the Creator for those who could use them, and in God's own time the men who could use them came. The choice men of the old world were brought to the new, and the free and constitutional races of Europe from England, Holland, and Germany, held the land and formed the dominant civilization of this continent. Our fathers did their best, but they adored as we do, the mysterious Power that rules over them and nations, and wrought through them results beyond their fondest dreams. God has made our country to be one, and he who tries to divide its domain impiously opposes His will. His hand hath uplifted the mountains, and poured out the rivers and lakes, that bind us together. They that would divide North and South should tremble as they hear the rushing tide of the Mississippi, that Father of waters, that cries in every wave, "What God hath joined together, let not man put asunder;" and the same protest is thundered against them who would sever the East from the West, by the roar of Niagara, the mighty bond of that great chain of lakes that binds the Rocky Mountains to our Atlantic coasts. Our fathers surely found a goodly domain, and He who gave them the land and its treasures, did not withhold from them the divine gifts.

They had their laws and their prophets, and they had them from God himself. Not only has the essential law of the Bible been always devoutly recognized by the leading American fathers, but the new legislature that founded and guarded our republic, embodied the best results of Christian civilization, and moreover answered to those instincts of natural right which the gospel ever quickens and confirms.

The great legal acts that made us a people, we can lay before God with thanksgiving, as we do this day, as being His work as well as our own. The great Declaration that marked our Exodus or Passover, and the Constitution that made our civil Pentecost, we lay before the mercy-seat to-day, and ask the God who gave them to us to bless them now and evermore.

Our prophets too we have had, and still have. —for such are they who speak from the spirit of God, whether naturally or supernaturally— the men and women who from the beginning have been divinely moved and, not by mere tradition of the letter or the dogma, not by cold prudence, or base calculation, but out of a living soul, lighted and fired by God's trust and love, have spoken to the heart of this nation of things past, present, and to come. We have had and have now prophets, and they have given the nation its progressive life as our laws have given its wholesome stability. Some of them have been seers into nature, and have read her secrets and have opened to us new and mighty powers in the mines, and prepared the way for our marvellous dominion over the elements, the water, the air, the lightning. Others have been seers of education, humanity, patriotism, religion, and touched with their sacred fire the heart of the nation, at the bar, in the senate, the school-house, the pulpit, the press. Certainly the American mind has been and is alive with inspiration, and whilst not all eloquence can be called divine, we should offend our sober sense and our Christian faith, were we to deny that the Spirit of God has been with us in our best thinkers, statesmen, orators, poets, moralists, and divines. Surely the tongue of fire has not been withheld from this continent, nor has its gift been by any means limited to the bishop's mitre that imitates and symbolizes its cloven flame. The free churches have had their full measure of the gift, and apparently more; and the conspiracy of despots who are trying, like the ancient priests of Baal, to destroy our nation by destroying our fundamental law, have been and are confronted by a moral sense that they fear as much as they do the armies of our constitutional republic. The conspirators cannot bear our clergy, and say that they are their greatest enemies. No wonder that the ministers of Christian civilization should be the enemies of military despotism, and the apostles of divine ideas should be the foes of barbaric force. I have sometimes in this place taken exception to what seemed to me to be the extravagance of certain of the more radical preachers of this country, and have always maintained that the law of the land should be respected by good citizens, and its imperfections should be corrected not by violence, but by peaceful legislation, under the influence of the higher law. I have little respect for the habit of thought that treats statutes as waste paper, and makes each man his own legislator and judge. Yet as between the radicals, who set the higher law above the statute law, and the conspirators, who are most bitter against them, I hold the balance to be wholly in favor of the former. For whilst such men as Garrison, Parker, and Phillips, have nobly vindicated the rights of conscience and humanity, although sometimes despising the statute of the Constitution, these conspirators have committed both transgressions at once, and have trodden under foot the laws of the land, and the great instincts of humanity. Well may such men fear the voice of our prophets, and seek shelter under the covert of defunct superstition. No wonder that the fear should deepen now that the conservative clergy have kindled into indignant flame, and they who do not deny but who respect our constitutional law, speak out for it with something of the fire of the prophets. Our brethren have done, and are doing their part, and the pulpits that God has gifted with such prophets of liberty as Mayhew and Channing have not lost their fire. Our preachers this day are lifting up their voices among the camps of the Capitol whither they have followed our citizen soldiers; several of our own ministers are chaplains of regiments from their own homes, and the men of Massachusetts who were fired on in Baltimore, had with them one of our preachers who is as gentle as brave; and all California lights up with the glowing eloquence of our gifted young brother, whom we cheered and blessed as he last year went on his way to bear the pearl of great price to those gates of gold that open our America westward still, as if to invite Asia our mother to come and dwell with her more than queenly daughter, who has a continent for her heritage. But why speak of any creed or class when the whole Church of our loyal Republic is visited with tongues of fire? This great city to-day keeps its Pentecost, and its clergy and people acknowledge the bond between our law and our prophets, our constitutional heritage, and our living inspiration. Here within sight, from spires and towers marked by different creeds, the flaming symbol of patriotism is borne aloft in the rushing wind, and this Church of the Messiah interchanges word with Trinity and St. Paul's with her tongue of fire.

Surely we are a people and God has made us so. There is a world of comfort in that thought, and the comfort will be double if we follow its promise to the end.

II. Follow it to the end, and dwell upon the brave and quickening words of the great Hebrew prophet Isaiah in their application to our needs and trials. Speak ye comfortably to our Jerusalem, and cry to her that her warfare is accomplished, her iniquity is pardoned, for she hath received of the Lord's hand double for all her sins.

Her warfare—it is already accomplished in its earlier stages, and its final triumph is begun. Our people have fought two great battles, one over nature, another over man. The contest with nature began when European civilization first touched these shores, and has been continued wherever the pioneer's axe has felled the primeval forest, and home, and school, and church have risen from the howling wilderness. How magnificently it has been accomplished, and the banners of its victory float upon ten thousand masts, and its jubilee sounds from chariots of iron that are borne by steeds of fire from land to land, and sea to sea. Glory to God for the warfare and the victory! Glory to Him for this great realm, His gift, and our trophy. The contest with man began when the savage crossed the first white man's path and denied him his share of this great heritage, which God intended for higher uses than for the hunting ground of savages, and has been continued wherever French or British despotism has wounded our liberties and laws. We have had the Frenchman for our foe, and we overcame him not only with the weapons that are carnal, but with the powers that are spiritual, and he fought with us, not against us, in the battles of our emancipation. Again he may be with us, and if England again plays false, France may give proof that she can defend the nation she helped to form. We have had England twice for our foe, and she has become our friend, and never as this very year had such testimony of the good will we bear her, and the love that should go with kindred blood. We wish her friendship, but do not depend upon her power, and will not brook her dictation. We have the heart of her people, but care not for the oracles of her grasping markets, or her aristocratic cabals. There is to us more of Heaven's thunder in any honest citizen's voice than in all the pretentious decrees of her great time-serving press that insults the land of Milton and Hampden by its base materialism and ill-disguised sycophancy at the footstool of wealth and power. We have not feared England in our day of small things, and shall not begin to tremble at her now in this day of our greatness. Enough valor has been shown and enough advantage gained to make us bold in face of the new aggressor, and to defy and defeat the new tyranny that dares to threaten our national life. What this new enemy is, it is not easy to say with entire definiteness, so changing is his face and so shifting are his arts. His movement, however, is clear, and he assails our National Union, not only by attacking our flag, but by denying that allegiance of the States to the Nation, which was the source, and is the life of our Constitutional Republic. His motive also is clear, and to the ungodly lust for power among the political leaders of the slaveholding oligarchy, we ascribe the origin of this foul treason. Our war is against the movement, or against disunion, and not against slavery except as far as slavery is arrayed against the Union. Prospectively slavery is undoubtedly doomed, and the doom is near at hand, and must come as soon as the slaveholding power as such unites in assailing our National life; for the Nation must and will be preserved, even if it be necessary to free every slave in the land. But without pushing this point to extremes, we are evidently now in conflict with a conspiracy of despots who are striving to win to their side the fears and passions of the whole South, and the interests and ambition of the great trading powers of Europe. We have beat them heretofore in the race of civilization, and the census is the field-book that records our forces and our trophies. We shall beat them in the new issue, and tread on the new traitors as on the old. Benedict Arnold, Daniel Shays, Aaron Burr, John C. Calhoun, the last the most seditious man that ever escaped unhung in America, in turn have felt the power of our republic in its wrath, and the day of reckoning is not far distant for the new crop of conspirators who are insulting the country after being pampered upon its bounty and honors. Already judgment is pronounced before the tribunal of our people against them; and the great army that has risen as by magic at the word of our rightful President, is but the armed magistracy that is marching forth to execute the solemn verdict of the public conscience.

If great deeds are done when great purposes are formed, the present warfare is accomplished, as at the old day of Pentecost, before Rome was attacked by the apostles of the Cross, she was virtually defeated in the rise of that fellowship of spirit that made the Eternal City its seat, and in the coming of those tongues of fire that consumed the old heathenism and kindled the new civilization with the flames of a divine charity. Great purposes as well as ideas are prophetic, and both purposes and ideas originate not with man alone. Certainly a victory is won when its germinal purpose is rooted, and all brave deeds are the fruit of that mysterious and mighty seed. God comforts us with the hope that our final warfare is accomplished.

How is it with our iniquity? Surely ours as a people has been great, and we have sinned especially in our social and our political life. We have lived too much as if Mammon were god, as if wealth were the great, if not the sole good; and what is won by engrossing care should be spent in enfeebling self-indulgence. We have tested institutions and laws too much by a material standard, and been willing almost, like Esau, to sell our birthright, if not for a mess of pottage, for a bale of cotton. Our politics had become depraved, and principles were sacrificed to policy, the spoils of office set above its duties, and party leaders have combined with unscrupulous crowds to pervert and estrange the people. The iniquity came to its head this very year, when a feeble and time-serving politician in the highest seat of power found himself surrounded by a clique of traitors, who, serpent-like, stung the hand that warmed and fed them, and showed the absurdity of the alliance between Northern democracy and Southern despotism. Can God forgive such iniquity? If not in view of our merit, certainly from His own mercy towards a people who meant well, and who spurned the treason when they saw the wolf stripped of his sheep's clothing. In our worldliness, moreover, we had not been godless, and the country from the Atlantic to the Pacific coast is covered with the schools and churches that consecrate wealth to humanity and religion; and our senate halls, in spite of their too frequent faction and venality, have rung with appeals as noble and patriotic as were ever heard in the great days that gave us our republic. God seems to have forgiven us for our worldliness and our self-seeking, and to have remembered what self-sacrifice was shown of old for this nation, and what noble characters and inspirations have gone forth from our time, and embodied themselves in our institutions of science, humanity, and faith.

Shall we dare to repeat the last clause of the text, and to say, " she hath received double for all her sins?" It is not wise surely, for any man to play the prophet in respect to developments so complex as those of nations; but I am moved to affirm a blessed future for our nation, as the fruit of this great uprising of faith and loyalty. We shall triumph anew in the breadth of our domain and the greatness of our spirit. The land that we now hold shall be doubled in yield and worth, because held by a nobler industry, and as our republic confirms its laws and its liberty, new domain will open to us beyond our wish, and realms, closed against the filibuster's invasion, will solicit the presence of our liberating hand, and the protection of our powerful flag. But the greatest victory will be in the kingdom of ideas and national enthusiasm. The consciousness of the people will be, and is stirred as never before. Society rests upon a mysterious ground of emotion and impulse, as well as upon definite ideas and interests, and the beginning of all great social movements, like creation itself, is in darkness. The experience that founds the home by mating the heads of the future family, and the experience which makes the birth or the new birth of a human soul, is hidden from analysis. It is so with the origin of great fellowship, civil or religious. The origin of the Christian Church is a mysterious fact; and Peter's sermon at the day of Pentecost no more explains the regenerating power at work within that fellowship, than a lecture on the prism explains the creative fiat, "God said let there be light, and there was light." What this great experience of our nation means, or what is its cause, I do not pretend fully to know; its occasion is clear enough, but its cause is deeper far. We know what set fire to our national feeling, but what constitutes that national feeling is more than we can say. A rude blow gave the kindling spark, but the fuel had been gathering for years in depths beyond our fathoming, and we cannot but believe that the heart of a great nation is now new born by the Holy Spirit and by fire. We may be tempted to hate a foe, but surely we are moved to love our friends, and it would be hard to find in all history so signal a dismissal of party names and feuds, and jealousies of race and country, as we have seen within one month. Our Union Square saw a Pentecost of patriotism that fused all parties and nationalities together, and the majestic face of the Father of our Country looked a blessing upon the multitude of his children there met together to own and defend the heritage that he bequeathed.

We have learned some valuable lessons in social philosophy as we note the defeat of schemes of bargaining compromise, and the success of movements of vital fellowship. Where are the old parties now—especially the two great parties which under various names have divided the republic since the days of Adams and Jefferson? The spell has been broken that bound the Democrat to the Southern despotism, and our great democratic party, essentially humane and loyal, in spite of its domineering policy, and unscrupulous methods, finding itself betrayed under the stolen banner of State rights in the hands of despots, who have set the bayonet of mercenaries above the ballot-box of the people, has turned upon the betrayers, and is waging, with terrible force of numbers and courage, the war for the Union against its destroyers.

The European races that have been marked as strangers, and whose swarming millions had sometimes been looked upon by cautious patriots with misgiving, are now strangers no more. Our country is the home of all who inherit it by the covenant sealed with their own blood, and I can call no man foreigner who is willing to lay down his life for our mother-land. The Irish, Germans, Scotch, French, and Italians are marvellously possessed with the spirit of our nationality, and a single spark of patriotic fire has fused into fellowship heterogeneous elements, races, and characteristics that a century of careful culture and conciliation might not have drawn together. How different is the way of God's spirit from the way of our policy. We aggregate, but God assimilates the elements; we put them together in one mass, but he unites them in one life. We are like the huckster who thinks to make the pile of copper, tin, zinc, and lead on his counter, pass for bronze. God's spirit is the fire which melts them into one rich metal in the furnace, and in due time fills the clay mould with the precious tide, and lo! when the mould is broken the eye of the beholder starts with amazement as God's own image looks out from the finished work, and a Washington or Franklin rises up to be called blessed by the people.

But why limit the assimilating work to living parties, races, and sections? Why not be open to the great conviction that every profound experience brings the living and dead together; and as Abraham, Moses, David, Isaiah, and all the great heroes, saints, and fathers of Israel seemed to commune together at the solemn feasts, and to chant together the thrilling Psalms of faith and patriotism, why not cherish as noble a thought at this Pentecost of our people when we so tenderly feel the beating of the pulse of national life that makes all true Americans one? We each cherish the memory of our favorite representative men, and each State feels the spell that rises from the dust of its own heroes, and calls the people to go forth to finish the work which they began. On their marches and voyages, on the deck of transports, and in the camp, our soldiers, with their war songs, do not forget the old hymns of devotion, and on this day, at the capitol, our New England troops, under the ministry of their chaplains, lift to God's mercy-seat under the open heavens the majestic strain of Old Hundred, that so often rung through our primeval forests. It is not hard to believe that the Pilgrims of the Mayflower with the fathers of the Revolution join in the swell, and a deep and solemn voice from the groves of Mount Vernon gives its Amen. Nay the dead do live with us, and within us, and the life that we call our own bears within it the continuous and associate life of the nation and its fathers. Our great father's presence we consciously feel, and nothing cheers and strengthens us more than the conviction that Washington now heads our armies, and his name and spirit designate the characteristic principle and secure the victory of our Constitutional Republic. Our erring brethren at the South whose good we seek, and whose worthy traits we revere, may well cherish this sense of fellowship with the dead, and let the voice of their own patriots reclaim them from the hands of the conspirators who are undoing precisely what those patriots lived and died to do. South Carolina and Virginia, the leaders in the mischief, have their best wisdom in that region of the dead, and we could easily forgive their recent sins if they would with us render due honor to their own great fathers, and cease to insult their dust by honors to the crew of despots whose madness rules the hour.

The fellowship will be complete when the lost sheep return—when the wanderers are reclaimed from deceivers' wiles, when Saul, breathing threatenings and slaughter, becomes Paul the Apostle, and the noble hearts not with us, catch the prevailing fire, and whatever have been their party or sectional dialects, all hear in their own tongue wherein they were born. That consummation would be a Pentecost of religion, as well as patriotism; and not only the love of country, but the charity that is born of God, and hath promise of heaven, would be mightily inflamed and perpetuated.

Why may it not be thus, and the nation and the church be friends as never before, as a more generous type of citizenship allies itself with a more rational and genial faith? Why not harmonize as we have never done as yet our Christian with our national type of consciousness? Ought not the two to rest upon the foundation of divine truth, the same law of righteousness, and rise up in the same fellowship of the spirit? The Word of God is not only in the Bible, but in all truth, and in all just law, and the Spirit of God is in all true union, working in nature in the order of the elements and the globes, bringing families and nations together in kind and free civilization, and giving all filial souls good fellowship on earth and in heaven. Why not acknowledge devoutly the Holy Spirit as the living bond of all union, and implore His presence to stay the hand of sedition, and to make us now and ever one people? Our fathers surely brought to the public councils minds disciplined and assimilated by divine grace, and we can enter into their faith as well as their heroism. We will do it—nay, we are doing it, and we feel to-day that our country and our religion are one in our hearts. Our flag floats from our church tower, and why may I not interpret it as it must seem to the whole world when what is best in its promise is restored, and America becomes the shelter and home of the oppressed, the seat of humanity, and the garden of God. When her warfare is accomplished, her iniquity is pardoned, and she hath received double for all her sins, the patriot and Christian who looks upon those stars on a blue field, emblem of the heavens, may read in them the call to give "Glory to God in the highest," whilst the white, the color of the Prince of Peace, says "Peace on Earth," and the red, the color that for ages has decked the Whit-Sunday altars, shall symbolize the flaming heart of divine love, and say, "Good will to men." Look this day, as we leave the sanctuary, to the flag of our country on our church tower, and ask the Holy Spirit to read to us, and to the new ages, the meaning of the Blue, the White, and the Red, by putting all the symbols together till they chant with tongues of fire in the rushing wind that plays with their folds, the anthem of the Messiah's birth: Glory to God in the highest, peace on earth, good will to men.

THE RE-UNION OF THE STATES.

A Sermon preached at Boston, Mass., Sept. 26, 1861.

BY REV. NEHEMIAH ADAMS, D.D.*

"The word of the Lord came again unto me, saying, Moreover, thou son of man, take thee one stick and write upon it, For Judah and for the children of Israel his companions; then take another stick and write upon it, For Joseph, the stick of Ephraim, and for all the house of Israel his companions: And join them one to another into one stick, and they shall become one in thy hand. And when the children of thy people shall speak unto thee, saying, Wilt thou not show us what thou meanest by these? Say unto them, Thus saith the Lord, Behold, I will take the stick of Joseph, which is in the hand of Ephraim, and the tribes of Israel his fellows, and will put them with him, even with the stick of Judah, and make them one stick, and they shall be one in mine hand."—*Ezekiel* xxxvii. 15-19.

EITHER the last days of the world, with the unutterable woes of prophecy, are at hand, or this nation is in some way to cease from its sectional alienation, and from the consequences of that alienation—perpetual hatred and wars. For self-defence against each other, if for no other reason, the North and South must be one people. If the things which have driven us apart are to remain, or if they are to be violently terminated, the prospect is like that dire-

* Printed from the Boston Courier, with corrections by the author of the sermon.

ful history of Israel and Judah, after secession had ripened into civil wars, ending in the ruin and captivity of a people who were preëminently the people of God. In promising those captive tribes that they should again be one people, (alas, how changed!) God makes known to them and to us that national Union is, in his view, essential to his idea of national happiness and prosperity. That which God did to Israel and Judah, after long civil wars and foreign subjugation, we must beseech him now to do for us. One thought, one desire, one prayer, may well take possession of you to-day, fellow-Christians and fellow-citizens— The re-union of the States.

We are beginning now to estimate the blessings which we have enjoyed as one great united nation. As the shadows of mountains, or the shadow of the earth projected on the moon, reveal their dimensions, the shadow of our national happiness, now flung like a pall over every thing and reaching across the earth, shows us what we have been and are ceasing to be. Oh, for the world's sake, remain, ye States, and still be one people! If we come out of this trouble one nation, it will settle the question of capacity for self-government. Must it, then, become like a logarithm in navigation, that human nature needs monarchs and the pomp and show of forms and rank to govern it? Just as we seem to be at the summit of our great enterprise, to have the mighty work become a byword, and to see that our system of self-government, so beautiful in theory, is too perfect for human nature, and that Delfthaven, Mayflower, Plymouth Rock, and all such names and memories, are forever to be like those sad but transcendent outlines and sketches of unfinished pictures by Allston in our Athenæum, while coming generations passing by shake their heads at our grand ruins, saying,—"This man began to build but was not able to finish," what true American citizen would not die a thousand deaths to prevent this? Whoever shall prove to have been the destroyers of such a fabric as this American Union, will have a fearful account to settle with the human race and with the God of the whole earth.

We have got beyond argument. Moreover, there is a stage of passion in which the subject of it becomes emotionless; the rapids are hushed, and the immense volume of feeling bends over to the abyss seemingly without a ripple. "To God the Lord belong the issues from death." A dying nation! Is it so with us? If we are drawing nigh to the tomb of nations, that land of silence, would that we might have spent this day alone, in silence. Words seem out of place. I despair of reasoning on this subject after the ordinary manner, and must ask you to turn aside and walk with me, in some paths which for the time may seem to you a little strange and out of the way.

Feeling sick with every day's report of the war, I had no heart to take the usual vacation this summer, till the time for it was half expired. But remembering how bad a symptom as to health is an apathetic indisposition to a change of place and scenes, I left home for a tour among the White Mountains, and happened to arrive there the day before the new carriage road to the top of Mt. Washington was opened to the public. Looking from the window of the Glen House the next morning about daybreak, I saw men harnessing four horses to a six-pounder rifled cannon, which had entertained us the evening before with echoes. A saddle was girt upon the cannon, which then started for the summit. A hundred and fifty people, including the directors of the new carriage road, assembled at the summit of Mt. Washington, and the cannon began to celebrate the inauguration of the road. But with great respect for the cannon, as one of the powers that be, one could not help feeling that the great symbol of violence and war is out of place in such scenery. All that world of sublimity and beauty, changing its forms every moment, now appalling, now delighting, subduing and then exalting you, passes on with perfect silence. As the Hebrew has it, "No speech, no language, their voice is not heard." So that in those chambers of eternal silence, where every thing around you knows so much, but forbears to speak, and where you yourself would not speak too loud, the cannon, dare I say it? seems impertinent. Our predictions, however, were true; for it was sublime and beautifully appropriate that the gun awoke not a single echo. Far above the reverberating sides of all the hills, in a rarified atmosphere, the report was only a quick, sharp bark. It was good to be for a little season where the voice of war met with no responses. The nearer we get to heaven, cannon are more and more out of place. We are yet a long way distant. The cannon must yet traverse our fields of earthly happiness. Among the Alpine passes Napoleon once eagerly said to the engineer employed on the Semplon, "The cannon—when can we get it over into Italy?" The spirit of that question is for the present the spirit of the times.

We, in this section of the country, did not desire it—we did not seek it. The opinion is not without foundation, that when our military forces were concentrated at Washington, it was the expectation of our Lieutenant-General, that with a sufficient military force, it would be easier to make terms and end the controversy; and neither he nor we supposed that we should so soon try the wager of battle. One in authority said, two weeks before the battle at Manassas, (and I know to whom he said it,) "I mean to finish this war without bringing in a butcher's bill." We all know how he and we were disappointed. We have no proof from the beginning that those who are charged with our military affairs have desired the evil day. On the contrary, there is reason to believe that as soon as duty to the Constitution will permit, they whose place it now is to be the first in war, will, of all the citizens of the free States, be first in peace. A good man, if eminent in military affairs, is made eminently humane by war. But to-day the cannon of the North is pointed against our alienated and embattled South; the cannon of the South is pointed at the foundation stones of our Republic. Quoting the Apostle James, who wrote, among other things, of war, we feel disposed to say, "My brethren, these things ought not so to be."

Going up Mount Washington, along the "Gulf of Mexico," as they call it, you see standing together, but more distinct than they seem from the plain, and yet buttressed one by the other, Mounts Jefferson, Adams, Madison, with Mount Clay between Mounts Washington and Jefferson. Glorious fellowship of Southern names given to Northern mountains! What a story does this contain! What mighty witness and what great reproof does it bear! We were designed to be one. These mountains have an eternal covenant of baptism joining the South and North. You find yourself making your longest pauses before that august companionship of the hills, and it is because faith and hope make the wish father to the thought, if you also find yourself saying there to your country, your whole country, in the name of our covenant-keeping God: "For the mountains shall depart and the hills be removed; but my kindness shall not depart from thee, neither shall the covenant of my peace be removed, saith the Lord that hath mercy on thee. O thou afflicted, tossed with tempest, and not comforted! behold, I will lay thy stones with fair colors, and thy foundations with sapphires. No weapon that is formed against thee shall prosper."

Five thousand people have passed the tollgate from the Glen to the top of Mount Washington the past summer. Few—so few that a child can write them—were from beyond the free States. What a day that will be in our land when that mountain top shall gather again representatives from all our latitudes. We shall see them vicing in courtesies, learning from each other, and again constituting bonds between the different parts of the land stronger and more enduring than ever. Then the mountains will bring peace to the people, the respective natural peculiarities of the various sections drawing them one to another. The idea that those of the South are to have no part in the White Mountains, and that we of the North are to be shut out of their equally charming and wonderful land, seems preposterous. We must have a "South," and they must have a "North." We will insist that we were made to be one nation to the end of time, and we shall be, if the prayers of millions in this land and around the globe, can prevail. It has been deeply interesting to find, as I have done, in this month of travel, among people of all parts of the North, notwithstanding all the intense feeling which there is against secession and on the subject of slavery, what deep-seated love there is for the South as a part of the nation, and what unaffected sorrow in having been obliged, if for no other reason, in self-defence, to be at war with her. We all understand that their seizing the military works was merely a consequence of a preceding step, for having made secession, they say it would have been simple in them to allow their adversary the use of his own guns at their very doors. So, as the French proverb says, "It is the first step that costs." But though the taking of Sumter united the North as one man, it was a speech at Montgomery that night, or the night after, as to ultimate designs on Washington, with the additional mention of Faneuil Hall, which left us no alternative but flying to arms. So that those who had defended the South found themselves, by their action, like men that would hold the arms and tie the feet of a near relative, who, in a paroxysm, is seeking to destroy the house. It looks like angry coercion, but I have seen strong men come near to weeping while they earnestly took part in it. We are not an enemy to the South. Multitudes in the two sections are now in a false position toward each other. This we must bear till the two swords now crossed have had their fill of blood. We have sinned against each other in the two sections; but that our Government has sinned against the South, or given them occasion for their action, we all steadfastly deny. They have always had more than their proportional share of influence at Washington; they alone are responsible for not at this moment having in the Presidential chair some one of their own nomination. They divided, and could not agree, and they should not find fault with the consequence. It is not uncharitable to say that powerful men among them did not wish the consequence to be other than it is.

The South might always have had more than their due proportion of influence in the Government, if they did not demand it. They are naturally a great conservative element in the nation—an agricultural people, bound together by one great interest; the other part of the nation would quietly forego some privileges, and, perhaps, rights, unless imperiously demanded of them, for the sake of that one large conservative element which the South would always furnish, if they could agree among themselves—somewhat as the land quietly allows the waters of the globe a preponderating influence—it being for the interest of the globe that the waters should be united, for thus only are they a conservative power. Very many true friends of the South at the North, left their respective parties, and voted for the present incumbent of the Presidency, for the avowed reason that they believed his election would best secure the peaceable fulfilment of all our Constitutional duties to the South; and their votes were not a declaration against that section. While the South misjudges us in this thing, we are also mistaken if we ascribe all that has happened to the loss of political power. President Lincoln said in his message to the special Congress, that probably two-thirds of the Southern people, if left to themselves, would be for the Union. If this is a sound opinion, it must follow that two-thirds of the South do not hanker after political power, and therefore they are moved to this war by some other cause. Many among us ascribe Southern alienation to the influence of demagogues. But some of you are too well acquainted with men at the South who have no superiors in all goodness and intelligence, not to know that it is sectional opinion and feeling which led to our present trouble. "Grievous words stir up anger." "Surely the churning of milk bringeth forth butter, and the wringing of the nose bringeth forth blood, so the forcing of wrath bringeth forth strife." Far down below questions of "tariff," "free-trade," "Calhoun's doctrines," "Missouri Compromise," our opinions, feelings, and language about the South, and theirs in retaliation about us, constitute the volcanic furnace in which these present swords and shields of Mars have been wrought. As the fist in a brawl is to the tongue, so is this war to our respective speeches and pens. It once seemed to many of us that in the eloquence of abuse some of our Northern people had won and borne the palm. But after reading many extracts from Southern papers, as you have all done, you must acknowledge that in the power of expressing themselves to suit any and every frame of mind in a controversy, our brethren have left us little reason for pride and boasting. They are naturally, by their warmer temperament, an eloquent people, and in the accumulation of new phrases when you thought the topic exhausted, the choice of a very pointed word, now and then, to prick the sides of attention, volubility, rapid transitions, and all the other arts of speech, they throw our most accomplished traducers into shadow. And so the admonition of Holy Writ is made pertinent to our case: "But if ye bite and devour one another, take heed that ye be not consumed one of another." Those have never seemed to go deep enough into human nature, who impute the action of these ten or twelve States to disappointed political ambition. The great original of all this trouble is the conscientious opposition of the people of the free States to the relation of ownership in man. It is this repugnance and opposition which make it difficult for us to see how we can do otherwise than repel and alienate each other, for two generations at least, if in the mean time we do not both perish. We all, perhaps, have some theory about the issue of this war, and one is, that let who will conquer, the greatest and most important result will be that the North will at length leave to the South the whole moral responsibility of their present relation to the colored people, and to time and Providence the question as to that people's destiny. Until we are willing to do this, no matter what our relations may be, united or divided, we shall be mutually hateful, and hating one another. Bitter experience may instruct us, as nothing else would, that the only terms on which we can escape destruction would be either for the North generally to adopt such views as the candid, Christian people at the South generally entertain, or to consent that they shall, unmolested by reproachful and irritating words, perpetuate, or change, their social state; and if the latter, in their own time and way. Since I can say it, and you can hear it, without improper feelings, I venture to suggest that because it has been so extensively received and acted on among us as a religious truth, that the relation of the South to the negro constitutes them unrighteous, a state of mind has been created, of which this war is the fruit. Considering ourselves when we are tempted, we cannot be surprised that such a people as they should feel and act irregularly, passionately, imprudently, unconstitutionally, and even wickedly. Take the most innocent and natural of all the forms in which our opposition shows itself—our discussion of the cotton monopoly, and our apparently sincere and earnest wish that India or Africa, or some other portion of the globe will yield cotton in sufficient quantities to make slave labor impossible. If we may not be allowed to discuss such a subject, we have no liberty of thought and speech. Yet it is easy to see if the South were thus discussing by what means Lowell and Lawrence, Lynn and Haverhill, and other centres of manufacture, could be rivalled, and that, too, from moral considerations, good neighborhood and kindly feeling would be likely to suffer a chill, even in our philanthropic dispositions. Then if we, as a manufacturing people, should be held forth to the world's hatred in novels translated into every tongue, be prayed for, and if indictments were filed against us at the mercy-seat, the name of our system made a synonym for "all villanies," I submit whether we should not be more or less than human, if we did not at length go mad and dash with our fist at every body and every thing having a Southern imprint. Then suppose that the South should explain our conduct by the use of such terms as "high tariff," "protection to our manufacturers," "losing control of the Government," "designing men working on the passions of a semi-barbarous people," and after years of such intercourse there should be a Peace Conference, and the South should introduce a resolution, proposing that we should be called upon to state our grievances on paper;—it would not be strange if we behaved ourselves unseemly, unconstitutionally, and made it necessary for the rest of the nation to muster armies and fight us, in their own just self-defence. All this time, be it remembered, the Government is leaning to our side; we have a majority in Congress, in joint ballot, and if we will but stay in the Union, and trust ourselves to Him that judges righteously, we shall in time be vindicated. So that we could clearly be put in the wrong by the best of logic. But human passions do not follow the laws of logic nor the rules of reason. We have sinned against each other, North and South, and in one thing most heinously—in the violation of charity.

There are no laws of men which can effectually govern free speech, but there is a law of God which can do it—and that is Charity.

If a man has charity, he may say any thing, at any time, in any way, about any body, and it may do no harm; but even though he has truth on his side, yea, though he speaks with the tongues of men and of angels, if he has not charity, he is become like sounding brass and tinkling cymbals. The tongue has principally made this war; now we must fight it out; now we must seek to destroy each other, for a season; now the blood of the South and North must run in the same brooks; now bankruptcy must visit happy homes; now widows and orphans must be multiplied; now life-long sorrows must brood over dwellings which never would have known grief except as the ordinary lot of man. The accidental discharge of a gun destroys the face of a dear and honored Christian gentleman, who dies and is buried amidst the tears of the community. But every day the gun is mutilating faces as dear as his to loved ones, North and South. Any body can tell you in a breath half a score of the proximate causes of this war of secession: but let us go back, and go further down, and the cause of it, unjustifiably made so, I repeat it is found to be here—that Christians at the North do not admit that Christians at the South are as acceptable in the sight of God as we. This is the tap-root of our Upas tree. If our relative position could be changed, and Christian men and ministers and religious editors at the South felt and spoke toward us as we do toward them, and we could build a wall as high as the impassable Himmalehs between us and our Christian judges, we should be tempted to do so. Secede? We should be provoked to break compromises, covenants, constitutions, unions, and then pay most bitterly for our passion. But it is the way that nature, and human nature each relieves itself—through convulsions. Now blood must flow. As the sin of the world could only be taken away by the Lamb of God, great sins of men against each other can sometimes only be expiated by blood. We are both to suffer greatly, and the greatest suffering in the end will be to have wasted and destroyed life. Whichever side destroys the most, will afterward weep the most freely, and so He who made peace by the blood of his cross may save us by blood. For where natural affection survives and pleads, the infliction of pain deepens love in him who inflicts it, as every parent knows, and as every one may see in the beautiful philosophy in those soliloquies of the Most High: "Is Ephraim my dear son? Is he a pleasant child? for since I spake against him, I do earnestly remember him still; therefore my bowels are troubled for him; I will surely have mercy on him, saith the Lord."

There is one state of things which will be worse than the present, one which will be likely to put every State of the Union into the condition of Missouri—which of all our States to-day is most to be commiserated. If this war is turned by our Northern people into a war for emancipation, we have not begun to know what trouble is. I will not ask you to say whether such a war would be just or not, wise or unwise; I only say that if the issue becomes changed from constitutional grounds, where our Administration has placed it, and is determined to keep it, thereby uniting loyal men in every State, North and South; if, I say, by reason of any great tide in our affairs, or if, in doubling any cape, we meet a running sea which we cannot stand, and philanthropy for the negro mounts the fiery car and takes the reins, scenes will pass before us of which neither history nor any of our dreams have given us a type. We might then possibly see General Scott and General Beauregard fighting under one flag for the Union. In helping your Government to maintain this Union of States —helping it, I say, not only with men and money, but with your moral influence, and with your prayers, you are doing a work of whose magnitude no finite mind can adequately speak. Ere long we may all have to accept as the issue, union and toleration, or disunion. It never can be that God will require of us the sacrifice of principle—never. But how far may the limitations of human responsibility make it justifiable in me to believe, and to act on the belief, that Christian people at the South may properly be left, without accusation, to meet their own responsibilities to God? If we had been willing to do this for the last thirty years, there would have been at least fewer pretexts for secession. The thirteenth chapter of first Corinthians will save us, if it can enter into our hearts, North and South.

Let me illustrate my meaning. I will select a few Christian men of the South, whom I have in mind, who, for intellectual and moral worth, have nothing to fear in comparison with their fellow-men. You would intrust your all to them; you would love to have them at your side in the last hours of life. Whatever those men say to us with regard to their conscientious convictions about the relation of master and servant at the South, ordinary Christian charity would make it proper for us to receive, so far, at least, as to keep us from accusing and reproaching them. But the reply will be, Must we, then, lay aside our opinions, because men as good as we differ from us? On that principle there never could be any result in a deliberative assembly, where there was much difference of opinion; for then good men must all yield to each other, and there could really be no decisive opinions on either side. The objection is plausible, but this is the answer: When personal conduct and motives are concerned, the known personal character of others makes it obligatory on us to be charitable. But need I say what a heresy this declaration, as applied to Southern Christians, is held to be by a large part of the clergy and Christian people of the North? And now we must do battle, probably, till either the relation of the South to the black man is forcibly changed, or the North generally concludes that Christian consciences at the South are as enlightened as ours. This is truly a war for the Union, and many believe that it will be successfully a war for Christian union. This war will make us charitable, lead us to know each other better, fear each other with a wholesome fear, respect each other; and we may yet be proud of each other before the world. It may be that foreign aggression will hereafter trouble us; if so, the experience we have had of each other in arms will make us more than allies, and the old fields where Northern and Southern blood mingled in defence of our young Republic, will supplant in our memories all our Great Bethels and Manassas. There is an amazing strength in reconciled affection. One deep impression made on you in the woods is, the manifest kindness of Nature to all its parts, hastening to bind up the wounded, to cover the fallen, to compensate for desolations. There is one noticeable feature in our wild places—the light purple flower on a high stalk, the "Fire Weed," springing up wherever there has been fire. You meet whole fields of it, covering up the unseemly looks of the burnt district, so giving it "beauty for ashes." The wild raspberry, with its remarkable flower, is another of those sisters of charity with which Nature abounds. These things find their counterpart in such a feeling as this, (of which I know you are all conscious,) a dread of having any portion of our country, here or there, subjugated, broken down. If a man's arm has nervous movements which indicate disease, he would not have his arm destroyed, to be carried as a dishonored member the rest of his lifetime; he seeks the alleviative and restorative process, feeling that if one member suffers, all the other members suffer with it. The desire for re-union is growing intense, and there is getting to be as impatient a feeling toward Northern disunionists as toward Southern. The noble stand which our Administration maintains on this subject, puts strength and courage into every loyal heart.

If, in the providence of God, the relation of the negro to the white race here, becomes changed by this war, consistently with his good and that of all concerned, who, South and North, will not say Amen? But deal violently, and "that which is crushed breaketh forth into a viper." O that God would in mercy raise up some who shall turn us into the ways of peace! We shall soon forget that we have quarrelled, if we agree in good season. After the war, if the South were not, as they are, a rich people, and it could be suitable that we should aid them in their care for the wounded, and for the widows and orphans made so by our hands, you are such a singular people here in New England, that while providing for your own wounded, and widows, and fatherless children, it would be like you if some subscriptions in token of sympathy for the other side should be as large in Boston as could be obtained in the South.

The opinion may yet gain general currency among us, that in love to God and man, in self-denial, disinterestedness, in charitable institutions, in attendance on public worship, in Christian experience, in morality, in all that constitutes a high state of civilization, the cities of the North have no more occasion for gratitude to God and his infinite grace than Charleston, Savannah, Richmond, Augusta, and such like cities. A smile would play round the lips of every Southerner who should hear this. The war will put an end to sectional fanaticism, and "what the law could not do," and what we could not make each the other do, may yet be yielded as gracefully as the soil enriched with the ashes of its tangled woods and snags, generously yields, as you are aware it does, for its first crop the very finest of grain. We shall yet have intermarriages, North and South, and bonds sometimes denominated silken, but stronger than iron will bind us one to the other part. Sectional manners, when we are again mixed together, will be like the rough stones which become agates by the silent chastisement of the waves. "O, scenes surpassing fable!" Because there is a God in heaven, and He a God of love, we dare to say these things. Surely, to-day we are like the prophet's "two sticks," but we are in the hand of God, and as it required the Babylonish captivity to make those two sticks one, this war may be appointed for the perpetual re-union of these States. Break forth into joy! sing, ye waste places! for the Lord will yet comfort Jerusalem. And when our Southern friends revisit us, they will find neither man nor nature retaining any memorials of unkindness. The North Star will still lie directly over the road in the Glen, the Northern Bear sleep quietly along the ridge of the mountains, and the Peabody River sing its low, sweet song at their feet, as they did when we were at peace; so will they, when peace again, like a river, makes glad our holy places of the tabernacles of the Most High.

In the accidental visit to the mountains, which has given a coloring to the thoughts and feelings in this discourse, I seemed to find every thing protesting against unkindness and disunion. Standing where you can see the ground almost covered with fallen trees, you perceive that each has become a bed for moss, which kindly gathers over it, and makes its decay and deformity graceful and even attractive.

On the largest boulder that I ever saw, there was no room upon its perpendicular sides for any thing but lichens to minister their love and care, except that in the only crevice visible, and that but a fraction of an inch, one harebell had succeeded in getting a foothold, and was showing kindness to the solitary wanderer from the glaciers. But why should I be musing after this manner, when the war news already arrived may change the whole current of our thoughts. "There is a time to embrace and a time to refrain from embracing." I will adopt the recent sentiment of a Kentucky Union legislator: "If the alternative is forced upon me to conquer or be conquered, I prefer to conquer." He expressed the sentiment of his noble State and of our Administration. And so you have my imperfect, desultory thoughts on the times, meditated on Mount Washington. If it were only later in our present contest, and if any one else were speaking these things to you, I would join with you and say, "How beautiful upon the mountains are the feet of him that bringeth good tidings, that publisheth peace, that bringeth good tidings of good, that publisheth salvation; that sayeth unto Zion, Thy God reigneth."

SERMON

On the Divine Origin of Civil Government, and the Sinfulness of Rebellion: Delivered in the Ebenezer M. E. Church, at Philadelphia, Pa., Sabbath, June 30, 1861.

BY REV. P. COOMBE.

"Let every soul be subject unto the higher powers. For there is no power but of God: the powers that be are ordained of God. Whosoever, therefore, resisteth the power, resisteth the ordinance of God, and they that resist, shall receive to themselves damnation. For rulers are not a terror to good works, but to the evil. Wilt thou then be afraid of the power? do that which is good, and thou shalt have praise of the same.—For he is the minister of God to thee for good. But if thou do that which is evil, be afraid; for he beareth not the sword in vain: for he is the minister of God, a revenger, to execute wrath upon him that doeth evil."—*Romans*, xiii. 1-4.

Among the many evidences of the inspiration of the Bible, there is no one more significant than the fact, that considered as a code of law it is of *universal application*. While all systems of human jurisprudence apply only to certain localities, the Bible system is adapted alike to every clime and nation. The laws of men define the duties of certain classes of citizens, but the Divine law details the obligations belonging to every relation in life. The parent and child, the husband and wife, the buyer and seller, the ruler and the subject, all have their duties defined and their obligations set forth.

As a minister is the teacher of the people on all matters of religious duty, his position requires that he should explain and enforce the duties which God has imposed upon men. This is especially the case, when peculiar circumstances direct public attention with more than ordinary interest to any particular department of religious obligation.

On next Thursday, we shall be called upon to celebrate our National Sabbath,—the anniversary of the nation's independence. For eighty-four years we have observed its return amidst increasing prosperity, and with renewed causes of gratitude to God. That sacred day will, this year, make its advent among us, surrounded by the horrors of *civil war*, and an extra session of Congress will meet to adopt measures for the protection of the Government. Under these circumstances, I call your attention to the duties which belong to the hour, and I have selected a portion of Scripture which treats of the origin and objects of Civil Government, while it defines the duties of its subjects. I propose, therefore, to discuss two general propositions, viz.:

I. The doctrines of the text in regard to civil government—and,

II. The application of its principles to our present condition as a nation.

The doctrines taught are: 1. *Civil Government is a* Divine Institution. It is evident that civil government did not originate with man, because Adam was created the subject of the immediate government of God. All other men have been born under a government already in existence.

The text teaches that government originated with God, hence it says, "There is no power but of God,—the powers that be are ordained of God." This is also the record of history. The *first* form of government known among men was the Patriarchal, in which the parent, as head of the family, was the ruler, by the appointment of God. Among the Jews, who were his special people, God established, at different times, several forms of government.—He gave them Rulers, Judges, and Kings.

We have here two general facts established: God established civil government among his own people, thereby declaring His will on the subject and setting an example for all nations to follow. Through all past time this example has been followed, and all civilized nations profess to pattern after the divine form and laws.

As God established *different* forms of government among his own people, it is clear that no particular form is binding on men, but each nation is left free to choose that form which is best suited to its necessities. Hence Peter says, "Submit yourselves to every ordinance of man for the *Lord's sake*, whether it be the king as supreme, or unto governors, as unto those that are *sent by him* for the punishment of evil doers, and for the praise of them that do well." We have the additional fact, that God, in his Word, has given laws for the government of all kinds of rulers, thereby recognizing all the different forms of good government, as of divine origin.

2. *Civil Government has a* divine purpose. It is designed for the *protection of good men*. "Rulers are not a terror to good works,—do that which is good, and thou shalt have praise of the same,—he is the minister of God to thee for good." From this language it is evident that God did not intend civil government simply for the protection of the rights of property

and the peaceful pursuits of business; but also to secure to good men their *religious privileges.* Religion prospers most under that form of government which protects the rights of conscience, and God is thus acknowledged.

Civil government is also designed to *restrain and punish evil doers.* The text declares a civil ruler to be "the minister of God, a revenger, to execute wrath upon him that doeth evil." Civil law often restrains men when the law of God has no influence over them. They are "afraid of the power, because he beareth not the sword in vain." If left to the restraints of religious principle alone, wickedness would abound and virtue be sadly hindered. It is evident, therefore, that civil government is a *religious agency* designed for the glory of God as well as the regulation of society.

3. *Obedience to Civil Government is a* RELIGIOUS DUTY. Obedience to lawful authority does not arise, as some suppose, from *expediency,* nor from any "social compact" formed among men, but from *divine authority.* God's Word says, "Let every soul be subject to the higher powers," and places the obligation, thus imposed, upon the fact that "the powers that be *are ordained of God.*" This obedience embraces several particulars.

The strict observance of all proper laws is specially enjoined. The Apostle says, "Submit yourselves to every ordinance of man for the Lord's sake." This implies that we not only keep the law ourselves, but that we *permit the law* to punish offenders. Men have no right to take the law into their own hands, while there is power in the government to punish those who violate its precepts. Peter says that civil rulers are "sent for the punishment of evil doers." He who undertakes to punish offenders *without legal process,* strikes a fatal blow at the very foundations of government, and is himself a violator of law. There can be no security to society under *mob law.*

The payment of tribute or taxes, is another duty. Government cannot exist without officers to execute law,—officers cannot be employed without expense,—that expense should be met by those who enjoy the benefit; therefore, the support of the government is the duty of the governed. Hence the Scriptures say, "For this cause, *pay ye tribute* also, for they are God's ministers, attending continually upon this very thing."

Reverence, or respect for Rulers, is also enjoined. Those in authority should be *respected* by the people, in order that they may exercise a proper control over them. Any act or word which tends to destroy the confidence of the people in those who are in authority, weakens the power of government, and is a sin against God. His Word declares, "Thou shalt not speak evil of the ruler of thy people."

Prayer for all in authority, is another duty. Government being a Divine Institution, good men should pray for God's blessing upon it. An Apostle says, "I exhort, therefore, first of all, supplications, prayers, and intercessions, be made for kings and for all that are in authority, for this is acceptable in the sight of God."

4. *Resistance to Civil Government is a sin against God.*

This position is so self-evident that it will not admit of serious argument. If God has established government for the accomplishment of his own purposes, and commanded men to be subject to the higher powers, then it follows, in the language of the text, that "whosoever resisteth the power, resisteth the ordinance of God, and they that resist, shall receive to themselves damnation."

There is only one condition of things which can justify resistance to civil government, and that is, when the power is used *in opposition* to the purpose for which God ordained its existence.

If men in authority employ the powers of government in protecting the wicked and oppressing the good,—in promoting vice, and opposing virtue,—in the destruction of civil, political, or religious liberty, then, and then only, is resistance to "the powers that be" excusable in the sight of God. Even in such a case, *force* is not allowable until all *legal* means of redress have been tried *in vain.*

II. THE APPLICATION OF THESE PRINCIPLES TO OUR CONDITION AS A NATION.

The position of our national affairs at the present time requires that every citizen should understand and perform his duty to God and to the Government. A portion of the people of this nation have attempted the destruction of the Union, and are now in arms against the Constitution and the Laws. The Government has pronounced this movement to be *Rebellion,* and calls upon all good citizens to aid in defeating those engaged in it. *What is our duty in the case?*

To decide this important question, let us inquire into the CHARACTER *of our National Government.* Is it a *compact between the several States,* which may be dissolved at the pleasure of the parties, or is it a *consolidated* government, formed by *the people of all the States* and designed to be *perpetual?* Upon the answer to this question, the duty of all good citizens turns. If it be a "compact between the States" which may be dissolved at the pleasure of the States, then it is a mere question of *expediency* as to whether the Government should allow a peaceful separation. If, on the other hand, this Government was formed by *the people of all the States,* and intended to be *perpetual,* then no *State, in its corporate capacity,* can destroy the Union, and any attempt of this character is *rebellion, and should be resisted.* The following facts of history will settle these questions and teach us our duty:

Previous to the Revolutionary War, the thirteen original States were colonies of Great Britain, and subject to her laws. In throwing off the authority of the mother country and assuming the powers of self-government, these colonies constituted themselves free and *independent States.* On the 2d day of July, 1776, the general Congress of these colonies separated from Great Britain by the adoption of a Resolution which declared that "These United colonies *are,* and by right ought to be, free and *independent States.*" On the 4th of July, this separation was fully consummated by the adoption and publication of "The Declaration of Independence," in which the same language is employed, and the position of *independent States assumed.* Here observe, from colonies they became *States,* free from Great Britain and *independent of each other,* the laws of no one State having jurisdiction over the people of any other State. During the Revolutionary War, these thirteen States formed themselves into a confederacy or league by the adoption of a compact which contained the following words, viz.: "The said *States* hereby enter into a firm league of friendship with each other." This league, or, more strictly speaking, this *treaty,* was ratified, *not* by the *people* of these States, but by the State Governments *in their corporate character.* This Confederacy of States continued until 1788, each State forming a separate government, independent of all the other States. It is a remarkable fact, going to show the difference between the *character* of the Government then and now, that though England acknowledged our independence in 1783, and made a treaty of *peace* with these States, she positively refused to enter into a *treaty of commerce,* on the ground that there was *no General Government* which could guarantee the enforcement of treaty stipulations.

From 1783 to 1787 was a dark and disastrous period in the history of these States. They had secured their independence, and were free from the dominion of Great Britain, but that very independence became the source of discord and difficulty. As each State was sovereign in itself, conflicting interests soon brought them into contact with each other, and there being no general government with authority to settle these disputes, they began to quarrel among themselves. It therefore became evident that some plan must be adopted by which all the States could be united in a form of government duly authorized to regulate conflicting interests, or ruin and desolation would be the inevitable result. To show the truth of this position, we give the following extract from a letter written by George Washington to Thomas Jefferson, dated May 30th, 1787:

He says: "That something is necessary, none will deny, for the General Government—*if it can be called a government*—is shaken to its foundations, and liable to be overturned by every blast. In a word, *it is at an end,* and unless a remedy is soon applied, anarchy and confusion will inevitably ensue."

This state of things produced its legitimate result, and it was determined by Washington and Jefferson, with other fathers of this country, that the thirteen independent States should be consolidated into one *great nation,* and a government constituted, having general control, while the authority of each State should be *so restricted* as to bring it into harmony with the powers vested in the National Administration. For this purpose, a Convention of Delegates from the several States met in Philadelphia, in the month of May, 1787. George Washington presided over that Convention, which, after a long and painful deliberation of four months, adopted, Sept. 17th, a *Constitution,* by which these independent States were to be formed into one *consolidated* Government, under the title of "The United States of America." This Constitution was afterwards submitted to a vote of the people in all the States, and by them adopted "*as the supreme law of the land.*"

Several facts connected with the adoption of this Constitution demand particular attention at the present time. It was adopted by the *people* in their sovereign capacity, and *not* by the States in their corporate character. Hence, the Preamble said, "*We, the people* of the United States, to insure a *more perfect union,* and to secure the blessings of liberty for ourselves and our posterity, do ordain and establish this Constitution." The Constitution thus adopted by the people, *limited* the powers of the several States, and *transferred* to the General Government certain prerogatives formerly possessed by each independent State. "No State was allowed to coin money, emit bills of credit, pass *post facto* laws, or laws impairing the obligations of contracts." They were also prohibited from "maintaining armies or navies, granting letters of marque, holding intercourse with foreign nations, and granting titles of nobility." The Constitution also contains this clause: "This Constitution shall be the supreme law of the land, any thing in the Constitutions and Laws of the States to the contrary notwithstanding."

From these facts it is evident that the Government thus formed was the consolidation of these States into one great national power, to which each State, in its corporate character, was subject, and that no act or law of any one of the States can absolve a citizen from his duty to the General Government. Nor can the States, in their corporate capacities, break down the Constitution, it being "the supreme law of the land, any act or law of theirs to the contrary notwithstanding." It follows, further, that as this Union was established by the *people* of these States in convention assembled, that the *people alone*, in like manner assembled, can destroy the same, and that the action of any State or States, or that of a *part* of the people, declaring themselves separate from and independent of the General Government, is *null* and void. The Union *cannot* be dissolved but by the action of the *whole people.*

This fact was not only well understood at the time the Constitution was adopted, but it was made the ground of opposition to it. Mr. Henry, who violently opposed the consolidation of the States, said: "That this *is* a consolidated government is demonstrably clear. The language is, '*We, the people*,' instead of '*We, the States.*' It *must be one great consolidated national government of* ALL *the people—of* ALL *the States.*" The doctrine of "State Rights," as now claimed, had, therefore, no existence in the minds of the framers of our Government, and cannot now be used for its destruction.*

IS THIS REBELLION SINFUL?

That this question must be answered in the affirmative, we think is evident. This rebellion has been marked by actions which are forbidden by the law of God, and held in universal detestation by honorable men. Among these is *official dishonesty.* It is a fact which should not be lost sight of in determining the character of this rebellion, that it originated with, and has been carried out by, men holding official positions under the General and State Governments. The *people* in the seceded States have had but little to do in the matter except to follow the bidding of their leaders, without any fair opportunity to consult their own wishes upon the subject. Officers in the Cabinet, Governors of States, Members of Congress, and officers in the Army and Navy, have been the principal actors in this rebellion. These men have turned the Constitution against itself, by prostituting their official position to the destruction of the Government which it created.

The Secretary of the Treasury, to whom was committed the financial interests of the country, employed the powers of his office in squandering the funds of the nation, so as to leave the Government nearly bankrupt, for the purpose of destroying its power to put down the

---

* Luther Martin, of Maryland, when in the Philadelphia Convention of 1787, proposed to make a reservation in favor of those who should resist the national authority in obedience to the command of their respective States. The proposition of Mr. Martin was as follows :

"Provided, That no act or acts done by *one* or *more* of the States against the United States, or by any citizen of one of the United States, under the authority of one or more of the said States, shall be deemed *treason* or *punished as such ;* but, in case of war being levied by one or more of the States against the United States, the conduct of each party towards the other, and their adherents. respectively, shall be regulated by the laws of war and of nations."

This was rejected, for the reason, to quote Mr. Martin, that it was "too much opposed to the great object of many of the leading members of the Convention, which was by all means to leave the States at the mercy of the General Government."

rebellion which he and his fellow-traitors were plotting.

The Secretary of War employed the latter part of his term of office in distributing arms and ammunition through the Southern States, for the purpose of leaving the Government without the means of defence, while the rebels were supplied with the most improved weapons of war. *Members of Congress*, while occupying their seats, have plotted treason, and communicated the secrets of the Government to its enemies, being at the time under oath to support the Constitution and the laws. *Officers in the Army and Navy*, without even resigning their commissions, have surrendered troops and delivered vessels of war into the hands of the rebels, to be used against the Government to which they had sworn allegiance. Nearly one-half of the officers from the South have resigned their commissions when the country most needed their services, and most of them have joined in the rebellion against the Government, and are now leading troops to destroy their former companions-in-arms. The extent of this official corruption among men so high and honorable in point of position, is an undeniable proof of the demoralizing tendency of the doctrine of secession. Verily, it is a *very wicked thing*.

Perjury is another crime of which the leaders of this rebellion are guilty. Men who hold office under the General or State Governments, together with all officers in the army and navy, are under oath to support and defend the Constitution. There is no provision anywhere to release them from this obligation, and unless it can be shown that the Government has so abused its power as to justify its destruction, these men are guilty of wilful perjury in the sight of God and all right-thinking men. As the right of secession is claimed upon no ground of abuse of power by the Government, there is no excuse for having rejected the Constitutional means of redress.

This rebellion is *unlawful resistance* to a divinely authorized Government. This is a crime of no ordinary magnitude. God has said, "Let every soul be subject to the higher powers; the powers that be are ordained of God, and he that resisteth the power, resisteth the ordinance of God." Our Government has special claims to Divine origin and sanction. The country was founded by men who fled from religious persecution and established a home for the express purpose of serving God. The Constitution was adopted amidst prayers and tears for God's blessing, and up to this time we have furnished a home for the oppressed of every nation, where every man is at liberty to worship God according to the dictates of his own conscience. As a consequence, we have received special marks of Divine favor. God has fought our battles and given us prosperity equalled only by that of His ancient people— the Jews. If resistance to any government be resistance to God, then this rebellion must be a crime of fearful magnitude. They have set at defiance all the laws of God and man, in the fact that they have *rejected all the Constitutional modes of redress*. When men live under government, common honesty requires that, when grieved or oppressed, they should seek redress by the methods described in the Constitution. The leaders of this rebellion acknowledge this by now claiming, with most singular inconsistency, protection from the Constitution, every feature of which they have ignored, violated, and despised. They have rejected the mode of Constitutional *amendment*. If the interests of the South required any change in the organic law of the land, special provision was to be found in the Constitution for that purpose, and a large majority in the North were ready to grant all necessary modifications. Instead of seeking to secure any such change, they have madly rejected all offers of assistance, and attempted to destroy the Constitution itself.

They have also abandoned the legal mode of *preventing* oppression and wrong. The Constitution wisely provides for the correction of any oppressive policy on the part of those in power through the medium of the ballot-box. Men may be elected to office whose policy is in accordance with the wishes of a majority. If the people *refuse* to unite for the defeat of a President whose principles are those of the minority, it is their own fault, and furnishes no just cause for rebellion against the Government. It would be useless to deny that the South had this matter in her own hands in the last Presidential campaign, and that her delegates to the Charleston Convention deliberately divided the party on which they could have relied for protection to their rights. They thus threw the Government into the hands of men whom they denounced as their foes. If this result was not intended, it was at least foreseen, and having rejected the only method of defeating an antagonistic party they were bound in all honor to abide the result.

They have rejected the means of *protection*. When a majority in Congress is opposed to the policy of the President, he can do but little injury to the country by any measures of his own. The South and her friends were largely in the majority in the Congress, and this was an unanswerable argument why she should have adhered to the Constitution and the laws. Instead of doing this, these men ungenerously abandoned their friends by vacating their seats, and by this act threw the entire control of the Government into the hands of the present Administration. Such an insane and wicked policy can only be explained by the fact that, according to the sacred record, blindness has happened to them that forget God.

They have rejected the only method of *dissolving* the Union. The intention and desire of these men was to separate from the North by a dissolution of the Union, and they might have succeeded had they had the patience to wait and the wisdom to adopt the proper plan. There was a strong disposition, among both the friends and foes of Southern policy, to consent that the cotton States should try the experiment of a separate government. So strong was this feeling, that had a proposition for a National Convention been seriously made, it would in all probability have been adopted. It is a well-established principle of constitutional law, that "the power that creates can destroy," and as a Convention of the people formed this Union, a similar one could have abolished it, if, in the judgment of the people, it had failed to secure the object for which it was brought into being. Instead of adopting this plan, the leaders in this rebellion proceeded to erect an unholy despotism, and have trampled upon the rights of the people by attempting to destroy the Government without asking their consent. They have thus defeated the object they so earnestly desired to accomplish—the people of this country are not to be bought, sold, or transferred at the pleasure of their leaders.

But of all the wicked acts committed by the leaders of this rebellion, that which filled their cup of iniquity to overflowing was their *infa-* *mous attack upon Fort Sumter*. In that one act rebellion culminated—the claims of a common brotherhood were ignored—the rights of humanity were sacrificed, and the authority of God and man set at defiance. Major Anderson was a gentleman, a Christian soldier, and a *brother from the South*. From his fortress home, which he occupied by the orders of his Government, and which had been erected for the defence of their own city, he had watched for weeks the erection of batteries by those traitors without firing a gun or interfering with their preparations for attack. The Government, with great propriety, might have ordered him to disperse the men employed in the erecting of the first battery. This he could easily have done, but with a forbearance which amounted almost to a crime, they were permitted to collect thousands of troops and cover the shore with batteries at every available point. They were also aware that the garrison was in a starving condition, and had been officially notified of the intention of the Government to provision them. There was no necessity, therefore, of their attempting the reduction of the fort, as they had forces enough to prevent any vessel from reaching it with provisions, and hunger would have compelled its surrender in a few hours. Under these circumstances the ordinary dictates of humanity should have induced them to avoid the shedding of a brother's blood. But with a madness which amounted to frenzy, and a cruelty which was absolutely diabolical, they fired upon an unoffending garrison, and struck the *first* blow at the heart of the nation. In that blow,

"Man's inhumanity to man
Made countless millions mourn,"

and raised a shout of indignation which will echo through all coming time. The heart of the nation burst with one loud cry to God for vengeance, and the people rushed to arms for the defence of the Government. A long wail of agony proclaimed to the world that the *fall of Sumter* was the last birth-throe of a spirit which should crush out treason and give protection to the loyal men of the land. Here, then, we see the features of this rebellion. If dishonesty, perjury, resistance to lawful authority, and cruelty be sins against God, then this rebellion is one grand crime in the sight of Heaven, the like of which is scarcely to be found in the history of the world.

Let us now turn our attention to some of the *results* of this rebellion.

First. Instead of destroying the Union, they have *broken up their own State Governments!* There is now no *legal* government in the seceded States. This is evident when we consider a few facts in the relation which a State government sustains to the Constitution. When the people of the thirteen original States formed "a more perfect union," they *transferred* the essential powers of sovereignty from the States to the General Government, and made the "Constitution and the laws of Congress enacted in pursuance thereof, the *supreme law* of the land." All the States which have been admitted into the Union since that time, have been admitted by an Act of Congress, and all State officers are sworn to support the Constitution of the United States. The State Government, therefore, exists *under* the authority of the General Government, and all State officers, both legislative and judicial, derive their powers from the Constitution itself. It follows, therefore, with all the force of demonstration, that, these men having thrown off their allegiance to the General Government, and risen in rebellion to the Constitution, they are no longer in possession of legal authority,—the seceded States have *no* duly authorized government, and the people are not bound to obey their new enactments. Each one is a despotism, and not a legal government.

Western Virginia has caught this idea and carried it out, by organizing a Provisional Government, which must of necessity be recognized as the only Constitutional authority in that State. The former officers have been legally deposed, and they are now without power, except that of force.

The General Government lives, but that of the traitors is broken, and thus God has "brought to naught the counsels of the wicked."

Second. They have forfeited all claim to protection under the Constitution and laws.

According to international law, one nation has the right to go to war with another nation, and they are mutually bound to treat each other according to the principles established by the Law of Nations. In such a case, the "rights of war" must be faithfully observed, and prisoners taken in arms must be treated with respect and kindness. They have the right to destroy life, to possess and employ the property of the enemy, without being liable to the penalties for murder and robbery. But when a portion of the subjects of any government rise up in rebellion to legal authority, they are not to be treated according to the Law of Nations, but according to the laws of their own land for the punishment of offenders. If *one* man rebels against lawful authority, and steals property or destroys life, he is held as a robber or murderer, and treated as such. If twenty men, or twenty thousand, do the same thing, it does not change the law in the case,— the principle remains the same. The punishment of offenders, in such cases, is *not the waging of war;* it is only the proper exercise of authority for the punishment of individual transgressors. It does not change the law nor the character of the offence, when the officers of a State employ their corporate powers in rebellion against the Government. They do not rebel *as a State*, but as individuals, and by the perversion of their official power they vacate their office, and become responsible to law, not as a government, but as citizens, guilty of crime.

This is precisely the character of this rebellion. It is not the rebellion of States, but of individuals, and each one is liable to the penalties of criminal law. In using force to put down this rebellion, the Government does not declare war; it only uses the power vested in it to punish offenders against its own laws. The rebels are, therefore, but an *organized mob*, and deserve to be treated as such. It is important that this distinction should be maintained in the popular mind, for the right of the Government to overcome an insurrection against the laws, takes away from the insurgents every legal privilege which is in opposition to that right, and leaves them liable to the punishment of the laws they have broken, when taken in arms against the authority of the State.

It is this fact, which has induced the insurgents to make such strenuous efforts to obtain the recognition of their so-called government. If our Government had received the men, sent as commissioners to Washington, it would have been compelled to treat the rebels according to the Law of Nations, and grant them all the rights of war. In refusing to receive them, it gave notice that it will hold these rebels as criminals in law. This being the case, their privateers are *pirates*, and the *leaders* of the men in arms *robbers* and *murderers*. The Government may deal mercifully with some of them, through motives of humanity, but they cannot claim it by right of law.

This state of things also clothes the Government with the *right* to use all necessary means to put down this insurrection, and its power is limited, not by the Constitution, but only by the laws of humanity and of God. It is perfect folly to talk about the Government not having the right to adopt any measure to prevent its destruction that is necessary. The whole structure of our Government is based upon the supposition, that such a state of things as now exists was an impossibility, and hence, there is no special provision in the Constitution to meet the case. Secession is not prohibited because it was not anticipated. The money of the Government has been lavished on the South and for its defence, because it was intended that we should always be one nation. Our forts were constructed to defend the South from foreign foes, with no means of defence against the attack of her citizens, hence Sumter fell because attacked from *behind*.

There is therefore *no law* for the General Government, but the law of necessity and humanity, and any and every measure which necessity or humanity requires to put down this rebellion, the Government has the right to adopt. It has the right to declare martial law all over the land, and to suspend every civil statute until the work be accomplished.

Third. It has strengthened the hands and developed the power of the General Government.

The power of all large nations lies—under God—in the union of the people, and their devotion to the principles of the Government. God has said, "A house divided against itself cannot stand;" and this truth applies with equal force to all associations, be they social, domestic, or national. If the people of a country be, to any great extent, divided in sympathy and feeling, the nation is feeble and cannot long resist its enemies, or prevent its destruction. There must be union or death.

It is a fact not to be denied by sensible and observing men that, for several years past, the sympathies of the people of this country have been growing painfully adverse. The bitterness of party feeling has been alarmingly on the increase. The questions which entered into our political contests have taken hold of the religious consciences of the people, and have become not only questions of political policy, but matters of personal morals. It has been contended that the laws of the land came in conflict with our duty to God. Political opposition engendered personal hatred, and political opponents were fast becoming personal foes. This was not only the case between different sections of the country, but it pervaded every part of the land, and entered all classes of society to a most fearful extent. The evidence of this state of feeling was seen in the bitter denunciations of the press,—the *abuse of the pulpit*, which was too often used to array brother against brother,—in the quarrelling of professing Christians, — in the divisions of churches, and in the breaking into fragments of political parties. Even the great Democratic party, which until lately had always been able to heal its disputes and present a solid vote at the polls, has shared the common fate, and now lies in ruins around.

Without attempting to explain the many causes which have led to this state of feeling, I refer to the fact to show, that as a nation, we were fast approaching a crisis in our history, which was to test the experiment of popular government, and decide the question of our national existence. It was this division of feeling in the Northern States on which, more than on any other one thing, the plotters of the present treason relied for support and encouragement. Had the leaders of this unholy crusade against the Government, for a single moment believed that they would have to meet a united Northern sentiment, in their battle against the Union, they would not have dared to commence this war against liberty and humanity. The mistake they made was in overrating the strength of our sympathy for the South, and in underrating the strength of our attachment to the Union. They supposed that our opposition to the ultraism of certain parties, was an opposition to the Constitution and general laws of the land. We were sadly divided, it is true, but it was a division between the love of the *whole* country on the one part, and the madness of sectional fanaticism on the other. Some great and startling event was therefore needed to show us our danger, to unite our rapidly dissolving sympathies, and by the intensity of its fires, to fuse into one solid mass the hearts of all true friends to popular freedom.

The fall of Sumter did this. Almost as quickly as the shock of a galvanic battery pervades the human system, it ran through the masses of the people, burying out of sight our former differences, and taking hold of the hearts of twenty millions of freemen; it moulded them all into one great national heart, fired with a deathless purpose to rescue the Government from destruction. The world's history furnishes no parallel to the spontaneous uprising of the people, which took place when the lightning brought the news of Sumter's fall. The nation rushed to arms, and *five hundred thousand men* offered themselves to a President, nearly one-half of whom had voted against him but a few months before. We are now united in the support of the Union, the Constitution, and the Laws, and though opposing armies tread our soil, the Government was never *so strong* as it is at this moment in the eyes of the world.

The statesmen of Europe are looking with amazement at this outburst of *practical* devotion and patriotism. They had given us credit for ingenuity and industry in all the departments of trade and commerce, but they never dreamed that a nation of farmers, mechanics, and merchants, would be so eager for the camp and the battle-field. They now discover that we can raise an army which *begs* the Government to accept its services, while they have to fill their ranks *by force*. A power has been developed which we were not supposed to possess, and we have thereby gained much greater respect and influence abroad. The same confidence, but to a much greater extent, pervades the masses of our people at home. They are quietly looking and waiting for the blow to fall on the enemies of the Union, without doubting the result—they know their power, and they feel secure. Let the Government but do its whole duty, and the Union cannot be broken. When this fact is established by the crushing out of this rebellion, the world will behold with astonishment, the energy with which it was done, and acknowledge the power of the Government which accomplished it. As a nation, we shall be "a terror to evil doers, and a praise to them that do well." These are some of the results which are plainly seen as growing out of this rebellion. Others, of still greater moment, are likely to follow, but as they are among the uncertainties of the unknown future they cannot yet be seen, and it may not be wise to speculate upon them. He who "maketh the wrath of man to praise him," has purposes to accomplish by this state of things, but they are hidden from mortal vision, in the counsels of the Eternal Mind. One thing is certain, and every Christian should rejoice— "The Lord reigneth: though clouds and darkness are round about Him, righteousness and judgment are the habitation of His throne."

That this insurrection will certainly lead to a permanent settlement of the slavery question, would seem to be a matter of necessity, as it has been made the occasion, if it be not the real cause, of all our trouble. It may result in gradual emancipation, by the adoption of some wise measures on the part of the General and State Governments. If thus left to ourselves, we will settle the question in favor of the Union among ourselves; but if other nations should interfere, it may involve most of the Powers of Europe, bring on a general war, and cause the battle of the world to be fought in the valley of the Mississippi. That great events in the history of the world are soon to transpire, is evident to every student of prophecy, and it is a fact of no little significance, that those who have studied this subject agree with great unanimity, that the "time is at hand." It is not improbable that this unnatural rebellion is among the great troubles predicted in the Scriptures, when "the Sun is to be darkened, and the Moon turned into blood."

Before this subject can be properly dismissed, one more point in the text must be noticed, viz.: *The duty of the Government* in the case. Civil Government has a *divine mission*, and woe unto the "powers that be" if that mission is not accomplished. The devotion of the people will avail but little in the preservation of the nation, if those who are in authority shrink from the responsibility which God has imposed on them. *The* LEADERS *in this rebellion* MUST BE PUNISHED.

We have already shown that God has ordained a Civil Government for a twofold object,—the protection of the good, and the punishment of the evil. If this be not done, the purpose of God is not accomplished, and "the nation that serveth not God, *shall perish.*" Rulers have no more power to disobey God in refusing to punish evil doers, than the people have to rebel against "the powers that be." The guilty must be punished, or the divine law is wilfully violated. Hear the words of inspiration on this subject: "But if thou do evil, be afraid of the power, for he beareth not the sword in vain; for he is the minister of God, *a revenger, to execute wrath upon him that doeth evil.*" Here then are both the *danger* and the *duty* of our Government. It has the power to punish treason, and if it fails to do so, it beareth the sword in vain. Instead of being the minister of God to execute wrath upon him that doeth evil, it becomes a party to the crime, and will be punished by its own destruction. The law must be executed, or the Government *will die.*

We are in great danger from a false sympathy on this point. Sympathy ceases to be a virtue when felt *against the innocent.* Mercy is a *crime* when it shields the impenitent. God never forgives the guilty unless they *repent.* Government must imitate his example, and punish those who persist in disobedience. There can be *no compromise* with treason, therefore, without incurring the Divine displeasure, and no thought of such a course should be entertained by any lover of his country. The guilty leaders in this rebellion have caused untold misery to thousands of innocent people. Gray-haired men and women are being sent to their graves destitute and broken-hearted. Thousands of our best business men have been robbed and ruined. Multitudes of industrious laborers have been thrown out of employment, and their families are starving. Wives are being widowed, and parents left childless in their old age. Every death of this kind is a *murder,* and the loss of property is *robbery.* Yet we are exhorted to have sympathy for the men who have caused all this evil, who are still attempting to destroy the Government to gratify their unholy ambition and hatred of free institutions. Away with such trifling with truth and justice. Let us think of the starving thousands who will next winter besiege our doors for bread, which we will not have to give them. Let us think of the mothers who will weep for their sons who have fallen in battle by the hands of traitors. Let us think of these sons and daughters of sorrow, and if we have sympathy to spare from our own sufferings, let the innocent have it, but let justice be meted out to the offenders.

If this be not done, it is mockery to ask God's blessing, and useless to implore his aid for a Government which tramples under foot his laws. Mercy may and should combine with justice in making the penalty as light as is consistent with the wrong, but it must be justice still. The dupes of these traitors may be spared, but the *leaders must be punished,* for nothing less will satisfy the purpose of God in ordaining the existence of this Government. I say again, this must be done, or the Government will have its record written among those nations which have forgotten God.

The Government must also *protect its faithful subjects.* "They must have *praise* of the same."

The duty of protecting those who do well, is just as binding on the powers that be as that of executing wrath upon those who do evil. In this case it is of the utmost importance. When this conflict began, it was greatly to be feared that the Government would have a *united* South to contend with, through the wicked misrepresentations of the leaders in this rebellion. The course of many persons and papers in the Northern States was well calculated to produce this result by their denunciation of *all* Southern people as traitors to the Government.

Before the true state of feeling in the Southern States was fully known, this course was simply imprudent and unkind. Recent events and better information render the continuance of this wholesale denunciation absolutely wicked, and it should be abandoned at once and forever. The strongest loyalty to the Union is now found in the South, where it costs something to be loyal, and where men are risking their all in standing up for the Constitution and laws. Respect for the feelings of men born in the South who are now engaged in supporting the Government, should prevent all such wholesale denunciation. How must Gen. Scott—that honored old veteran—who is a Virginian, feel when he reads and hears from a thousand different sources that *all Southern men are traitors.* We forget that the hero of this war, Major Anderson, is a Kentuckian, and has covered himself with glory and honor by his devotion to the Union. "Honor to whom honor is due," is a Divine command, and the Government, with all loyal people, should unite in praising and in protecting those who have done so well.

A late editorial in *The Methodist* is so appropriate to this point that I adopt the following language from it:

"It is only too much the fashion to speak of 'North and South' as if they perfectly divided the country between loyalty and rebellion. The real state of the case is far otherwise, and the language of the press and rostrum should conform to the facts. Men of Southern birth, living in the free States, who cannot annul the fact that they were born in a slave State, and would not if they could, are but little flattered at public meetings to find the whole discourse of the orators turning upon an invidious comparison between the North and the South. It is not a little wounding to their pride to be even eloquently assured that they sprang from a race of poltroons and ignoramuses.

"Is this the way to talk and write while we claim that the country is one and indivisible; while Maryland is electing a complete Union delegation to Congress; while Missouri and Kentucky are full of true patriots, and only hesitate because Jackson and Magoffin, their misgovernors, are traitorous; while East Tennessee is loyal by a majority of ten thousand, and while Western Virginia is not only in arms against secession, but is establishing a provisional State government, and degrading from office and power the rebels east of the mountains? No! there is no such division as North and South in this war: it is Union and disunion, loyalty and rebellion. The dividing line does not run between free and slave States, but wildly, and in some places yet invisibly, all over the country. And as the army moves forward, liberating the imprisoned sentiment and bringing back utterance to gagged patriotism, the true line will become more and more distinct.

"The loyal men of the South are the noblest of our patriots. With them adherence to the Union is no mere holiday parade, which demonstrates itself at the expense of a flag, and reaches its jolly culmination in a patriotic song. In an atmosphere hot with secession hate, they dare speak and act for the Union. Against the prejudices of education, against the current of their own blood, against a false theory of the Constitution, sugared with pleas for State rights, against the influence of the great and the power of the many, they dare stand firm for American nationality. We honor old Parson Brownlow now more than ever; he is the leader of the hardy mountaineers of East Tennessee; he stands firmly and defiantly at the head of his mountain legions.

"It won't do, then, so to draw our lines in the present struggle as to leave out of our political communion Brownlow, or Etheridge, or Nelson. If Tennessee is not in the Union, the Union is at least in Tennessee, and is likely to stay there.

"What has been said of Tennessee may be said with equal or even greater truth of Kentucky. Notwithstanding all the unmeaning talk about neutrality, the Union is there. Prentice represents a Union constituency whose name is legion. And Crittenden, and Guthrie, and Thomas Clay, though slow to act, have spoken boldly and well.

"But the noblest devotion to the Union to be found in any Southern State is now developing itself in Western Virginia. Precisely in proportion to the madness of Eastern Virginia, has been the patriotic courage of the Western portion of the State. If the East received Davis, and staked its all upon the issue, the West has accepted Union troops from Ohio, and resolved, both by the sword and the forms of law, to wrest authority from the seceders at Richmond. If Virginia has been disgraced by Wise, and Floyd, and Mason, and Pryor, she has been honored and almost redeemed by the men of the Wheeling Convention."

Who is a better patriot than Andrew Johnson, of Tennessee, who said, a few days ago, on his way to Congress:

"I know that rewards have been offered for my head, and that it is even said that warrants have been issued for Etheridge, myself, and other Union men. But, my friends, I am no fugitive, much less am I a fugitive from justice. I am not flying from my home. *I am on my way to execute a holy mission.* I am willing to place every particle of property I possess at the disposal of the Government, if she needs it, in this strife; and if this is not enough, I am willing to pour out my life-blood a libation on the altar of my country. If I fall in this strife, all I ask is, that my corpse shall be carried to my home in Tennessee, wrapped in the Stars and Stripes, and that I shall be buried among her mountains. And if the Union shall fall with me, all that I ask is, that, wrapped in the flag which is her emblem, I shall be buried in the same common grave. I ask no greater glory."

Let all, therefore, cease talking about the North and the South as separate divisions of the country, and unite in honoring and protecting those, no matter where they live, who stand up for the Union, the Constitution, and the Laws. May the Almighty bless these faithful men, and grant them a speedy relief from all their sufferings.

My work is now nearly done. I have shown from the Scripture that Civil Government is the institution of God for the protection of good men and the punishment of evil-doers,—that obedience to "the powers that be" is a duty to God,—that this rebellion is a fearful crime,—that Government violates the Divine Law when it neglects to punish the guilty; and, therefore, it is the duty of all good citizens to aid the Government in putting down this rebellion, and in restoring the Union to that perfection in which it has been handed down to us by the Heaven-directed fathers of the American Revolution.

In doing this, I have avoided the discussion of all side issues, about which men may honestly differ, because they were not necessary to the proper understanding of the subject. I have introduced no party politics, because the pulpit is not the place to discuss such questions. I have confined myself to the explanation and application of the principles of the Divine Law, because of that I am a duly authorized teacher. If I have been severe upon traitors and their treason, it is because I am authorized by the law of God to follow the example of Christ, who said to a much less guilty class of men, "Ye generation of vipers, how shall ye escape the damnation of hell?"

And now, in conclusion, I exhort all good men to nail the Star-Spangled Banner of the nation just below that banner on which shines the Star of Bethlehem, and on their knees before God—with a full purpose of heart to live and die true to the Union, the Constitution, and the Laws,—let them say,

"The Flag of our Union, O long may it wave
O'er the land of the free, and the home of the brave!"

SERMON,

Delivered in the Second Baptist Church, at St. Louis, Mo., on the evening of April 21st, 1861.

BY REV. GALUSHA ANDERSON.

Let every soul be subject unto the higher powers. For there is no power but of God: the powers that be are ordained of God. Whosoever therefore resisteth the power, resisteth the ordinance of God: and they that resist shall receive to themselves damnation.—*Rom.* xiii. 1, 2.

BEFORE entering on the discussion of the subject presented to us in the text, we will notice briefly a few facts. It has often been said in our day, that the minister of the Gospel has no right to introduce into the pulpit any political question. This objection has frequently been made, in Christian candor and love, and we should be most ungenerous if we did not meet it in a similar spirit. It is in part right and in part manifestly wrong. In the first place, every Christian pastor must himself determine what topics shall be introduced into his pulpit. He feels imperatively bound to choose those subjects for discussion which are best adapted to the times in which he lives, and to the necessities of his congregation. When a church call a man to be their pastor, and he accepts that call, neither he nor they, by forming this relation, determine what themes shall be presented in his pulpit ministrations. Confident that he agrees with them in reference to the fundamental doctrines of the Gospel, they give into his hands their pulpit, and so long as he continues to occupy it, it is his throne, from which he utters that truth which his conscience, the word and the spirit of God, teach him to speak. The *pews*, therefore, cannot determine the right of the *pulpit* in any given instance, to discuss or not discuss, even a political question.

If, however, by politics are meant either those questions of *minor* importance, which often divide men into parties, or those schemes resorted to by demagogues to obtain office, we agree with our objectors, that they ought never to appear in the pulpit; or if by politics is meant the science of government and law, however commendable may be their study, we again agree with our objectors, that a pastor would be most unwise, if not recreant to his trust, to introduce them into his pulpit as subjects of discussion, to the exclusion of the great themes of the Gospel. But we must not forget that many political questions have a moral basis. They sustain most intimate relations to the spiritual life of our churches. These questions a Christian pastor has not only the right to discuss, but he would be unfaithful to those to whom he ministers, if he neglected to discuss them. He has taken the most solemn vows upon himself to declare the *whole* counsel of God. In the Scriptures, the duties of citizens to the State are pointed out; he could not, with a conscience void of offence, meet his church and his Judge at the day of final account, if he should neglect to enjoin upon his flock the faithful performance of these duties.

We have been told again, that a pastor ought not to introduce into his pulpit any political question on which his congregation are divided, lest he should wound the feelings of some and drive them away from the house of God. There is something of truth in this statement. The judicious minister will avoid, so far as it is compatible with his duty, all irritating controversies. And he who discusses any topic for the *purpose* of wounding the feelings of others, is unworthy the name of a Christian pastor. But the feelings of men are not the guide of the herald of the Cross in his pulpit ministrations. He must always interrogate the Word of God and his own conscience, and act in accordance with their decisions. If, in treading the path where they lead him, he wounds the sensibilities of men, he is not responsible for the result. We must also remember, that those truths which please men most do not always benefit them most. He who leaves the house of God, expressing his admiration of the sermon, and declaring that he has been edified, because he has heard that which accords with his previous notions of truth and duty, has often been only confirmed in some cherished sin, while he who has heard that which struck at long-cherished principles, or loosened in the hard soil of his heart some deep-rooted prejudice, so that he writhes in pain beneath it, has received that which will be to him a rich and lasting blessing. God has commanded his servants to tell the people of their sins, and such announcements are usually distasteful.

But those who may be irritated by the plain utterances of the pulpit in reference to national sins, claim the right of freedom of opinion and of speech for themselves, and they would be most ungenerous, not to say unjust, if they did not accord the same right to their pastor. And surely every high-minded man, who desires to know the truth, whatever it may be, would rejoice to learn the views of those who differ from him, when they are expressed honestly and in Christian love. But he who is offended by the honest utterances of a Christian brother, upon questions in which we have a common interest, and undertakes the task of dictating what those utterances shall be, has not yet learned the first principles of the Gospel or of religious liberty. There are those here who have assumed the task of dictating what this pulpit shall say. They belong to a class of men who suppose that when a man becomes a minister he ceases to be a man—he ceases to be a citizen—he ceases to have an opinion—he gives his conscience and judgment up to the pew-holders—he speaks, just as the puppet moves on the stage, when some one in the pews pulls the wire. I belong not to that class of ministers; I was not conscious, when I became a Christian pastor, of laying aside my manhood. Permit me to say to all such dictators, that I shall not bow down to them nor serve them, for the Lord whom I serve is a *jealous* God.

Paul, when he entered Corinth, as he afterwards wrote, determined to know nothing save Jesus Christ, and Him crucified. A too narrow interpretation is often given to these words. The minister who reiterates, from Sabbath to Sabbath, the story of the cross, is supposed to act in accordance with this noble determination of the Apostle, when a heathen might read with admiration and yet without profit this wonderful story. He only truly preaches Christ *crucified*, who sets forth the claims of the cross upon the hearts and lives of men—unfolds the doctrines which cluster around the cross, and enforces upon the consciences of men the duties of the Christian life. Paul never broke his sublime resolution, yet he places before us all the great doctrines of the Gospel; the duties which we owe to each other as brethren and to the world without; the duties which grow out of the relations of the household, and the duties which we, as citizens, must render to the State.

There is no duty that we should more carefully determine, at the present time, than our duty to the Government under which we live. We have an infallible guide. To the law and the testimony let us resort and hear what God says.

We learn, first, from the text, that human government is ordained by God.

Human government is a necessity. Men are wicked and corrupt; left to the guidance of their natural propensities, might, without regard to justice, would soon be the controlling principle of society. The innocent, feeble, and defenceless would be stripped of all their inalienable rights. Government is necessary to hold the passions of men in restraint, and without it the earth would be a vast arena of oppression, injustice, and strife. God has amply provided for this necessity. He placed His own chosen people under a national government. He was Himself its head and lawgiver, but men were appointed to judge the causes of the people, and to enforce the law which He gave into their hand.

When Israel chose for themselves a King, contrary to the will of Jehovah, He enjoined on the people strict obedience. The King was His representative on the throne. To rebel against the King, was rebellion against Himself. And when Christ came, He taught the same lesson in reference to heathen governments. Judea had been unjustly subjected to the Roman yoke; the government of Cæsar was rigorous and exacting; but Christ said to the Pharisees and Herodians, "render to Cæsar the things that are Cæsar's;" and once he wrought a miracle, causing a fish to be taken, in whose mouth was a piece of money, which was to be used to pay the tax of himself and a disciple to the Roman government. Thus, by word and act, Christ has taught obedience to civil authority.

We should observe, however, that God has not ordained any special form of government, only government in its essence. The form has been left to be determined by men, according to the condition of the people to be governed. The command, therefore, is to obey the established and recognized government, whether it be aristocratical, monarchical, or republican.

We notice, in the second place, the limits of the powers of government. God has marked out these limits: He has said, Thus far shalt thou go, but no further. He was too wise to put into the hand of corrupt man, who loves to rule others, such vast power, and then permit him to use it without restriction. Such a privilege would always end in tyranny, for which there would be no redress.

What are those limitations? We have them placed before us by the pens of Apostles. Paul writes: "Rulers are not a terror to good works, but to the evil." Peter confirms this teaching in the words: "Submit yourselves to every ordinance of man, for the Lord's sake: whether it be to the king as supreme, or unto governors, as unto them that are sent by Him for the punishment of evil-doers, and for the praise of them that do well." We are thus clearly taught that the powers of government are legitimately exercised only when used for the good of the governed. They are to be employed to foster and honor that which is good, and to curtail and repress that which is evil. The ruler who does not labor for this end, unlawfully uses the power given into his hand.

By thus limiting the exercise of power, God has provided, on certain conditions, for the right of revolution. It is clear, however, that it cannot justly be resorted to except for the most weighty and conclusive reasons. Both Christ and his apostles taught obedience even to a tyrannical government.

When a Government has long persisted in transcending the limits of its powers, lifting up that which is evil and honoring it, treading down that which is good and repressing it, disregarding every petition and remonstrance of the oppressed, cutting off all appeal to the suffrages of the people, till it has become the general conviction of all good citizens that the advantages of a revolution would far outweigh its necessary evils; then, and not till then, a people may rise up in their might and shake the unjust Government from their necks as a lion does the dew-drop from his mane. But such a step, usually fraught with dire calamities to the masses of the people, should be the *last* resort in redressing the wrongs of a nation.

In the second place, to oppose Government in the legitimate exercise of its powers, is exceedingly wicked. It is so, in the first place, because it is deliberate opposition to God. "Whosoever, therefore," says Paul, "resisteth the power, resisteth the ordinance of God," and he further declares " damnation " to be the fitting retribution of such a crime. To lift up the hand of rebellion deliberately against the authority of God, is the most daring impiety, and the penalty which the Scriptures here pronounce on the deed, reveals to us its terrible wickedness and how abhorrent it is to God, the author of government and law.

In the third place, we see its dire wickedness by the woes which it drags in its train. It dries up commerce and trade, turns the clerk and artisan penniless into our streets, and fills their houses with want and starvation. It breaks the bonds of peace by which society was held together, and makes friends and neighbors implacable foes; it unsheathes the sword, fills the land with anarchy and conflict, and covers many a field with carnage and blood. No human mind can adequately estimate the wickedness of rebellion against government, when it bears such horrid fruits.

It has been asked, Shall we obey the enactments of Government when they are in opposition to our consciences, and the word of God? Certainly not, for by the latter all human enactments are to be tested. It is that law which is above all human laws and constitutions, and its clear utterances are final and decisive. Any requirement of human government that conflicts with it, must be disobeyed. But, by such disobedience, we need not resist the authority of Government; having disobeyed its laws, in so far as they are in conflict with our consciences and God's word, we may honor the Government, by carefully obeying all other of its enactments, and by receiving, without opposition, the penalty of the law, which we have been compelled, by the demands of conscience, to violate. So Daniel acted. Darius sent forth the edict that any one, who should pray for thirty days to any god save the King, should be cast into a den of lions. But Daniel, led by his conscience and the law of God, prayed as he had done before, three times a day; yet he did not resist by act or word the king, and received without complaint the penalty of the law he had broken. So acted Peter and John. For their preaching at Jerusalem they were apprehended and thrust into prison. They received the penalty of the law without uttering a word against the Government, and when they were commanded "not to speak at all nor teach in the name of Jesus," they boldly replied, "whether it be right in the sight of God to hearken unto you more than unto God, judge ye." Paul, who wrote our text, violated continually the Roman law in preaching the gospel, but always honored the Government by receiving without opposition every legitimate infliction of the penalty of the law, and by enjoining on the disciples to pay, without complaint, tribute to the Government. While, therefore, we disobey a law, in obedience to God and our consciences, we may honor the government which framed it, by refusing to resist its authority, even when we deem it unjust, and by sustaining it in the legitimate and rightful exercise of all its powers.

Let us now apply this truth. We see all around us insubordination to law. First, it appears within our city. We have at last a city government which, with even hand, is enforcing the law of the Sabbath; our candy shops, grog shops, and beer saloons are to be shut up, and our ears will no longer be pained, on the Lord's Day, by the shouts of drunken revelry. At this event the heart of every good citizen swells with joy. Our municipal officers will be sustained by the prayers of all true Christians among us. There are those, however, who show signs of insubordination, and are ready to resist the enforcement of the law. Many of these come to us from lands where they have been taught that one day is no more sacred than another, and that the Sabbath is best spent as a holiday. Their education should make us lenient in our judgment of their conduct, while by a rigorous enforcement of the law, we should teach them the practical lesson of obedience to the powers that be. We have received them among us with open hearts and open arms, and they should be early taught to be cheerfully submissive to the laws of that land which has so generously welcomed them.

In the second place, we see direct and positive opposition to the General Government and the Federal laws, in many States of our Union. It does not belong to me to discuss all the causes which have produced the present anomalous condition of affairs. I could not, however, be true to my country, to my conscience, and to my God, and keep silence on this point. You who may differ with me in judgment on this question, have your opinion and the free expression of it, and *I shall have mine.* There is no sufficient reason for this rebellion and revolution. Has any constitutional right been denied the seceding States? None whatever. Have any unjust exactions been made on them? None, whatever. If they were suffering any injustice, could it not have been redressed by an appeal to the ballot box? No such appeal has been made. The rebellion is the most wicked and condemnable of any recorded in the history of nations. The anarchy, conflict, and bloodshed which it has brought upon us must rest upon the heads of those who, without any just cause, have inaugurated and carried forward this mad revolution.

A few months since a voice of condemnation came up from these rebellious States against men in other parts of our country, for the violation of a federal law, (the fugitive slave law;) but where now is their professed loyalty, when, instead of violating a single enactment of the Government, they trample on all its authority, and lift up the red hand of revolution, without a just cause, in rebellion against it?

Let us notice two of the causes which have produced this insubordination to law, so fearfully prevalent throughout our country. We discover one cause of it in the laxity of our family governments. Boys of sixteen cast off the authority of their parents, and become their own masters; having never learned the first principles of obedience at home, it is not strange that we see their insubordination manifesting itself in the State. Heathen minds clearly apprehended this truth. Plato wrote a dialogue to set forth a model republic. Men have sometimes turned to it, expecting to find in it all the parts of a republic placed before them, nicely adjusted to each other, and in harmonious operation. They have been surprised, however, to find instead that Plato insists on the study of science and music, and also on obedience to parents and the gods. He was wise enough to see that if children were taught to obey these at home, they would in maturer years be law-abiding citizens of the State. Let us learn, then, from this heathen, if we will not from the Bible, how to produce among us loyalty to Government and law.

Another cause of this growing insubordination to Government, is the manner in which we have discussed before our children, the characters and measures of the officers of our Government. The Government is democratic; the governing power is "near the soil," in the nut-brown hands and honest hearts of the people. It is necessary, therefore, that the people discuss the measures of men in office; by such discussions they become intelligent and capable of discharging their duty as voters; but while we jealously guard this sacred right, we must not forget that we are obligated not to speak evil of the rulers of the people; that an Apostle has taught us to both fear and honor those holding places of public trust. Here we have greatly erred. A man no sooner appears as a candidate for office, than the press and the popular orator dissect mercilessly his character, and pour forth upon him the vilest vituperation and abuse. The highest officers of the land are not shielded from this disregard and contempt. The manner of the press and the political orator has obtained within our homes. A generation has sprung up who have no regard for the rulers of our land, nor, by a natural and easy transition, for their authority. Beardless youths in our streets discuss, in the most contemptuous language, the acts of Presidents and Cabinets. All restraint is broken through, and men, without a thought of its wickedness, regard it simply as a matter of choice whether they shall obey or disobey the powers that be.

In conclusion we ask, how is this disregard of government and law to be remedied? We must produce, in some way, a public sentiment in favor of obedience to the established authorities. This can be produced only by speaking out against insubordination and rebellion. The pulpit must speak honestly and fearlessly in unfolding and applying God's truth. All good men, by both act and word, must sustain their Government in the legitimate exercise of its authority. This lesson must be taught our children both in public and private. This will create a Scriptural sentiment in reference to the duties of the citizen to the State. Men say, often, that it is wiser to keep still, lest we unduly excite those who cherish sentiments different from our own. But this festering wound can never be healed until it is probed, however painful the process. We should be careful, also, to guard inviolate the right of freedom of speech everywhere. Our Baptist fathers, of Virginia and New England, asserted this God-given right through persecutions the most bitter, and we would be most degenerate sons of theirs to tamely give it up. Assuming this privilege, let all high-minded men speak out for the right, till it bears sway in the hearts of the people.

I wish to bear my own individual testimony, to express the feelings of my heart. I love my country—I love the Government of my country—I love the freedom of my country. It was purchased by the blood of our fathers, and when I become so base, so cowardly, so besotted, that I dare not speak out in behalf of that for which they so bravely fought, I pray that my tongue may cleave to the roof of my mouth.

But, brethren, we need have no fears as to the ultimate issue. The Lord God Omnipotent reigneth! In this conflict your property may be swept away, and all may be reduced to a common level. Your life and mine may be sacrificed on the altar of our country, yet, Jehovah, who presides over the scene, will bring the nation forth from the ordeal wiser, purer, nobler. If the scythe of rebellion is swung over our whole land, mowing down all of our free institutions, leave us the Christian family, the Christian Church, and the time-honored Bible, and in the track of the destroyer, they will spring up with new life, new power, and new glory. "The Lord reigneth: let the earth rejoice; let the multitude of isles be glad thereof."

GOD'S CONTROVERSY WITH THE PEOPLE OF THE UNITED STATES.

A Sermon, delivered in St. Stephen's Church, Baltimore, on the National Fast Day, Sept. 26, 1861.

BY REV. JOHN N. McJILTON, D. D.

Thou shalt not escape out of His hand.—*Jer.* xxxiv. 3.

It is well that, in our present condition as a nation, a day of Fasting, and Humiliation and Prayer, should be appointed. We are in the hand of God. We cannot escape from it. But for our sins, in His hand we were in safety. On account of them we may fear—and trembling may take hold upon us. The controversy of an outraged and offended Divinity is with us, and the dust is our place—the sackcloth our humiliation, and honest, earnest, faithful prayer our duty.

It is generally conceded by those who are accustomed to the consideration of the dealings of God with men, that our present troubles, and the civil war in which they have resulted, have been permitted to come upon us as a national scourge, applied on account of our offences and offensive character in the view of the pure Being who has given us our existence and our blessings. Against Him have we offended, and our appeal should be to Him, in the very depth of penitential sorrow, for the intervention of His power in our behalf. It is now clearly evident that our hope is not in man, for every effort that has been put forth for the removal of the evil, has failed in the accomplishment of its purpose, and instead of inducing the desired relief, has served only to aggravate the feud, and sharpen the desire of the opposing agencies in their resistance of each other, until they are provoked even to the shedding of each other's blood.

Hitherto the efforts of the General and State Governments—of Congress and the State Legislatures—have been sufficient to prevent any serious difficulty from disagreements between the States and the General Government, and among the political parties of the country. But in this issue the General and State Governments, Congress and Conventions of the people, have proved powerless. Congress has been twice invoked in vain for the interposition of its authority; the Peace Convention, composed of delegates from a number of the States, labored for weeks to effect a compromise. The Virginia Convention did the same, and eminent statesmen of different sections of the country interposed suggestions and plans of settlement. The exertions of all the parties have been unsuccessful. They have not removed the cause of the difficulty, nor arrested for a moment the progress of the feud. Harmony has not been restored. The working of the Constitution of the United States has been arrested, and the laws of Congress are not effective in their execution in all the States.

Perhaps the worst, certainly the most fearful, form in which a scourge from heaven could be presented to a nation, is that of a civil war—an intestine feud, in which a brother's hand is raised against a brother's life. In this form it has fallen upon our land, and we are terribly straitened in the calamity. When God's favorite among the kings of Israel committed a high offence by numbering the people in opposition to the Divine will, he was peremptorily ordered to an account for the deed. Failing to justify himself, he was allowed a choice of one of three modes of punishment. He was directed to say whether he would be scourged by the horrors of war, the ravages of the pestilence, or the wasting effects of famine. In the war he was to flee three months before his enemies; the pestilence was to pursue its ravages three days; and the famine was to continue seven years. The test was too severe for the penitent king, and he exclaimed, "I am in a great strait. Let us fall now in the hand of the Lord, (for His mercies are great;) and let me not fall into the hand of man." (2 Sam. xxiv. 14.) The Lord was merciful in sending the pestilence, and there died of the people seventy thousand men.

Truly, like the people of Israel, as a nation, we are in a great strait. We could not choose the mode of correction necessary for our reformation, and God has chosen it for us. He has appointed the calamity by which we are to be humbled before Him. In the dread issue of civil war we are now struggling. Our works are those of destruction, and our only hope of deliverance is the hand that afflicts us, and from it there is no way of escape. The extent of the calamity must be determined by its continuance, and the violence with which it is pursued, and knowing that our only hope is in our Great Father in heaven, it is becoming and proper that we should appear in His awful presence with reverence, and in the depth of humility; and if in our penitence we be sincere, in our confession honest, and in our faith sufficient, we shall surely find that our appeal shall be effectual, and our safety secured. As a nation, and as individuals composing the nation, we have our work to do; and that work cannot be omitted. It *must* be performed. It is not so much to prepare for the battle and to pursue the work of destruction, as to submit our case to the Divine counsels, and in the righteousness of faith abide the issue.

While in the depth of his trouble, the afflicted king of Israel saw the angel of the pestilence standing by the threshing floor of Araunah, the Jebusite, and he was directed by the prophet of God to go up and rear an altar to the Lord on the spot where the angel stood. He purchased the site of the threshing floor, erected the altar, and offered upon it burnt offerings, and peace offerings. "So the Lord was entreated for the land, and the plague was stayed from Israel." (2 Sam. xxiv. 25.)

If it be true, as it surely is, that we are now suffering under the hand of our outraged and offended Divinity, our appeal to man and our trust in ourselves must be in vain. We must provide the place, and erect the altar, and offer thereon our burnt offerings of bleeding, penitent hearts, and the peace offerings of elevated holy purposes. We must reform our guilty characters, and change our offensive habits. We must cease from worshipping the idols of our own making and adoption, and worship in sincerity and truth the great Author and Giver of every blessing that we enjoy. If we now pursue the path of obedience, the Lord will surely be entreated and this plague shall be stayed from among us. The race is not to the swift, nor the battle to the strong, but the victory is in the hand of Him that hath mercy upon the penitent, and holds out the reward to the faithful among His people.

It is not necessary that we should now enter upon an inquiry in regard to the manner in which the war has been brought upon us. It is enough for us to know that, like the people that the Almighty Jehovah chose for His own, and sanctified to Himself in choosing, we have been rebellious, and for our rebellion we are scourged; and that, like those people, we must become penitent, obedient, and faithful, before the desired relief will be afforded us.

Like the scourges that were visited upon the Jews, our national calamity has been applied as a natural result of the course we have pursued, and the character we have formed. There are noble features in our character as a nation, and the world will ever hold those features in high esteem. Our bravery is undoubted, and we are dignified, and honorable, and patriotic. But it is not with those features that we have to do to-day. There are other traits which are prominent among us, and for these we are brought to the scourge. We leave the better lineaments of our nationality for occasions of rejoicing, and consider those that have reduced us to our condition of humiliation. We are selfish, and self-willed, and proud, and obstinate, and revengeful. These offensive properties cling to us, both as individuals and communities. The evidences of our fall from purity, are everywhere around us. Society bears the marks of the evil in all its departments, insomuch that, in all history, there is not to be found a more ungrateful and disobedient people.

Neglect of God's worship and the worship of other gods was the great sin of the Jews. For their often repeated transgressions, they were frequently punished, and when found at last to be ungovernable their nationality was destroyed, their beautiful country desolated, and although the chosen of the Lord, the people themselves were driven out as outcasts and as homeless wanderers, to be a byword and reproach among every nation upon the earth. The boasted nationality of the Jews is a ruin that the centuries have marked with every variety of vicissitude; and long since the mingling of the dust of prophets, priests, and kings, is beneath the tread of the foul idolater. Pæans of impiety have ascended from the hills and vales that were once vocal with the songs of Jehovah's praise, and the sacred mount on which the temple stood, is desecrated in its dedication to the use of the followers of the false prophet. The basest and the blackest idolatry—the idolatry of which man is the subject, has assumed the worship of the Lord Most High, and the land is withering under its oppressive rule.

It is remarkable that, in the face of warning and reproof and punishment, the Israelites, like an ill-starred nation, pursued their way of transgression. They were threatened with calamity, and the threat was executed, and while the threat was unheeded, the calamity failed to effect their reformation. They pursued their way of rebellion in the very face of affliction, and while they were in the endurance of its scourge, the strong arm of the Almighty was held out in their view for protection and punishment; protection in obedience, and punishment in transgression. They preferred the evil before the good, and went on through trouble and sorrow until their career of guilt as a nation was terminated in their final overthrow.

In comparing our national progress with that of the Jews, it is difficult to tell which received most of blessings from the hand of their Heavenly Benefactor. Both have shared largely of His favor, and no other nations of the world were ever placed under equal obligations with them to love and honor their Omnipotent Protector. Like God's ancient people we are guilty of the abuse of His blessings, and of the impious violation of His commandments. Our offences have appeared as a thick cloud before heaven, and they now hide the face of our kind Father and Friend from us. We look upon the past but to trace His merciful interposition for our support, and His hand of power for our protection. He has given us a goodly land, wherein we have eaten bread without scarceness, whose very stones are iron, and out of whose hills we may dig brass. (Deut. viii. 9.) We have built goodly houses and dwelt therein; our flocks and our herds have multiplied; our gold and silver have multiplied, and all that we have had has multiplied, and our hearts have been lifted up, and we have forgotten the Lord our God, that gave us all these blessings. (Deut. viii. 13, 14.)

Measuring our fall by the rule of God's commandments, there is not an article of the Decalogue but we have practically and habitually violated. And as a people we are now living in the indulgence of our selfish desires, regardless of the order that has been issued, once for all, for the obedience of all men, and which there never was a nation under the same obligation that we are, to respect and obey. The commandments engraven upon the two tables of stone which Moses delivered to the Israelites, were given for our obedience as well as theirs. They sum up the whole duty of the man and the citizen, to God, to the government, to society, and to the family. We are directed to show our obedience to God in our intercourse with our fellow-men; and in this obedience is included our love to God with all our heart, and soul, and mind, and our neighbor as ourselves.

We not only do not exhibit in our lives such love to God as the commandments require, but it really appears as if it were a matter of indifference to us whether we have any interest in Him, or He in us. We not only do not show our love to our neighbor, by doing to him as we would have him to do to us, but we selfishly appropriate whatever of our neighbor's services and property we can secure to our own use, almost utterly regardless whether we do him any service in return or not. We live for ourselves, and concern ourselves but little whether we worship God or serve our friends, as we are commanded, or not. We have other gods than the Great Jehovah, which we prefer to worship, and heart, and soul, and mind are given to them. Our gods are not those of the hills and groves, and of the host of heaven. They are those of our own hearts, and of the household, and of society. But they are the gods of our idolatry as much as those of the hills and groves, and the host of heaven, were of the idolatry of the Jews. They employ our thoughts; they absorb our affections; they increase our cares, thoughts, and affections, and cares that should be dedicated to the honor and service of Him who is God alone, and the only true object of our worship. Not more thoroughly did the gods and goddesses of the Jews monopolize their interests and services than do these idols of our hearts monopolize our affections and attract our services. We have not Moloch, and Ashtaroth, and Chiun in wood and stone. But we have them in our desires and passions, and in our ungovernable will. They appear in our selfishness, which is satisfied only when we secure to ourselves the advantage over others with whom we may have to do. They are in our desires, which always run before us and claim all the resources of nature and art in their gratification. They are in our pursuits and purposes, which must be carried out, even in the face of peril, and at any cost or hazard. We do not place our children in the arms of the sculptured divinities, from which, as if by some magical motion, we cause them to fall into the furnace that consumes them; but we rear them for the idolatry of fashion, and selfish enjoyment, and folly, equally destructive with the flame through which the offspring of our ancient brethren were forced to pass; a practice which, perhaps, more than any other, is condemned and forbidden in the Scriptures. Thus, instead of loving our Creator and Preserver with all the heart, and soul, and mind, it is clearly evident that we have many other gods besides Him, all of which we worship before we think of Him.

In this pursuit of the various forms of our practical idolatry, we have lost the reverence that is due to the name and character of the Most High God. The commandment declares that we shall not take the name of the Lord our God in vain, and that we shall not be held guiltless by Him if we so offend. And yet in the very face of this order, how almost universal is the habit of the prohibited profanity? The name of God is blasphemed by multitudes who are never troubled with a thought in relation to the criminal nature of their deed. From the earliest periods of youthful indulgence the habit is encouraged with impunity, until it is fixed upon the subject, and the commonest of household words are those in which the awful name of Deity is irreverently spoken. But not only among the profane by habit is this offence committed. In refined society and among the educated the impropriety is indulged; and there are those among the worshippers of God's temple who lightly speak the name once ineffable among the chosen few that were permitted to tread its hallowed courts. When the incense of abomination was burned upon the mountains, and the name of God was blasphemed upon the hills, (Isa. lxv. 7,) the iniquitous habit was transferred to the House of the Lord, and the vengeance of the Highest followed it until the land was made a desolation.

In the indulgence of this debasing practice we have greatly damaged our national character and name. The members of our national and State councils are generally men of profane habits, and the halls of our country's legislation are frequently desecrated by the irreverent use of the name of God. For this form of our guilty character, if continued, we shall certainly be brought to judgment. If the complaint be renewed that was uttered of old, "My name continually every day is blasphemed," the judgment of the Almighty will not sleep, and we shall surely answer for the crime.

In connection with the varieties of our idolatry and profanity, we have systems and plans for the violation of the day that God has reserved in the commandments to Himself, and which He has declared shall be kept holy. As a people, we do not obey this commandment. The Sabbath, by multitudes, is used as a day of labor, and of business, and of pleasure. It is well known that in many of the cities of the United States, both of the North and the South, places of business are kept open just as they are in the working days of the week. Concert rooms, gardens, theatres, and other places of amusement, are advertised with attractive bills of entertainment, and every possible effort put forth to gather in the crowds and render the desecration profitable. The violation of this commandment, although a light offence in our city when compared to the extent to which it is carried in other cities of the country, is sadly subversive of the teachings of religion and morality, and ruinous of the characters of many of our youths. We close the restaurants, and confectionary and tobacco stores by law, but sales of the prohibited articles are effected secretly, and the tobacco stores are attended by crowds of young men and others whose engagements are not always conformable with the rules of morality. Were the authorities sufficiently strict in the enforcement of the law, and the law-makers as conscientious as they ought to be in the protection of the public morals, these practices would not be allowed. The command is clear that we shall keep holy the Sabbath day, and, as a people, we ought to render it a willing obedience, simply because God has so ordained it. That there are multitudes that do not enter the sanctuary of the Most High on this day is clearly evident, from the fact that there are hardly seats enough in all the churches of all the cities to accommodate more than half their population. Like every thing else for which provision is generally made, the number of places in the church is determined by the demand. If but half the people design to worship God in His temple, it is useless to make provision for more. There are multitudes of American citizens that pollute the Sabbaths of the Lord, in the occupancy of its hallowed hours anywhere and everywhere else than in His sanctuary, and in any and every pursuit but that of His worship. Is it a small thing that we pollute the Sabbaths of the Lord? "What evil thing is this that ye do and profane the Sabbath? Ye bring more wrath upon Israel by profaning the Sabbath." (Neh. xiii. 17, 18.)

While we thus forget the Lord our Maker, and worship other gods, and profane His Sabbaths, we cannot be bound together in the bonds of love and fellowship that should bind us in union as brethren and friends; nor can we consider properly our own in considering the welfare of others, as members of the same great household of which all men, especially those of our own nation, are parts, and of which God is the head and governor.

A sad mark of our degeneracy as a people, is witnessed in the indifference allowed in relation to the law that requires the honoring of parents. It is doubtless the fault of the parents themselves that the children are inconsiderate and blameworthy in regard to this order. There is evidently the lack of proper instruction; and this neglect, together with the absence of propriety of character, and dignity of demeanor, induces the violation of the most affectionately ordered commandment of the decalogue—the commandment ameliorated by the promise that the days of the obedient shall be prolonged.

The commandment that parents should be honored, is of much more importance than the mere respect and reverence children should exhibit towards their fathers and mothers, would indicate. The respect for parents, so kindly ordered, is indicative of the reverence that the young should entertain and practise before God, and it leads naturally to the proper estimation of His august name and person. The law is linked with those requiring that God's name and Sabbath shall not be polluted, but held in hallowed esteem by all the people of the land. As a part, therefore, of the obedience that should be rendered the Almighty Sovereign of the Universe, the members of every household are to be instructed and directed to render due honor to father and mother. The pledge of lengthened life to the obedient is given to every household, and is, therefore, the nation's property. That pledge is annexed in order to secure the nation's obedience, and to enforce it more emphatically upon all the people. That the non-observance of this commandment leads to the profanation of God's holy name and Sabbath, none can doubt; and the end of pollution thus induced may be readily anticipated. The most terrible curse is denounced in the word of God against it. "The eye," says the proverb, "that mocketh at his father and despiseth to obey his mother, the ravens of the valley shall pick it out, and the young eagles shall eat it." (Prov. xxx. 17.) Surely, if this terrible premonition were carefully enforced, and at the proper period, it would prevent the calamity denounced against the fault so forcibly condemned.

As an expansion over the community and the nationality of the order of the household, we are forbidden to destroy or hurt one another. The utterance is as fearful as it is brief. "Thou shalt do no murder." During the later years of our history we have seemed in a considerable degree to disregard this law; and we have become so familiar with the crime of homicide, that we are hardly shocked at the recital of acts of cruelty, nor startled when the announcement is made that a fellow-creature has fallen by another's hand. The period is not far in the retrospect, when the report of a murder would startle the neighborhood, and send its thrill of horror throughout the city. But that period has passed away, and, with it, the keener sensibilities of our more refined and less hardened nature. The rehearsal now of the terrible particulars of the murderous scene can be listened to almost without emotion. There is an alarming proof of degeneracy in this change of character. The frequent occurrence of the murderous scene has rendered us familiar with the deed, and with the loss of the sensitive impression, our sensibilities have been blunted, and we have not only lost the grade in civilization and enlightenment we had attained, but we have retrograded towards the barbarous condition from which we supposed we had long ago emerged. We have been so free in the enjoyment of our liberties, that we have become licentious, and so well are we pleased with ourselves, that we do not discover that we have fallen so far below the standard of virtue we had reached.

The sins of debauchery and dishonesty are denounced in the decalogue in plain and forcible language, and yet among the records of crime, the repetition of such offences is frequent. With the news of every day comes the intelligence of deeds that shock humanity. There are revelations that disclose in a thousand forms the alarming truth, that the flame of moral purity burns dimly upon the altar that was once hallowed in its consecration to civil and moral purity. The domestic sanctuary is invaded by the footsteps of the destroyer, and the marauder's hand, already gilded in the successful practice of its wiles, is closed in its relentless grasp alike upon the fortunes of the millionaire, and the pittance of the poverty-stricken subject of his artful practice. The name of the felon of the social circle is coupled with that of the felon of the till; and the grade of the crime is all that prevents them from being the equals of each other, in the infamy they have earned. In the magnitude of the offence there is a sort of amelioration for the offender, and while society is satisfied to retain in its fellowship the felon of the higher offence, it consigns the mean villain to the cell. In this partiality of the social circle is the proof of its corruption. It is the fearful evidence of a sad departure from the rule of virtue, that once regulated its operations, and fixed the estimate of its character.

With the baser forms of human depravity, are linked the false witness against his fellow's character, the creature that covets his neighbor's property. The word of the Great Lawgiver proclaims that these wrongs shall not be committed. The prohibition is unmistakable, yet the tongue of the slanderer and the defamer is everywhere in society, and every man seems to covet some feature of his neighbor's character, or some part of his possessions. Within the knowledge of every member of the social and domestic company, is the person who has suffered in the disparagement of his good name. His character has been filched from him, or damaged in some way by the rumor that has been started and circulated, and that has gathered volume and strength as it progressed, until it became necessary that it should be arrested and counteracted. And in almost every heart, there is the lurking desire that property should be possessed for which men have never labored, and for which they do not think of rendering an equivalent. The desire is not unfrequently the father of the action by which the effort is made to secure the possession without the return of its proper value.

We may thus include every commandment of the decalogue, in the charge that we are a disobedient and rebellious people. The charge is applicable to us as a nation, and involves in some degree or other, almost every individual citizen in the offence. Few, if any, can claim entire exemption. All are to a greater or less extent involved in the accusation; and the acknowledgment will be made by every one that enters personally into the examination. To the inquiry, "Is it I?" will the ready response be given, "Thou art the man." The hearts of the multitudes are open to the eye of God. To His view, their secret plans and purposes are exposed. How then shall they escape out of His hand? Shall He not be avenged on a nation that hath not respect for His laws, and that will not be obedient to His commandments?

As a people in our constant practical violation of God's commandments, we exhibit two prominent governing qualities,—Selfishness and Self-will. Throughout every department of society, from the highest to the lowest, these qualities are exhibited. They control our intercourse; they determine our conduct; they disclose our character. In two general features they affect us in our various personal and national relations. Our self-will has reference to our desire and purpose of exercising control over others. Our selfishness inclines us to a personal monopoly of every desirable object; while through our self-will we claim control over the sentiments and actions of others. In our selfishness we pursue wealth, and fame, and pleasure. In our self-will we would possess power, and exercise authority; and in pursuit of our purpose, we would rush forward in the overthrow and destruction of every opposing element, either of lawful or unlawful restraint.

There are various shadows under which our selfishness and self-will appear. It is under these shadows that our national name and character are now suffering. We may notice a few of the more prominent of our faults; and in passing them in review, we shall perceive how greatly we have disfigured our national escutcheon in our disregard and violation of God's commandments. We have abused our national name and character by the variety of defects which appear most plainly to the view, and afford convincing proof that we have sadly degenerated since we secured our nationality and assumed our place among the independent powers of the earth.

These defects appear in the following forms. They show themselves in

I. Our Habits of Dealing.
II. A Reprehensible Practice of Boasting.
III. A Distinction for Falsehood to which such Boasting Naturally Leads.
IV. An Unduly Excited Curiosity.
V. The Degrading Sin of Drunkenness.
VI. Our Fast Living.
VII. The Violence of our Sectional Divisions, and the Bitterness of Party Spirit, which have Contributed their Full Share in Reducing us to our Present Condition of Misfortune.

I. Our Habits of Dealing.—In this department of our intercourse, we exhibit a degeneracy of character which is alarmingly reprehensible, and of which we would be most heartily ashamed, did we fully realize the force of its degrading tendency. The desire and determination to secure the advantage, are apparent in all our issues of trade and labor. We must have the most for our property or service, and we would give the least for the property and service of others. We must, in all cases, whether we sell, or buy, secure the advantage. We must obtain the better of the bargain. In this desire and purpose, how clearly is it seen that the idea of fairness and honesty is entirely lost sight of?

For the system upon which we conduct our pursuits of trade we have a characteristic title. We call it jowing. Upon this system the seller purposes to obtain, if possible, much more for the article he sells than it is worth: while the buyer designs and endeavors to possess it for "much less than it cost." Both the seller and the buyer exercise ingenuity and talent worthy of a better deed, in the effort to overreach each other. It matters not whether the article of sale and purchase is a plantation or a yard of tape, the jewing process is pursued, and the number of falsehoods uttered, and false issues exchanged between the parties, would utterly destroy the characters of both, were society in a better condition. But the practice is universal, and society surrenders itself to its control. Every one seeks the advantage. Every one must secure the bargain, and he is considered the most fortunate, and the best man of the community who is most successful in effecting his purchases at the lowest and his sales at the highest prices. The seller "deceiveth his neighbor, and saith, Am I not in sport?" (Prov. xxvi. 19.) "It is naught: it is naught, saith the buyer, and when he is gone, he boasteth." (Prov. xx. 14.) It is the advantage, the best of the bargain that is sought both by the buyer and seller, and between them the principle of fair dealing and honesty is sacrificed—it suffers immolation by the selfish desire of personal benefit. We call the process jewing, but if the Jews were ever more formidable in the pursuit of personal benefit, and more thoroughly devoted to the practice of deceiving one another by misrepresenting and cheapening in their dealings than we are, they were not worthy of the protection of their Heavenly Benefactor, and richly deserved the calamities their deceitful character brought upon them. And in this comparison, in which we are evidently worsted, what can we say for ourselves? Where is our excuse? By what process can we justify ourselves? To such inquiries we can make no satisfactory reply. In our own judgment we condemn ourselves. It were therefore wise in us to make the acknowledgment of the wrong, and renounce it. It were greatly to our credit that we should confess the sin and forsake it. A moment's reflection would satisfy any one that it is an unmanly and mean practice, and none can consider properly its meanness without being ashamed of it. To obtain more for property than it is worth, or to undervalue it in the cheapening process for personal advantage, is simply deception. It is so much like the practice of a cheat, that if properly intimated neither of the parties engaged in the traffic would be willing to acknowledge the deed. It is a remarkable species of imposition that, as a people, we are practising upon ourselves in our commercial relations. We must possess the advantage in every respect, or we are not satisfied. To fail in an attempt at a bargain is a source of regret and mortification. Our exchanges are frequently affected by the effort to speculate upon the necessities of the community. The practice prevails in every department of our commercial intercourse. We acknowledge the deceit, and yet we most determinedly pursue it. We repudiate and denounce the artifice, and yet fortunes are lost and won in its employment.

The evidence of wrong is clearly apparent in this selfish pursuit of personal advantage. The wrong is an offence to purity, to justice, to honesty. It ought to be removed. The corrective ought to be applied. It must be if we would obtain favor and blessing from God. What we admit as wrong, He shall most certainly condemn. What we denounce as error must be judged in righteousness by Him.

The plan may be readily presented upon which the evil, or rather the multiplied evils that arise from our habits of dealing, may be corrected. We must look the wrong in the face. We must own the error and renounce it. We must cultivate and encourage a better spirit. Fairness must be substituted in place of the desire and purpose of securing the advantage. The idea of the equivalent, upon which the law is based, must be fully and fairly admitted and practised. The proclamation of value received must be realized. The face of the account must be true to the transaction, and the living profit must be allowed between man and man. In the sale, the seller ought to fix the price of his property in accordance with its true value, and require but a fair profit for his capital and labor in the trade. In the purchase, the buyer ought to be willing to allow a fair and honest remuneration for the services rendered by the vender. The equivalent—the value received—should be precisely what the law, in equity and propriety, demands. In such pursuit of trade, both seller and buyer get what is properly and fairly and honestly their own; and both ought to be satisfied with the result. The plan is based upon an old but familiar idea, that of each dealer securing a living for himself, and affording the opportunity to others for doing the same. "Live and let live," is the trite old adage long since obsolete, which must be revived. Its revival will doubtless bring back the good old times, when neighbors could rejoice in each other's prosperity, knowing that each had contributed his share in producing it. It was under that old regimé that forty-eight out of fifty dealers realized fortunes in the pursuit of business, sufficient to support them when the infirmities of age rendered the pursuit of business impossible. Two of the fifty made the failure, and left off in a worse condition than they were in when they started. But under the new rule of working for the advantage, and being satisfied with nothing less, the forty-eight out of the fifty make the failure, while but two are successful in realizing a competency sufficient to sustain them in the decline of life. The proportion of failures here given, in comparison with the successful pursuits of trade, is drawn from the records as they are reported for the City of New York,—the greatest commercial emporium of the United States. There is no doubt of its correctness.

In the pursuit of the old custom in dealing, each man contributed his proportion to his neighbor's prosperity, and he was enabled to rejoice in the deed, knowing that it produced the equilibrium of trade, which rendered nearly the whole community prosperous. In this success his own opportunities were included. In such custom the idea of over-reaching was unknown, and the shrewd dealer that sought his advantage in the ignorance or lack of enterprise or energy in his customer, was generally the man that made the failure. The shrewd dealers have multiplied in modern times; hence, the increase in the number of failures among the mercantile communities. It is the pursuit of the wrong that secures its own defeat. The result is inevitable, and can only be prevented by the removal of the cause.

II. Our Habits of Boasting.—Not more prominently in other habits of dealing does our selfishness appear, than it does in our habit of boasting. This habit is almost universally indulged, and by it we have rendered ourselves ridiculous. We have boasted of our freedom, until we have run it into licentiousness. We have vaunted ourselves of an invincible prowess, which has led us into the defiance of the opposition of each other and of the world. In the encouragement of our sectional feelings, we have arrayed one part of the country against another; and one State against another; and one part of a State against another; and one part of a city against another part of the city. We have practised this boast until we have ceased to remember that we are all friends and brethren of the same great commonwealth, and we imagine that we are the enemies of all that we oppose, or that may be opposed to us. In our divisions thus induced, we have so far forgotten ourselves as to issue threats of a revengeful character, and in some instances, have attempted to put those threats in execution. In the temper and spirit of such boasting, there is more of the disposition of the savage, than of the civilized man. It has induced the mob and the riot by which our domestic peace is sometimes disturbed. There is no section or party in any part of our country, but in its brag of superiority is wiser and better, and stronger than any other section or party; and the vaunt is sometimes issued, that the test will be hazarded with the odds of two or three, or five to one. It is in our halls of national, and state, and city legislation, as well as among the communities of different sectionalities, that this habit has been exhibited, and its purpose to rule or ruin has been plainly apparent. Had not this sectional spirit, in its party boast, been overruled by some conservative power, almost mysteriously interposed in some instances, it had long ago accomplished our national overthrow. It is now doing its terrible work among our States, and the extent of its ravage cannot be estimated. Doubtless this unfortunate habit has effectually performed its part of the dread issue that now afflicts us so severely. And it is by this practice that we are imperceptibly led into trouble.

III. THE DISTINCTION WE HAVE ATTAINED IN FALSEHOOD.—We have reached a point in this particular, from which we ought to be able to estimate the degradation to which it has reduced us. The false issues of society are everywhere effective in their work of deception. The glitter of gold that we see is but the gilding of the surface. It is defaced by the touch which reveals the deformity beneath. The gilding is put on in the family, and in the school. Instead of being trained and educated for substantial life, in the open and honorable, and candid intercourse which should ever be the characteristics of a free people, our children are taught to vaunt themselves in their superiority of position, or character, or strength, or other supposed advantage. They are encouraged in the pursuit of a fictitious fame, by hiding the true condition under an assumed ideal of superiority.

The falsehood shows itself most fearfully, in the suspicious development apparent in our intercourse. Scarcely any thing is believed upon representation, and for very good reasons. It is because our representations are generally misrepresentations, and we are frequently deceived by them. We take the word of but few of our associates as truth, and unless we examine the statement for ourselves, we find that, in some way or other, we have been deceived and wronged.

Rumor, with her thousand tongues, but seldom speaks the truth. The narration of an occurrence of trifling import, and the detail of the startling event, are alike filled with falsehood. We should suppose that if the truth might be expected in any records, they should be those of the battles of the present war, in which all are so greatly interested; and yet there are very few persons, if any, that down to this moment can rehearse, as they really occurred, the scenes of the battle-field, or tell the actual result of a single battle that has taken place. With the falsehood of our character and condition, we are practically writing the falsehood of our history. The charge of falsehood thus preferred, may be run through every department of our intercourse, and it is threatening us, name and nation, with the most fearful consequences.

IV. OUR UNDULY EXCITED CURIOSITY.—Like our boasting and falsehood, our unduly excited curiosity is a fault of universal notoriety. It begins with the earliest period of observation, and is increased with the occurrences of every day, both in the family and in the school. One of the most dangerous, and perhaps destructive forms in which this curiosity appears, is in the feverish anxiety almost universally experienced to hear the news. And to this anxiety the sensation press is ministering to an extent unknown. If the newsboy adds "another battle" to the announcement of the paper he has on hand, the extra is sure of sale, and the purchaser may be deceived again, as has frequently been the case before, although in his disappointment he most heartily denounces the deceiver. And how frequently is it the case, that the purchaser of the penny extra had rather read the intelligence that tells him of the battle and the destruction of his fellow-citizens, than experience the disappointment. With the detail of the battle he is satisfied; but he is vexed, and disappointed, and mortified if it be no part of his penny's purchase. What is to be the end of this feature in our character, if not checked, it is impossible to determine. It must either be in idiocy or some form of insanity. It has already very nearly reached the degree in which insanity begins, and if it is preparing its subjects for the madhouse, as a nation we are working our way to destruction with a rapidity, of the extent of which we are not aware.

V. The Defect of Drunkenness a Degrading Sin.—That drunkenness is on the increase among our communities, must be evident to every observer. The quantity of spirituous liquors consumed in the United States is immense, and its destructive work is terrible to think of. It is a moderate computation that includes every third family of the Union in the fearful ravage it is making. But a short time ago a proposition was started for the establishment of an inebriate asylum in this State, and before the organization of the Board of Managers was effected, hundreds of applications were made for admission, and from some of the best families of the State. It has become fashionable for young men to visit drinking-houses daily, and hundreds of thousands of them are now tippling their way to destruction. Better were it for these that they should fall upon the battle-field than that they should drag along their slow passage to the desolation that awaits them. The present war of Providence with our nationality, terrible as it is, may be a merciful intervention compared with the ruin that we are working among our communities in the indulgence of this degrading, desolating propensity.

VI. Our Fast Living.—The evils here enumerated may all be included in our fast living, which is an invention of the later periods of our history. Our forefathers were men of moderation, and lived frugally and plainly, and exhibited their sterling worth of character in their families, and in their intercourse with society, and in their labors among the community. The modest beauty and intelligence of the household needed no trumpet-tongue to boast of its preëminence. Their quiet and gentle communion with each other, and the honor and honesty that characterized their intercourse, required not the falsehood for the concealment of imperfections, nor the gilding for the covering of internal deformities. The true native dignity of their day has been left far in the rear of the present generation, which is hurrying on with lightning-speed to the end of its career. Impatient of restraint, defiant of consequences, madly determined upon the uncertain result, we are rushing forward in the annihilation of time and space, and helping each other out of life in the use of every agency we can bring to bear upon the effort. The most important inventions of the present time are those which assist us in our eating and drinking, and in the destruction of each other's lives. The discoveries of science are those of a past period, and we now use them in our pursuits of pleasure. The steam-engine, the rail-road, and the telegraph are but the subservients of the dinner, and the dram, and the latest news. We are rapidly outrunning ourselves, and unless arrested in our course, our fall is inevitable.

VII. Our Sectional and Partisan Divisions.—If not the worst, certainly not among the least, of our national faults we must class our sectionalism, and the violence of our political party dissensions. Doubtless to these more immediately are to be attributed the evils we are at the present time enduring. One of the most conservative features of our free institutions is the freedom of sentiment which they admit and encourage. Properly used, this feature forms a kind of safety-valve for the preservation of our liberties. In the guarantee of the Constitution of the United States, of a republican form of government to every State, and to every citizen of every State, every citizen is rendered a sort of sovereign in his own individual right; and if this right were properly maintained, with a due regard of every citizen for the sovereignty, and sovereign rights of every other citizen, our republic would be safe, and all would be happy in the use of its unequalled institutions. But if every individual citizen regards himself as a sovereign, and treats every other citizen as a serf, we must expect dissensions and disasters,—a final overturning of our Government, and a general crushing out of its free institutions.

As sectionalists we are bitter in our opposition against each other. There is no impropriety in our local attachments. It is right and proper that we should love the places of our nativity,—the homes of our childhood, and that our affections should cluster around the familiar scenes of our earlier years. But in the entertainment of this native feeling and interest, we are not to interfere with others in their possession and enjoyment of the same happy privileges. It is rather our bounden duty, as fellows in our citizenship, each to regard and protect the others in the possession and use of these native rights. In the variety of climate and production, our widely extended territory affords us every thing that is necessary to our prosperity and happiness as a people; and it is our interest to sustain and support each other in the interchange of the productions supplied by the varying sectionalities, which are doubtless providential in their distribution. In the friendly intercommunion which the exchange of supplies requires, we are a peaceful and prosperous nation. But in the encouragement of sectional jealousies, and the provocation of sectional divisions, and the indulgence of embittered sectional feelings, we convert our national blessings into sectional curses, and destroy ourselves in the destruction we bring upon others.

And our political party privileges which are admitted in our constitutional freedom, are blessings if properly employed. And the proper employment and use of these privileges, is in the respect and maintenance of the rights of others equally with our own; and in the fairness and honesty, and honorable dealing which should ever characterize our political party operations. This honorable dealing is especially necessary in the preservation of the purity of the ballot-box. The dearest and most sacred rights of the freeman, are those which he has the privilege of exercising in the choice of the agents of his government. Corruption in this department of the freeman's rights is ruin. And corruption is apparent in every undue advantage that may be sought or secured in the effort to contravene a just expression of the will of the majority.

That we have become shamefully corrupt in this department of our national character, is obviously certain. The political parties of past years have been laboriously engaged in their efforts to secure the party triumph, almost without regard to the means used in the accomplishment of the object. Bribery, deception, violence and bloodshed, have disfigured and stained the paths over which the parties have proceeded to the attainment of their successes. "Rule or ruin," has been the motto of the times, and it has ruled to our shame and sorrow, in the ruin it has brought upon us. Through the violence of the party disputes and dissensions of the past, we may trace our present misfortunes. These misfortunes are the natural result of the causes that have produced them, and it is becoming in us, that we should search out the corruption, and remove it.

OUR RELIGIOUS DISSENSIONS.—It is a most lamentable consideration in our estimate of this sectional and partizan contest, that we cannot exempt our religion. Religious denominations have entered the arena of strife, and after fierce and furious contests, they have separated into factions and set the example of disunion before the nation. The members of the same denomination in different sections of the country, have proscribed each other on account of their conflicting sentiments, doubtless honestly entertained; and the official decision has been sent forth to the world that the parties had no desire to affiliate with each other any longer. The feud of the religious assembly has heralded the feud of the nation, and we have now before us the most anomalous mixture of religious, and political, and domestic and social heresy and schism, that the world ever witnessed. The church, on account of this unbrotherly, and unchristian, and unmanly raid against the freedom of opinion, has cause for the deepest humiliation. She cannot answer for her sin, and until she is ashamed of it there is but little hope of her reformation. Where was the gentle and forbearing spirit of her high Exemplar, when she sat in sectional judgment upon her membership, and rent her bosom in twain because she could not be as tolerant as the gospel required.

It is the pursuit of the wrong in these defects of our national character, that has dishonored and disgraced us as a people. The seal of the Almighty's displeasure is upon our courses, and its condemnation is written. The escape from His hand is not to be effected while the violation of His precepts and commandments, is encouraged and practised. The failure must ever succeed when His law is contravened, and when the hope of success for the enterprise is based upon fraud and falsehood. The commandments must be acknowledged and respected, in the pursuits of every department of life, and when overlooked, or abused, the consequences must be endured. The individual must pay the forfeit of his offence, and the nation must endure the ills that the forfeiture of heaven's favor and protection may produce.

OUR HOPE IS IN THE PURSUIT OF THE RIGHT AND THE TRUTH.—While the failure, and the disappointments, and the mortification must generally succeed the wrong, the pursuit of the right, in fairness and honesty, must be attended with the gratifying assurance that the consciousness of duty, properly recognized, and faithfully performed always suggests. This is an order of Heaven's own ordaining, and its application is as universal as any law can be to the varying vicissitudes of life. In the rule of Providence, the right must prevail, although the wrong may sometimes seem to possess the advantage. The triumph of truth is ever in its progress, notwithstanding the apparent advantages that error occasionally secures. In our intercourse as a people, the right has been obscured, and the wrong admitted, for a series of years. Truth has been crushed under the foot of the prevailing selfishness, and error allowed to assume its place. But while the nation has suffered for the fault, and is suffering still on its account, the right and the truth, in their essential qualities, have sustained, and can sustain no damage; they are as pure and as true as they ever were, and may be restored to their reign of propriety and peace. In their encouragement we may re-introduce the honest and honorable customs of more primitive times, when men were more prosperous in their business, and more happy in their social relations, because they were more candid, and more upright in their dealings, and more frugal in their habits, and more simple in their manners and manner of life.

THE REFORMATION OF THE EVILS OF OUR CHARACTER.—To be successful in this patriotic, this religious enterprise, we must educate our children for their nationality, and not as sectionalists and partizans. The noisy patriotism of the holiday must give place to the more quiet and sober patriotism of the settled nationality which should be taught in the school. The rising citizen must be prepared for the exercise of his freedom, and for the maintenance of the purity and prominence of the free institutions, which are the only true boast of his citizenship.

The introduction of the reformation necessary for the performance of the great work before us, must be begun by every man and woman, and it must be carried out effectually in every place of business, and in every household. No man or woman can be exempted from the obligation. It is society, the community, the state, the country that demands the sacrifice, and he and she must be traitors to their country and their God who hesitate to make it. The treason involved in this issue is the treason of the soul. It includes the physical, the mental, and the moral faculties in its overt act of disobedience to the commandments of God. As a nation we are guilty. The evidences are in every city; they are in every family; they are in every heart. The ruin has pushed its ploughshare over every foot of our inhabited territory, and the land is disfigured in every part. To assist in the restoration of its fair proportions, and its beauty, is the bounden obligation of the nation. In this obligation every individual citizen has a share. None can be excluded. Each has his count in the numbering of the people. Each has his place at the domestic board, and in society. Each is a member of the community, and takes his place in its pursuits and labors. Each performs his part in the traffic, in the boast, and the falsehood, and the undue indulgence of his curiosity, and if not in the drunkenness and the fast living, perhaps in the violence of his sectional feelings, and the bitterness of his partizan pursuits. Let the few that may consider themselves faultless not content themselves in inactivity and indifference. It is God that speaks to us. It is His controversy that we are called to meet, and from the northern to the southern, and from the eastern to the western limits of the land, the people should arise and own their obligations, and enter their services in the effort to remove the calamity.

History records but a single instance in which a people repented of their sins and humbled themselves before the threatened vengeance of the Almighty Jehovah. The people of the heathen city of Nineveh, at the command of the king, put on the sackcloth, and covered themselves with the dust. Their penitence was accepted, and the city was saved. It becomes the civilized, the enlightened, the christianized people of the United States to imitate the example of the obedient heathen. We have been called to the fast and to the religious service. In form, at least, the call has been obeyed, and to-day we own the sackcloth, and profess to be in the dust. God Almighty knows if we are sincere in the service. If we are, we will continue the effort to subdue our selfishness and self-will, and to conquer our improprieties, and we will labor most earnestly as a people to escape the hand of vengeance that is now held over us. We will labor to secure the merciful intervention of the kind Providence under whose hand of protection we have prospered so abundantly.

If we are not sincere in this show of our service, we will arise to-morrow in the forgetfulness of the duties of to-day, and we will sin yet more against God, and suffer yet more under the rod with which He is scourging us. We may be assured that the controversy under which we are suffering is not so much with man as it is with Heaven, and that it is on account of our unfaithfulness in not honoring and keeping the commandments of God, that were given for our continued obedience. The arm of man is not sufficient for our safety. It is impious to lift that arm against God, and for the impiety His vengeance shall be visited upon us. His voice of thundering eloquence is now calling alike to the people of the North and the South to submit to His all-powerful sway, and to cease to offend Him by the falsehood of their lives. The sooner this obedience is rendered the sooner shall we be freed from our present troubles. Doubtless among the offending multitudes may be found, as of old, the seven thousand that have not bowed the knee to the image of Baal. In them the power may be conservative, and through that power we may be saved. In our humility our trouble may be removed, and, by the blessing of Heaven, we may be rendered more prosperous than as a nation we have ever been. To labor to avert the curse and restore the blessing is the duty of every American, and performing it we may escape the hand of the Almighty's vengeance, and secure a return of his protection.

OBEDIENCE TO THE CIVIL AUTHORITY.

A Sermon preached in the South Presbyterian Church, Brooklyn, N. Y., April 28, 1861.

BY REV. SAMUEL T. SPEAR, D.D.

LET every soul be subject unto the higher powers. For there is no power but of God : the powers that be, are ordained of God. Whosoever therefore resisteth the power, resisteth the ordinance of God : and they that resist, shall receive to themselves damnation.—ROMANS xiii, 1. 2.

ON the Fourth of July, in the year of our Lord 1776, the Continental Congress adopted the Declaration of American Independence, as the basis alike in the principles involved and grievances alleged, upon which they appealed to the moral sense of the world for the justice of their cause, and to the God of battles for their hope of success. This was no hasty act on their part, no sudden ebullition of misguided passion. It was forced upon the Colonies by the administration of George III. They hesitated long and petitioned earnestly before sundering the political ties which had bound them to the mother country. Posterity and history have justified their course. The growth and development of a great and powerful people furnish the commentary of fact upon the wisdom and utility of the measure. Having fought the battles of the Revolution, and gained an honorable peace, our fathers soon discovered that a stable, efficient, and well-ordained government must be invested with central powers and prerogatives adequate to the wants of a nation ; and hence they called a Federal Convention, composed of the wisest and best men of the country, charged with the duty of drafting and submitting to the people a plan of national government. This plan being adopted by the people, superseded the Articles of Confederation, and became, as it has continued to be from that day to this, the Constitution of the United States of America. Under this Constitution George Washington was elected as the first President; and to his wise and patriotic hands the ship of State was committed for eight successive years. During his administration occurred what is known as the Whiskey Rebellion, which a prompt and efficient exercise of the Federal power very soon suppressed. Aaron Burr at a later period laid a plot for the subversion of the National Government. The loyalty of the country was shocked with the idea. Burr was indicted and tried for treason; and though not legally convicted of any overt act, posterity has branded him as a traitor. John C. Calhoun, with his false doctrine of State Rights, in opposition to Federal sovereignty, led the people of South Carolina into the attitude of nullification upon the tariff question, during the administration of General Jackson ; but when both leader and people found in the President a public officer not to be trifled with, they wisely concluded to abandon the conspiracy, and yield to the *supreme* law of the land. With a forecast almost prophetic, General Jackson said : " It is the tariff this time ; next time it will be slavery." Since that period we have heard much about dissolving the Union. Not a few Southern men have repeatedly threatened, that in certain contingencies they would dissolve this Union. They have, perhaps, thought that it would be a kind of holiday amusement ; they have accustomed their ears to this strange sound, till they have forgotten alike the enormities and the difficulties of the idea; they have succeeded in poisoning a portion of the Southern people with doctrines as ruinous to themselves as they are false to the Constitution; they have misrepresented the public sentiment of the Free States; they have made issues of fact out of fancy; they have deserted the platform and principles of the Revolutionary fathers, and demanded that the whole country should follow them in this apostacy; and yet, not until recently have they entered openly and actively upon the work of breaking up the national Government. A plan which has been slowly maturing for the last thirty years, has now culminated to its ignoble climax; and the great struggle of national life is upon us. We are in the midst of commotions that demand our most serious thoughts. We must now *think* as well as act, and act as well as think.

In these circumstances, I appear before you this morning to discharge the duties of a patriot to my country, of a pastor to you, and an ambassador of Christ to my God. This is the hour of the nation's trial and peril. The eye of Heaven is upon us. The spectacle we present to-day, commands the intensest meditation throughout the civilized world. We are in the midst of a great work; and if we do it well, unborn generations will bless us for the achievement. The scenes which so much excite our hearts will be *historic*, and exciting for a thousand years to come. Every thing that is vital in the structure of human society, is now placed in the providential scale that is to weigh this mighty issue. Our whole present and future national life hangs upon the questions of this momentous hour. We shall never again see such a time. Other nations have passed through similar crises, and have risen to a higher position, or gone down in dishonor and disgrace. If the fathers fought, and bled, and prayed, and planned to create the institutions of society under which we have lived so long, in which we have gloried so justly, and from which gathered such an ample harvest of national good, then Providence is calling us to the not less important task of *preserving* these institutions, and committing them unharmed to the generations that are to follow us. This is our work. This is now the great trust and duty of the American citizen. At such a moment, the pulpit would be treasonable to God as well as man,
if it did not open its mouth, and cry aloud, seeking to guide the public mind to a just estimate of the crisis, and the proper remedy for those evils that now darken our political heavens. This question is not to be left exclusively in the hands of the *secular* press. The pulpit is bound to coöperate with the Government in supporting the authority of law. It did a good service in the days of the Revolution, and it can do a good service now.

There is a Christian doctrine, a doctrine of the Bible and of right reason, in respect to civil government, considered in its nature and claims upon the obedience and support of the subject, at all times important, and preëminently so at the present moment—a doctrine deeper than any written constitutions of merely human origin—a doctrine that goes back to first principles as enacted by God himself. It is only by accepting and honoring this doctrine, that I see any hope for the salvation of this people from utter desolation and ruin. Hence my theme this morning is the doctrine of OBEDIENCE TO THE CIVIL AUTHORITIES.

The text, as you are aware, was addressed by Paul to the Church at Rome, composed of converted heathen and converted Jews, both living under the government of Nero, who was one of the most barbarous and cruel monarchs that ever disgraced the civil power. The magistracy was heathen, polytheistic, idolatrous, oppressive, and, withal, opposed in faith as well as practice to the principles of Christianity. It was doubtless very offensive to the Christians of that age. It did not at all represent their views; yet there it was, the government of the country in which they lived, the only government then existing, neither created by them, nor capable of destruction by their hands. Bad as it may have been in many respects, it was nevertheless the bond of civil and social order, and incomparably better than anarchy. Observe, now, that the Apostle had in his eye this very system of public authority, when he laid down the law and testimony of God as to the claim of civil government upon the obedience of the subject, stating the true doctrine for that age and for all ages. He proclaimed the *politics* of heaven as to the relation between the sovereign and the subject in the constitutiton of civil society. And if thus he wrote in respect to Nero's government, what, think you, would be the character of his message if he were now to address an epistle to those deluded men—some of them misguided Christians, others base and ambitious traitors, determined to rule or ruin—who have sought, and still are seeking, to overthrow the most genial and excellent system of public law which any people ever enjoyed? His language might not be essentially different from that of the text, yet the application would clothe it with an emphasis of unusual power. Let us then hear what the Apostle does say in—

THAT PART OF THE TEXT WHICH RELATES DIRECTLY TO THE PRACTICE OF THE CITIZEN AND THE SUBJECT. "Let every soul be subject unto the higher powers," is the language of this considerate as well as inspired man, substantially renewed in the fifth verse, when he says: "Wherefore ye must needs be subject, not only for wrath, but also for conscience' sake." By "the higher powers," he meant the civil authority, not as a mere abstraction of thought, but as a concrete reality embodied and set forth in a living and acting magistracy, in recognized possession of government, and performing the functions of law. Primarily, he meant Nero and all the officers who held authority under him. He told the Christians to pay *tribute* at the command of this magistracy, declaring the tax-gatherers to be "God's ministers, attending continually upon this very thing." In a larger sense, the precept refers to the government of any country in which one may be living. The fact that it *is* a government then existing, and not the rightfulness of its origin in the outset, or its form, or the general wisdom of its measures, brings it within the circle of the Apostle's conception. As to the subject, it is the Sovereign Power. Such a power exists in this land, and is, by the Constitution of the United States, committed to the national magistracy. This Constitution and all laws enacted by Congress in conformity therewith, form the *supreme* law of the land. The plain duty, then, of every man existing within the territorial jurisdiction of this Government, is that of subjection, including both the spirit and the practice of obedience to the laws of the country. The "higher law" of God makes the civil statute morally binding and authoritative. Whether we occupy official positions, or move in the sphere of private life, God imposes upon us the duty of subjection unto "the higher powers." This is the divine rule of action for the citizen; and if we disobey it, except in those instances which I shall specify in due season, we sin against God. Moreover, since government, whatever be its form, rests at last upon the bone and sinew of the people, depending upon their strong arms for the power of doing its work, whether in the infliction of penalty upon the guilty, or the resistance of aggression by foreign nations, or the suppression of unlawful assemblies of men who are disturbing the peace and order of society, or seeking to destroy the existence of the Government itself, it is clear that those who are subject to its authority, are bound to obey its call for any or all of these legal purposes. Law is nothing if it cannot be enforced, and government nothing, without the power of *coercion;* when ideas and commands cease to rule, then force must rule; and hence, when the civil officer has not sufficient power to defend the State, or execute the laws, and commands the people to help him, they must either obey the precept, or resign themselves to the reign of anarchy and confusion. If they wish to live under law, they must *support* the laws; and to do this, they must be ready to lift their arms for the maintenance of that which is the organ of law —government as established and administered by its legally appointed agents. Let them, however, not take this work into their own hands uncalled. I have no sympathy with that kind of zeal or patriotism, which proposes to supercede the civil magistracy in the execution of law. This gives you two anarchies instead of one, and looks to me very much like doing evil that good may come. The suggestion of one or two editors of the secular press, that the people should make a way through or over Baltimore, not waiting for the President's action in the premises, was the suggestion of mob law on the part of those who profess to be the supporters of law. Such a proposal may spring from a very patriotic impulse; but it is zeal without knowledge. I prefer to have Baltimore and every other city or State that resists the Federal authority, attended to in the dignified and legal way, as I have no doubt they will be in due season. I go for supporting the laws according to, and not against the provisions thereof. The country can be carried safely through this contest only by the hearty coöperation of the people with their constitutional rulers.

The President of these United States has recently issued his proclamation, declaring a portion of the people to be in a state of rebellion, and commanding them to lay down their arms, and return peaceably to their homes. Eighteen centuries ago, God issued his proclamation, directing every soul to be "subject unto the higher powers." If, then, these rebellious people would obey God, they must obey the nation's chief magistrate; and yet we are told that Jefferson Davis and his Cabinet read the President's proclamation amid roars of laughter, insulting the dignity of this Government, defying the God of heaven, and acting like men too much intoxicated with passion to be sensible of their own position. Before this contest is ended, they will, perhaps, learn that the authority of this nation is not to be trifled with.

As to the EXTENT of the precept we are now considering, I hold it to be universally binding in all cases, and under every form of civil government, with two *exceptions*, which, though not stated in the text, lie in the very nature of things; and that I may not teach a false doctrine in the effort to proclaim a true one, I think it well to pause a moment upon these exceptions.

The *first* is that of a *conflict* between the law of God and the requirements of the civil authority. Here, I admit that we must obey God rather than men. So the Apostles acted, and so we must act. There can be no doubt as to the rule of duty in such a case. Yet even here we must not pervert the rule. While we obey God, we must not add the sin of *resisting* the civil magistracy, when inflicting the penalty for that which the law of the land makes a crime. The true doctrine here is *obedience to God, and non-resistance to man*. As to the question which party is right, the individual or the State, in such an alleged conflict, let me say that neither party can determine this point for the other; and hence the question must go to posterity, and finally to the bar of God. On the one hand, the State cannot concede that the civil statute *is* in conflict with the law of God without confessing its own iniquity, and equally surrendering its own dignity and authority; and, on the other, the individual cannot obey that statute against the explicit testimony of his own conscience without being unfaithful to God. Hence the conscience of the State must govern the State, and the conscience of the individual must govern the individual. His conscience, however, is not the law of the land; nor must he claim that the law shall be staid in its action, because he cannot comply with it. In the issue that he makes with civil society, he must do what he regards as the will of God, and then meekly suffer for it; and whether he is a fool or a martyr, will be determined at another day. If he has not virtue enough for this, then his declinature to obey the law on the ground of conscience is little better than a mockery. And, before dismissing this point, let me seriously ask, whether those who are in open rebellion against the public authority of this land, can justify themselves to history, to posterity, and to God, on the ground of a *religious* conscience? Where is the law of God which requires this attitude on their part? Where is the statute of the national Government which they cannot obey, because it conflicts with the law of God? I know not by what sophistry good men at the South may deceive themselves on this subject; yet I confess myself utterly unable to see how they can ignore the claims of the Apostle's precept. Unless they can show that allegiance to this Government will be a sin against God, then the very law of God itself requires that allegiance. Moreover, on the theory that they cannot obey the nation's law, because this would be a sin, as they suppose, where, in the book of God, is their justification for overt acts of resistance and rebellion—their justification for plotting the ruin of the Government, for stealing its property, for raising armies, and employing them against the peace and good order of this Commonwealth? The apostolic theory of doing right, and then meekly suffering for the same, is manifestly neither the basis nor the spirit of this movement. There is no rebellion in that theory; but in this movement you have as glaring an exhibition of rebellion and treason, as the world ever witnessed. It is not, and it cannot be, founded upon the law of God.

The *second* exception to the general rule of obedience, is derived from what is termed the inherent right of *forcible* REVOLUTION, which means the subversion of an existing government by its subjects for the purpose of creating a better one. I cheerfully concede the *reality* of the revolutionary right; yea, I go farther, and say that its exercise, in certain circumstances, may be a solemn duty to God and man; and hence I take the Apostle's precept with this qualification. But remember, my hearers, that this question of revolution has more than one side to it; and that you may see it on all sides, I propose to state as clearly as possible the *principles* that are applicable in the case. If we are to go back to first principles, meaning to reconstruct the social fabric in this country, I wish to know precisely what we are doing. Let me then say to you:

In the first place, that the revolutionary right does not belong to the individual as such, or to the minority, but only to the *majority* of the people living under a government which it is proposed to supersede and destroy. By the very terms of the case, it is a *popular* right inherent only in the majority; and hence no individual, town, county, or section of a nation can forcibly make the attempt, without involving the crime of treason. Revolutionists against the popular will are traitors, and nothing but traitors, and should be dealt with accordingly. If a few disaffected spirits or disappointed demagogues may with impunity make this experiment upon the public peace, then civil society has no security. It may be disorganized at any moment. If such spirits do not like a government which a majority of the people do like, then let them peaceably emigrate, and keep on emigrating till they find something that pleases them. I am in favor of this kind of secession. This is just the thing which the Pilgrim Fathers did.

The right of revolution, in the second place, should not be exercised even by the majority, except in what are termed *extreme* cases. It almost necessarily brings with it all the evils of *civil* war. Society is dissolved into its elements, and thrown into a state of terrible confusion, and hence this expedient is justifiable only in *extreme* cases, where government is so oppressive as to be past all reasonable endurance; where, too, the evils of revolution are likely to be less than those of submission; where also there is a fair prospect of success, and where, again, all milder and less objectionable means of redress have been tried in vain. Revolution is in itself a prodigiously serious matter. It means death, usually, on a great scale; and it should therefore be the *last*, because the most terrible, resort of an injured and outraged people. In the outset it is a *rebellion*, and if sufficiently strong, a *revolution;* and hence, whether it be the one or the other, is purely a question of strength. *Might*, after a fair trial, must fix its character. Those who try the experiment, should open their eyes to the full consideration of this question of power. They will meet it in the process, and they had better think of it beforehand. It at once inaugurates the age of bullets and contending armies. It awakens the thunders of war.

I add, thirdly, that government as such, cannot recognize the existence of the revolutionary right without providing for its own death. The right can never be inserted in any written Constitution, or admitted by the administrators of law. It is itself a principle of destruction; and surely no organized civil society can exist on a basis that is fatal to its own being. Government must crush the rebellion by an armed force, or be crushed by it. It cannot reason or parley with a mob, whether that mob consist of ten men or ten thousand men. It must put that mob down, and demand unconditional submission to the forms of law, if necessary at the point of the bayonet, and by the authority of cannon-balls. Government can never concede that a rebellion is respectable by reason of the number engaged in it. The rebellion must make itself respectable, or perish under the due execution of law. The government that shrinks from meeting its own foe, is not to be trusted as the guardian of the peace and safety of human society. Brought face to face with those who repudiate its authority, it must command obedience, and enforce the command by the power of the sword. At such a moment I believe in fighting on the side of law and order, for the same reason that I believe in hanging pirates. The remedy, I know, is an awful one; yet I see no other course possible in the premises. It is fighting in a just cause, under the authority of law and the God of law. A people that will not, at any cost and at all hazards, sustain such a system of political and civil liberty as that under which we live; a people that will not respond to the call of the Government when the very life of the nation is at stake; a people that will permit anarchy and treason to stalk unpunished through the land; a people on whom the civil authority cannot depend at such an hour, are either revolutionists themselves, or a nation of *cowards*, destitute of all the elements of public virtue, without the fire of patriotism, without the love of order, alike incompetent either to preserve itself or command the respect of mankind. A nation made up of such a people has no soul, no organic life, no character, no attributes of effective sovereignty. Its ship of State is a miserable old hulk, and its Government nothing but a rope of sand. God forbid that we should accept this sad and helpless condition of the State, rather than fight for our institutions till every rebellious arm is palsied, and every traitorous machination is dead! God forbid that we should, in this nineteenth century, do what no nation can do without its own destruction! If any portion of the people insist upon trying the question of force under the revolutionary right, then Government must insist upon trying the same question under the high, solemn, and majestic attributes of sovereign authority.

I remark, fourthly, that a resort to the revolutionary right, under the guidance of wicked men, is quite certain to be disastrous. In such hands, the first stage is anarchy, and the second despotism; and hence the people lose vastly more than they gain, even if they succeed in prostrating government. The spirits that apply the torch to the civil fabric, are wicked and ambitious spirits, base wretches, often perjured villains, deceiving an ignorant and infatuated multitude to their ruin, serving themselves, and having no regard whatever to the public good. They are blind guides, fanning and fostering, and for their own purposes using the worst passions of men. It takes a great amount of moral integrity and political wisdom, added to a good cause, and combined with general intelligence and public virtue, to launch society upon the tempestuous waves of revolution, and then bring it safely into the harbor again. These conditions of success and advantage gave to our fathers their triumph, enabling them to pass through the dangerous struggle, and then construct a Government that has deservedly commanded the admiration of the civilized world. They had good leaders in such men as Franklin, Hamilton, Jay, Adams, Jefferson, and Washington. They were themselves the lovers of liberty and law; they sought to break, and not to strengthen the yoke of oppression; and for these reasons revolution in their hands became both a success and a blessing. In the absence of such reasons, it is always a failure even in its success; a curse in the beginning and a curse in the end; a fruitless and awful agony under which society bleeds at every pore, being left unprotected in every interest, trembling in every limb, yea, pierced to the very heart by the assassin's dagger. Such revolutions are inspired by the devil. A people delivered up to such convulsive movements, themselves mad, and led by others more mad and wicked than themselves, can accomplish nothing but their own destruction. It is a mercy to them to hang their leaders, and teach them, peaceably if you can, but forcibly if you must, the value of government. It is a mercy to them to put a stop to their proceedings. The conditions of a desirable success are not in them or among them; and hence they are fit neither to accomplish a revolution nor to make any good use of it. What a sad history is presented by the revolutions in Mexico! Since 1820 the Mexican people have had Presidents and Dictators, wars and rumors of wars, secessions and local dismemberments, till they have lost nearly all ideas of public order. One of the finest countries in the world has been laid waste by a constant series of revolutions. Not a single one of their Presidents has served out his whole time. A Presidential election in Mexico, first conducted by the ballot, is afterwards settled by the bayonet; and in some instances the latter mode of settlement has reversed the former. Mexico is wanting in the principles that give permanency and stability to government. Look, too, at France in the days of the Jacobins, in her Reign of Terror, in the hands of such men as Murat and Robespierre; see how the scaffold groaned with the weight of its victims; see the streets of Paris drenched with blood; study this lurid and profitless scene of human woe; and then tell me, ye restless disturbers of the public peace, ye despots in the disguise of friends, what society has to expect from revolutions over which such a spirit of evil presides. Those who without just occasion, put the knife into the very soul of civil order, and draw the life-blood of the State, are the greatest criminals on earth. They deserve to die. I abhor them with an intensity I want words to express. They are more detestable than the pirate upon the high seas. No other class of men do so much mischief.

I add, fifthly, that rebellion with a view to revolution in a Republican Government, like that of these United States, must always be utterly without excuse. In the very nature of things there can be no right of revolution against such a government. It is already a *popular* government, based on the representative principle. It recognizes no hereditary sovereign clinging to his throne; the voice of the majority of the people legally expressed, is the law of the land; the rulers are chosen by the people, holding their offices for limited terms; the Constitution provides for its own amendment at the call of public sentiment; all evils and grievances may be redressed in the peaceful and legal way; every possible occasion for resorting to the revolutionary right, is fully provided for; and hence any right of revolution against such a government means, if it mean any thing, the right "to overturn *all* government, to resist any and every law, and to dissolve society into its original elements." Whatever may be true in despotic governments, where the people have no voice in the selection of their rulers, and no voice in the enactment of their laws, and where they may be bitterly oppressed by the tyranny of a Pope or a king, without any means of redress except by violence, here, in this land of freedom, and under the Constitution of these United States, the revolutionary right can have no existence. Its equivalent is furnished by the Constitution itself. Voting is here the peaceful substitute for the natural right of revolution by fighting. Rebellion, here, is an effort to destroy the government of the *people*—a refusal of the minority to submit to the will of the majority; and this I pronounce to be the rankest form of treason that ever offended the eye of Heaven, or cursed the abodes of earth. It can rest on nothing but simple, naked wickedness. Those who are now setting the Constitution and laws of this land at defiance, insulting the flag of the nation and seeking to prostrate the Federal authority, are the crusaders of *sin*. The work is the work of *sin*. Why cannot they submit to the will of the majority? Are they to assume the character of rebels because they are outvoted? Are they to repudiate their allegiance the moment they cease to rule? Why cannot the chivalry of South Carolina yield to the popular will? Where are their grievances, either threatened or felt, that cannot be redressed under the Constitution? What yoke oppresses them? None, except the will of the majority. And in contending with them, if we must do so, we are fighting for that which is not only the vital principle of *every* government, but is also the essential life of the very best government under which a people ever lived. We are simply making good the declaration of the Fathers, that the Constitution of the United States shall be the supreme law of the land. We are simply insisting that the will of the majority under this Constitution, *shall* be paramount to the will of the minority. Meaning ourselves to be *loyal* subjects, we equally mean that all others shall be loyal, or answer for their treason at the bar of the nation's justice. This is the doctrine that now comes home to the bosom of the good citizen with such a weight of interest.

Let me add once more, that when the struggle between organized revolutionists claiming jurisdiction over a *section* of the country, and the established Government claiming jurisdiction over the *whole* country, is actually pending, there is an important problem of *allegiance*, which the citizen and subject must settle for himself upon his responsibility to both God and man. The question is this: When shall the subject, living in the midst of the rebellion, but at heart loyal to the Government, consider the revolution as a fact accomplished, or so certain of being accomplished as to be practically real to him? At what particular point does his allegiance to the Government under which he has hitherto lived, cease to be a moral reality, and become transferable to that which is the product of a revolution? You may call this a very nice question; yet in revolutionary times, it is a very *practical* one, often a very difficult question, not unfrequently subjecting the virtuous and patriotic citizen to the most terrible sacrifices. Of course, if the Government of his choice, and to which he has the heart of loyalty, be actually dead and gone, this ends the matter. He must then accept the fact as he finds it, however much he may regret it. But if the Government be not dead, if it be engaged in the work of suppressing the rebellion, supported by a majority of the people, evidently the stronger power, going forward and meaning to go forward in the due and proper execution of law, then I insist that, as a religious duty, he owes allegiance to the Government existing, and is morally bound to do every thing in his power for its support. He does not accept the proposed revolution as legitimate, for he condemns it; and in this status of affairs he cannot accept it as a fact accomplished, since it is not accomplished. The revolutionary government that disputes the authority of the established one, is to him a rebellion. His allegiance is therefore due to the powers that *be*, and not to those which are merely *trying* to be, and which as yet have no governmental character except that of sedition and lawless force. He must stand by the flag of his country till all reasonable hope of its salvation is gone. Surrounded as he is by a horde of traitors who are thirsting for his life, and ready to make loyalty a crime, his position is an awful one; yet he had better lose his life than save it at the price of dishonor. The man who is true at such a moment, absolutely true to his convictions, who can be neither bought nor frightened by traitors, has a noble spirit. His loyalty is something that it will do to talk about. Very often, too, a bold stand on the part of such men, promptly taken and firmly maintained, will roll back the rebellion, and crush it out without any great disturbance of civil society. The Union men of the South have, in my judgment, committed a grand mistake in not seasonably meeting the treasonable machinations which they now condemn and deplore. Those *so-called* Union men who are now taking sides with the new Confederacy, against protestations that have hardly yet become cold on their lips, who have abandoned the nation's flag in the hour of its peril, whose loyalty has been swept away in this hurricane of Southern treason, are equally committing a mistake. Yielding to the wild passions of the moment, they augment an evil which they might restrain, and greatly aid in removing. I know that breathing the bracing atmosphere of this political clime, it is much easier to condemn these men than to do better; but if the doctrine of the "Constitution, the Union, and the enforcement of the laws," was a good doctrine six months ago, I am not able to see why it is not just as good to-day. The new Confederacy has not yet so changed, and as I believe, it cannot so change the status of things in this country, as to make it wise or patriotic to ignore this national motto, and practically trample it under foot. It will be time enough for those who are Union men at heart, to give in their allegiance to the revolutionary government when it is really entitled to that allegiance. Let them remember that neither its Constitution, nor its officers, yea, that not a single fragment of it, has yet received the popular sanction in the legal way. It is a government of despots, of usurpers, of robbers, who extemporize their own laws, whom no nation on earth has yet acknowledged as legitimately invested with civil functions, and who are now sustaining themselves in what I trust will prove to be their transient career, by military force. Such a government, thus created, and withal disputed by the national authority, has no claim to any man's allegiance. The Union men in the seceded States may not, just at this moment, have sufficient power to overcome it; yet let them be careful how they rush actively, and against their own secret convictions, into this whirlpool of social disaster and public disorder, involving themselves in the crime of treason. They have a duty to discharge as well as the citizen in the loyal States. Take the case of Virginia, Maryland, the city of Baltimore, and let me ask, are the thousands and tens of thousands of Union men in these places passively to yield themselves to that which as yet is nothing but a *mob* on a great scale? Have they no country to save, and no Government to defend? Are the people of the Border States that do not mean to secede, so unwise, so untrue to their own interests, that they will be content with the doctrine of an armed neutrality between the Government and its enemies? Will they permit disunion leaders to cheat them into a virtual acceptance of the treason, and ere they are aware of it, make them parties to it? This doctrine of armed neutrality on the part of a State has the ring of treason in it. It is treason begun, if not intended. The Governors of the respective States are sworn officers, bound by their oath to support the Constitution and aws of the United States; and when the President, under a law of Congress passed in 1795, called for the State militia to suppress unlawful combinations of men and "cause the laws to be duly executed," it was the duty of these Governors to respond to this call, not in the language of insult, but in that of practical obedience. In refusing to do so, the Governors of the border Slave States violated their oath of office. In declaring the President's design to be the subjugation of the Slave States, they wantonly perverted the language of the Proclamation. And in proposing to put these border States in the attitude of an armed neutrality between the Government and the rebels, they virtually announced the purpose of resisting the authority of the Government. Armed neutrality is equivalent to rebellion against the laws of the land.

I submit then, in all candor, that honest Union men and Union Governors have something to do. This is no time for them to be talking about neutrality. They are either for the Government, or against it. I am equally of the opinion, that the Government ought to protect its friends so far as it can, and most of all, those friends that *need* the protection. It has no right to fold its arms and look on supinely, while the sons of loyalty are bleeding and dying on the unprotected altars of the Constitution. If necessary, it is bound to march an invading army to their relief, and suppress the reign of terror which is alike their alarm and their scorn. It asks for loyalty and pledges protection, and must do all in its power to fulfil this pledge. Shall peaceful and law-abiding citizens be forced into the armies of the insurgents: shall men, whose only offence is loyalty to their country, be persecuted, robbed of their property, driven from their homes and compelled to flee for their lives; and then shall the National Government say nothing, do nothing, attempt nothing in the premises? I confess, I do not so understand its duties. If it mean to recognize this rebellion as a revolution accomplished, then it ought to say so; but if it do not mean this, as it certainly does not, then it ought, at the earliest practicable moment, to stretch forth its arm and protect its own citizens against the outrages of these conspirators. They are entitled to the protection of the nation's flag. Let such enormities be perpetrated against an English subject in this country or any other, and you would soon hear the thunders of the British navy. I trust that our own Government will ere long teach rebels, that allegiance to the Constitution is not to be treated as a crime.

I have thus set before you the duty of obedience to "the higher powers," endeavoring carefully to qualify my statement of that duty, and going somewhat at large into the question of *revolution*, because of its special pertinency to the circumstances of our country at the present time. You are American citizens, and some of you Christian citizens; and to all of you permit me to say in the language of the Apostle: "Let every soul be subject unto the higher powers." This is as much your duty as it is to pray. To decline this duty, except in those cases which I have named, and which practically have no application to the present struggle, is to sin against God. Standing in this place as a preacher of Bible doctrine, I feel no difficulty in exhorting every man that hears me, to aid and obey the Chief Magistrate; yea, to support him in the exercise of his constitutional powers, and the performance of those duties which he is solemnly sworn to discharge. The language of Senator Douglas, recently uttered before the Legislature of Illinois, expresses not only a patriotic impulse, but equally that which God himself makes a duty. "The first duty of an American citizen," I am quoting the Senator's words, "or of a citizen of any constitutional government, is obedience to the constitution and laws of his country." Accepting this doctrine, let me now ask you to meditate for a moment upon—

THAT PART OF THE TEXT WHICH ASSIGNS THE REASON FOR THIS OBEDIENCE.—President Wayland, in his *Elements of Moral Science*, has furnished what I regard as a good philosophical argument to show that civil society, with government for its agent, is an INSTITUTION OF GOD. He derives this doctrine from "the original impulses common to all men, and from the necessities of man arising out of the conditions of his present existence." A wiser than President Wayland, made such by the gift of inspiration, has said to us: "For there is no power but of God: the powers that be are ordained of God. Whosoever therefore resisteth the power, resisteth the ordinance of God: and they that resist shall receive to themselves damnation." This is the Apostle's reason for telling us to "be subject unto the higher powers," "not only for wrath, but also for conscience' sake." He calls the civil ruler "the minister of God, a revenger to execute wrath upon him that doeth evil," declaring, too, that "he beareth not the sword in vain."

The doctrine thus stated is not the divine right of *kings* as to their *persons*, or to the perfection and wisdom of their official acts, but the divine right, authority, and appointment of civil government, *as such*, whatever may be its form, and by whomsoever administered. Some of the Revolutionary Fathers were a little jealous lest they should get government and religion too near together; yet the Apostle seems to have had no such fear. In this view, civil society, with government for its agent, is clothed with a *divine* prerogative. It does not exist merely by the grace, consent, and compact of the people, but rather rests upon the will and appointment of God, and derives its authority from this high source. It is an arrangement fixed in the very nature of things, through which God asserts, and intends to assert, his own authority over the children of men. It supposes human nature to be an organism of related parts, and not a mass of disconnected fragments, in the heart of which, and to its utmost extremities, is ever beating the pulsation of civil authority in the name of God. I had no hand in making this Government. I was not a voter when the Constitution of these United States was adopted. I found it here when I was born; and let me tell you, that I am glad that I did find it; and so far as I am able, I mean to keep it here. Considered providentially, the existing Government of this country is to me *God's* system of civil authority, and not the system of the Continental Congress, or of the Federal Convention, or of the people who voted in the adoption of the Constitution. I am bound by it, not because they made it, but because it is. As to the *form*, when this question is before the people, we may choose; as to the *ruler* we may choose; but government itself is a ministry of God, whether Washington or Nero be the administrator. The civil ruler, considered in respect to his *office*, and acting in its sphere, is as truly God's minister as was Paul, considered in respect to his office. Not his *personal* character, not the perfection of his administration, not the *form* of the government which he administers, but the fact that he *is* the ruler, makes him *officially* the minister of God; and as such, he is to be obeyed.

Proceeding on this basis, and bearing in mind the qualifications of the general rule of obedience already considered, you are prepared to accept the Apostle's inference: "Whosoever therefore resisteth the power, resisteth the ordinance of God." To disregard the mandate of the civil authority, or resist the due execution of law, is a *sin*—not simply a crime against man, but a sin against God. He so regards it, and will so treat it in the final day. The rebel is as truly a sinner as was Satan when he seceded from the realms of bliss, and made a vacancy in the ranks of celestial loyalty. This fallen angel is the first secessionist of whom we have any account. His fate is the commentary of Heaven's justice upon the wickedness of the theory. And if this be the general view of the Bible, what shall we think of that form of resistance to the divine ordinance which is in itself *treasonable*, which attacks the very life of government, and seeks to lay it in ruins? The offence is of the very highest grade—far worse than ordinary murder. I can look with some degree of allowance upon a lawless and unthinking mob, acting without premeditation or definite end; but the deliberate traitor against a good government, whether living in this city or in South Carolina, whether a Senator in Congress or a member of the President's Cabinet, I hold to be the enemy of all mankind. For such a man I have no honeyed words. Those who initiate the terrible reign of passion and anarchy are pirates against the peace, happiness, and prosperity of society. Well did Dr. Breckinridge say, in a sermon entitled, *The Union to be Preserved*, of those who have led the people into the grievous sin of rebellion and secession, that they "have no hope for good from coming ages half so great as that they may be utterly forgotten." Even this is a vain hope. There men will be remembered as long as history lives to publish the inglorious deeds of other days.

What now is the plan of God for the treatment of those who set the civil authority at defiance, and thus resist his ordinance? Are they to be merely reasoned with? Shall they be met with a flag of truce? Shall Government simply address to them a moral essay upon the duty of obedience? "They that resist shall receive to themselves damnation," says the Apostle; and the very lowest meaning that can be attached to these words is that they shall be *punished*, as they ought to be, for this sin against God's ordinance. That he refers mainly to punishment as inflicted by the civil authority, is evident from what he subsequently says. He adds: "For rulers are not a terror to good works, but to evil." He adds again that the ruler "beareth not the sword in vain, for he is the minister of God, a revenger to execute wrath upon him that doeth evil."

According to this testimony, it is the divine plan and purpose that civil government should wield the *penal* power, and employ all the force necessary to make that power effective. It is clothed with this power, not for its own sake, but for the good of society. In the legitimate infliction of penalty, it acts as the ministration of God against the guilty. It is a divinely-appointed agency for this purpose. This is Paul's doctrine, and equally the doctrine of right reason. "Law," says an able writer, "comes from the depths of eternity, and in its sublime sway is the nexus of the universe." Law at last has its support in penalty. Without this reliance it is a dead letter.

The text in its teaching is now before you. The Bible doctrine of civil government in its claim upon the obedience of the subject is now explained. I have supposed, too, that the circumstances of our country at the present moment, make this discussion very pertinent. Christianity is the religion of this land. As a moral power, it lies at the basis of our institutions. The American people have too much intelligence, too much virtue, and many of them too much piety towards God, to be led blindly into the great conflict that is now upon us. Not simply their patriotism, but their moral sense also, must be consulted. Hence, in placing before you the Bible doctrine of civil government, I have endeavored to examine the *moral* merits of the question now pending between the national authority and that portion of the people, who are in open rebellion against the Government of these United States. My mount of vision in this discourse has not been the Constitution but the Book of God. I wish to know where we stand in respect to that book in this struggle for a nation's life.

Let me then say very distinctly that, as I view the matter, this contest is not between two independent and sovereign nationalities, fighting about a boundary line, or the interpretation of a treaty; and hence it does not involve the considerations that are usually applicable to the question of war or peace. This is not the question now before the American people; and we should therefore not suffer ourselves to be deceived by a fallacious use of the term *war* or the term *peace*. The mere *physical* fact of fighting is not always war in the *moral* sense by any means. The police of this city are not engaged in an act of war, when fighting to suppress a rebellion in this city. And, my hearers, this illustration presents the exact issue, in kind, between the National Government and the secessionists. What is their attitude? Simply one of treason and rebellion, with a view to dissolve the Union and dismember the nation. What is the attitude of the Government? Simply that of an effort to assert its authority over its own citizens and subjects, to put down the rebellion, and restore peace to this distracted and suffering land. What is the army now marshalling under the new Confederacy? An army of traitors, called forth by traitors, and proposing nothing but the work of treason. What is the army now gathered in the capital, and to be gathered in other places? The military *posse comitatus* of the nation, coming forth at the President's call from their homes, from their firesides, from their workshops, from their peaceful industry, not to wage an aggressive war upon an unoffending people, but to defend their own country against traitors, to protect the capital of that country, to support Government against anarchy, to save the Union from dismemberment, the Constitution from disgrace, and society from actual dissolution. Such is the question with which we have to deal, considered in reference to its *moral* merits. The nature of the issue is as clear as the light of day. You know what it is, and I know what it is; the world understands it; and history will tell the tale to the end of time. The London *Times*, thinking for us across the water, makes the following remark: "It is quite possible that the problem of a democratic republic may be solved by its *overthrow* in a few days in a spirit of folly, selfishness, and short-sightedness."

Now, upon such an issue, with such a question up for settlement, so entirely different from the ordinary contests of war, I have no sympathy with that milk-and-water theology that chants peace at the expense of righteousness, that ignores the claims of God's ordinance, yea, that takes the robes of its sanctity, and rushes blindly to lay them down as a free-will offering upon the polluted altars of treason. In this place I will not preach it, for I do not believe in it. I will not ask you to act upon it in this controversy between law and anarchy, between your country's present and prospective weal and the dreadful vortex of dismemberment and disunion.

If there can be a case arising in human affairs, justifying an appeal to arms, then we have met it in this age. This nation can appeal to history, to the law of nations, to the moral sense of the world, to the scrutinies of philosophy, to the Bible, to the infinite Searcher of all hearts, that, in the effort to preserve itself and transfer the blood-bought institutions of civil liberty to coming generations, it is but discharging a duty, the neglect of which would be a crime, and the failure of which would be the greatest disaster that the world has ever witnessed. Let us then in the spirit of obedience to God, of loyalty to our noble Constitution, of generous and large-hearted patriotism to our common country, now settle this question once and forever, for ourselves and our posterity. We have met the foe, and the foe has met us; and now is the time to quit ourselves like men. Let this infamous secession theory, whose only principle is anarchy, and whose only end, if successful, is ruin and national death, find its doom on the soil it has dishonored, while the stars and the stripes shall be victoriously flung to the breeze, there to wave in undisputed triumph as long as nationality on this continent shall have a mission, as long as a free and happy people shall here live to rejoice in the "Constitution, the Union, and the Enforcement of the Laws."

Yes, let this question *now* be so settled that history will have nothing to do but record the fact; and posterity, nothing to do but read the record. Let it never come up again to disturb the nation's peace, to try its strength, or tax the arm of its avenging justice. We have this work to do; in the providence of God it is our present work as a nation; and if we do it well —if we suppress this rebellion—if we effectually rebuke the spirit of lawlessness and insubordination to public authority—if we cover every inch of this broad land with the motto of our national honor and safety, *E Pluribus Unum*— if we restore the seven wandering stars to their orbits, and gather them again around the central sun of the Federal power—if we teach the prodigal States both the folly and impossibility of our disintegration as a people—I say, if we do these things, we shall make this age the most illustrious in the annals of history. We shall place the question of our permanency beyond cavil or dispute. We shall solve the problem of a democratic republic, not by its failure, but by its glorious success. We shall retain our prestige among the nations of the earth. We shall connect the destinies of Christianity and civilization on this continent with one permanent, indivisible, powerful, progressive nationality. We shall restrain and ultimately, by causes as sure as the decrees of God, exterminate the furious insanity of slavery propagandism. We shall prevent the existence of a rival Confederacy, whose only motto is the despotism of slavery. We shall save the Southern people from destruction by their own hands. We shall keep within the nation's control, and subject to its authority and uses, the grandest territorial domain on which the sun ever shone. We shall avoid the multiplied inconveniences, perils, and wars, that will almost certainly follow, if we permit this nation to be broken into fragments. We shall leave behind us, for the blessing of our children and our children's children, a system of political institutions based on liberty regulated by law.

I believe, moreover, that the Government supported by the people, has power, all the power needful, to do this great and good work. Rather than fail in its accomplishment, I would have the Government spend hundreds of millions; I would have it employ the utmost military strength of the national arm. Yes, I would have it absolutely conquer a peace at any price, recognizing the now rebellious States as integral parts of this nation, entitled to all their rights under the Constitution, but retaining them in subjection to that Constitution by force, if necessary, till reflection and bitter experience shall make them wiser, or a merciful Providence furnish a new generation of men to deplore and forsake the folly of their ancestors, or a National Convention, legally assembled and peacefully deliberating, shall think it best so to alter the fundamental law of the land as to dissolve this Union. The point to be gained in this contest, I would have the Government gain, or by the failure demonstrate its utter impossibility. I would not have the Government disgraced by any inglorious negotiation with this wicked treason. I would have it assert its authority over those, and against those, who, for no reason under heaven, have engaged in this stupendous villainy of organized rebellion against the Federal power. I would have the Government accept of no settlement of this question, short of absolute submission to the constitutionally expressed will of the majority. Any other course on the part of the Government will, in my opinion, be an ignoble desertion of duty.

May God smile upon the effort, making the people strong to think, patient to bear, determined to do, valiant for the right, till law and order, out of confusion restored, shall scatter their blessings over the entire length and breadth of this land; till anarchy and treason shall have exhausted their unhallowed fires; till the music of peaceful industry again chants the supremacy of law; till in a providence of mercy through one of wrath, we come forth from this terrible discipline an instructed, a wiser, and a better people!

THE CHRISTIAN'S BEST MOTIVE FOR PATRIOTISM.

A Sermon Preached in the College Church, Hampden Sidney, Va., on a general Fast Day, Nov. 1, 1860.

BY ROBERT L. DABNEY, D. D.

Because of the house of the Lord our God, I will seek thy good.—*Psalm* cxxii. 9.

THE true Christian feels the claims of patriotism as sensibly as any other man, though he holds them subject to the limitations of justice and charity to others. Thus, King David resolves that he will seek the peace of Jerusalem, the capital city of the Hebrew Commonwealth; not only as a patriotic king, but from an additional religious motive. So the Christian has a motive for patriotism far stronger and holier than those of all other men. Additional to theirs, he has this reason to pray for the peace of Jerusalem; for his brethren and companions' sakes, and because of the house of the Lord his God which is in it. The kingdom of Jesus Christ—that blessed kingdom whose sceptre is peace, righteousness, meekness, and truth; in whose prosperity the hopes of a suffering race are all involved, which alone can arrest the flood of sins and woes which now sweeps generation after generation into ruin—is committed by its Divine Head to human hands, and is partially dependent on the course of human events. This spiritual commonwealth among us, as is proper, has no legal ties to the secular, and no other relations than those of mutual good-will and courtesy. But still, inasmuch as Christ is pleased to leave to second causes their natural influence over his Church, it is largely dependent on our secular governments. Now there are few things which can affect the interests of Zion so disastrously as political convulsions and war. Let the Christian weigh their influences.

First: We are taught, even by experience of customary party excitements, that a season of political agitation is most unfavorable to spiritual prosperity. Few experienced pastors expect revivals during excited presidential canvasses. The mind is absorbed by agitating secular topics, angry and unchristian emotions are provoked, and the tender dew of heavenly-mindedness is speedily evaporated by the hot and dusty turmoil of the popular meeting and the hustings. Few men who traffic habitually in such scenes exhibit much grace. We suspect that the Christian, returning from a day of such excitement, is little inclined to the place of secret prayer. But how much must all these evil influences be exasperated when the subjects of political strife assume a violent and convulsive aspect? When every mind is filled by eager, secular concerns—when angry passions rage in every heart, dividing brother against brother in Zion—when unscrupulous haste precipitates multitudes into words and acts of injustice and wrong, agitating and defiling their own consciences, and provoking the hot tumults of resentment on either side—what room is there for the quiet and sacred voice of the Holy Spirit? It has been remarked by wise historians, that a time of political convulsions is a time of giant growth for all forms of vice. And just to that degree it is a time of barrenness for the Christian graces.

But when political strife proceeds to actual war, then indeed do "the ways of Zion mourn." War is the grand and favorite device of him who was a liar and murderer from the beginning, to obstruct all spiritual good, and to barbarize mankind. To all the above agitations, distractions, and evil passions, raised now to actual frenzy, must be added the interruptions of Sabbath rest and of public worship, while the sacred hours are profaned with the tumult of preparations, marchings, or actual combats. Domestic life, that most fruitful source of all wholesome restraints, is broken up by danger, fear, waste of property, and separations. The youth hurry from that peaceful domain of humanizing and pious influences into the rude noise and gross corruptions of camps, whence they return, if they return at all, depraved by military license, unused to peaceful industry, and hardened to all evil, to poison society at home. Colleges and schools are scattered, the voice of science is silenced, the hopes of peaceful industry are violently destroyed, till recklessness and resentment turn the very husbandman into a bandit. And, above all, Death holds his cruel carnival, and, not only by the sword, but yet more by destitution, by vice, by pestilence, hurries his myriads unprepared from scenes of guilty woe on earth into everlasting despair below. Need we wonder that the Heavenly Dove should spread its gentle wings and fly far from such abhorrent scenes?

But civil feud has ever been known as the most bitter of all. "A brother offended is harder to be won than a strong city: and their contentions are like the bars of a castle." The very tenderness of brothers' love makes them more tender to the injury. The strength of the mutual obligations, which should have bound them to kindness, enhances the hot indignation at mutual outrage. When the twin lands which now lie so intimately side by side, parted by a line so long, so faint, so invisible, that it does not separate, begin to strike each other, the very nearness and intimacy make each more naked to the other's blows. How dire, then, would be the conflagration of battle which would rage along this narrow line across the whole breadth of a continent! How deadly the struggle, when the republican hardihood and chivalry, the young, giant strength, and teeming wealth, which begin to make the mightiest despots respectful, are turned against each other! Some seem to delight in placing the relative prowess of the North and South in odious comparison. Should we not, my brethren, rather weep tears of blood at the wretched and wicked thought, that the common prowess with which the North and South have so often, side by side, carried dismay and rout into the ranks of common enemies—that terrible prowess which, in North and South alike, withstood the force of the British Lion while we were yet in the gristle of our youth, and which ever since has overthrown and broken every enemy, with the lion's force and the eagle's swiftness combined —should hereafter be expended in fratricidal blows? And, then, this vast frontier must be forted and guarded. This hostile neighborhood, so dangerous because so intimate, must be watched on either hand by armies; and those armies become, as among the unhappy and suspicious nations of Europe, as much the machines of internal oppression as of outward defence. Our future growth of men and wealth would be swallowed up by the devouring maw of strife. These teeming fields, whose increase fills the granaries of the famishing nations, and makes their owners' bosoms to overflow with wealth, must go to feed the barren waste of warlike preparation and labor. The source of half the missionary activities which now gladden the waste places of the earth would be dried up. Farewell to the benign career of imperial *Peace*, by which we had hoped the Empire Republic would teach the angry nations nobler triumphs than those of war. A long farewell to that dream we had indulged—dream not unworthy surely to have been inspired by the *Prince of Peace*—that here a nation was to grow up on this soil, which God had kept till "the fulness of time was come," wrapped in the mysteries of pathless seas, and untainted by the steps of civilized despots, or organized crime; a nation composed of the strong, the free, the bold, the oppressed of every people, and, like the Corinthian brass, more precious than any that composed it; which should come, by the righteous arts of peace, to a greatness such as at last to shame and frighten war away from the family of kingdoms; which should work out the great experiment of equal laws and a free conscience, for the first time, for the imitation of the world; and from whose bosom a free Church, unstained by the guilt of persecution, and unburdened by the leaden protection of the State, should send forth her light and salvation to the ends of the earth to bring the millennial morning. This cunning machine of law, which now regulates our rights, would be wrecked amidst the storms of revolution. The stern exigencies of danger would compel both the rivals, perhaps, to substitute the strong, but harsh will of the soldier, for the mild protection of constitutions. And the oppressors of soul and body, from every stronghold of absolutism throughout the earth, would utter their jubilant and scornful triumph: "Lo! the vain experiment of man's self-government has drowned itself in its own blood and ruin!" The movement of the world's redemption might be put back for ages, and the enthroning of the Prince of Peace over his promised dominion, so long ravaged by sin and woe, would be postponed, while eternal death preyed upon yet more of the teeming generations.

Now, in view of this tremendous picture of possible crime and misery, would to God that I could reach the ear of every professed servant of Jesus Christ in the whole land! I would cry to them: Christians of America—Brothers—Shall all this be? Shall this Church of thirty thousand evangelical ministers, and four millions of Christian adults—this Church, so boastful of its influence and power; so respected and reverenced by nearly all; so crowned with the honors of literature, of station, of secular office, of riches; this Church, which moulds the thought of three-fourths of our educated men through her schools, and of all, by her pulpit and her press; this Church, which glories in having just received a fresh baptism of the Spirit of Heaven in a national revival—permit the tremendous picture to become reality? Nay, shall they aid in precipitating the dreaded consummation, by traitorously inflaming the animosities which they should have allayed, and thus leave the work of their Master to do the Devil's? Then, how burning the sarcasm which this result will contain upon your Christianity in the eyes of posterity! Why, they will say, was there not enough of the majesty of moral weight in these four millions of Christians to say to the angry waves, "Peace: be still?" Why did not these four millions rise, with a LOVE so Christ-like, so beautiful, so strong, that strife should be paralyzed by it into reverential admiration? Why did they not speak for their country, and for the House of the Lord their God which was in it, with a wisdom before whose firm moderation, righteousness and clear light, passion and folly should scatter like the mist? Were not all these strong enough to throw the arms of their loving mediation around their fellow-citizens, and keep down the weapons that sought each other's hearts; or rather to receive them into their own bosoms than permit our mother-country to be slain? Did this mighty Church stand idly by, and see frenzy immolate so many of the dearest hopes of man, and of the rights of the Redeemer, on her hellish altar? And this Church knew too, that the fiend had borrowed the torch of discord from the altar of Christianity, and that, therefore, Christians were bound, by a peculiar tie, to arrest her insane hand before the precious sacrifice was wrapped in flames. Then, shame on the boasted Christianity of America, and of the nineteenth century! With all its parade of evangelism, power, and light, wherein has it been less impotent and spurious than the effete religion of declining Rome, which betrayed Christendom into the dark ages; or than the baptized superstitions which, in those ages, sanctioned the Crusades and the Inquisition? In the sight of Heaven's righteous Judge, I believe that if the Christianity of America now betrays the interest of man and God to the criminal hands which threaten them, its guilt will be second only to that of the apostate Church which betrayed the Saviour of the world; and its judgment will be rendered in calamities second only to those which avenged the Divine blood invoked by Jerusalem on herself and her children.

How, then, shall Christians seek the good of their country, for the Church's sake? This raises the more practical question of present duty, and introduces the more practical part of my discourse.

And first: Christians should everywhere begin to pray for their country. "Because of the house of the Lord our God, let us seek its good." The guilty churches of all our land should humble themselves before a holy God, for their Christian backslidings, and our national sins. "Blow the trumpet in Zion, sanctify a fast, call a solemn assembly: Gather the people, sanctify the congregation, assemble the elders, gather the children, and those that suck the breasts; let the bridegroom go forth of his chamber, and the bride out of her closet. Let the priests, the ministers of the Lord, weep between the porch and the altar; and let them say, Spare thy people, O Lord, and give not thy heritage to reproach."

And along with this should go humble confessions of our sins, individual and social. And here, let me distinctly warn you, that I am not about to point your attention to sins of fellow-citizens of another quarter of the Confederacy, from whose faults some may suppose the present fear arises. Whether they have committed faults, or how great, it is not my present concern to say. Our business is to-day with our own sins. It will do our hearts no good to confess to God the sins of our fellow-men: He already knows them, and estimates them more fairly than perhaps our prejudice will permit us to do. It is for our own sins alone that we are responsible to God. It is our own sins alone that we have the means of reforming, by the help of His grace. Let each man then consider, and forsake his personal transgressions; for as your persons help to swell the aggregate of this great people, so your individual sins have gone to form that black cloud of guilt, which threatens to hide from us the favorable light of our Heavenly Father's face. But let us remember, and confess also, our social sins; that general worldliness, which hath set up the high-places of its covetous idolatries all over the good land God hath given us; that selfish profusion and luxury, which have squandered on the pride of life so much of the goods of our stewardship; that Heaven-daring profanity and blasphemy by reason of which the land mourneth. And let me not forget faithfully to protest, on such a day as this, against that peculiar sin of the Southern country, the passion for bloody retaliation of personal wrong, which has been so often professed and indulged among us, unwhipped of justice. You have allowed too often the man of violence, the duellist, professing his pretended "code of honor"—most hateful and deceitful pretence of that Father of Lies, who was a murderer from the beginning —to stalk through the land with wrongs upon his angry tongue, and blood upon his hand, while his crime was winked at by justice, and almost applauded by corrupt public opinion. "So ye have polluted the land wherein ye are; for blood, it defileth the land, and the land cannot be cleansed of the blood that is shed therein, but by the blood of him that shed it." Let us remember also, that our innocence or rightfulness in the particular point of present differences and anticipated collisions, gives no assurance that God may not chastise us for our sins by those very events. Often has His manifold, wise, and righteous providence permitted an unjust aggressor to make himself the instrument wherewith to lash His sinning people, even when he afterwards punished the invader himself.

Second: We would say, with all the earnestness and emphasis which the most solemn feeling can inspire, let each individual Christian in our land, whether he sits in our halls of legislature, or rules as a magistrate, or guides public opinion through the press, or merely fills the station of the private citizen, consider his own personal concern in this matter. We would affectionately individualize each man, and say to him, my brother, "Thou art the man. Consider what would God have *you* to do?" Every Christian man, whether law-maker or law-executor, or voter, should carry his Christian conscience, enlightened by God's word, into his political duty, in another manner than we have been accustomed to do. We must ask less, what party caucuses and leaders dictate, and more, what duty dictates. For the day is at hand, when we shall be brought to an awful judgment for the thoughtless manner in which we execute our civic function. My brethren, the Christians of this land are able to control the selection of reckless and wicked men for places of trust, if they please, and will do their duty. Here are four millions of men and women, chiefly adults, among a people of twenty-six millions of men, women, children and slaves —four millions who profess to be supremely ruled by principles of righteousness, peace and love, and to be united to each other in the brotherhood of a heavenly birth. If even the voters among these would go together to the polls, to uphold the cause of peace, they would turn the scale of every election. Where is the community in all our land, where the male citizens who are professors of Christianity would not give the victory to that party to which they gave their united support? But alas! how often have we gone on Monday to the hustings, after having appeared on Sabbath as the servants of the Prince of Peace, and brethren or all his servants, and in our political heats speedily forgotten that we were Christians! Let each Christian citizen have his independent political predilections, and support them with decision, if you please. Let them, if need be, render that enlightened and moderate allegiance to the party of their choice, which is supposed to be essential in free governments. But when their party demands of them that they shall sustain men of corrupt private morals or reckless passions, because of their supposed party orthodoxy, let all Christians say: "Nay, verily, we would fain yield all reasonable party fidelity; but we are also partisans in the commonwealth of King Jesus, and our allegiance to Him transcends all others. Unless you will present us a man who to party orthodoxy unites private virtues, we cannot sustain him." Then would their reasonable demand be potential in every party, and the abuse would be crushed. And this stand, if taken by Christian citizens, we affirm, would infringe no personal or associated rights. For, is there any party who would admit that it had not a single member respectable, virtuous, and sober enough to deserve the suffrages of Christian men? If there is, surely it is time it should slink away from the arena of political competition, and hide itself in oblivion. Here, then, is a prominent duty, if we would save our country, that we shall carry our citizenship in the kingdom of Heaven everywhere, and make it dominate over every public act. We must obey the law of God rather than the unrighteous behests of party, to "choose out of all the people *able men, such as fear God, men of truth, hating covetousness, and place such over them to be rulers,*" or God will assuredly avenge himself for our violated allegiance to Him. The Christians of this country must sternly claim that wicked or reckless men shall no longer hold the helm of State; that political orthodoxy shall no longer atone for that worst offence against citizenship, a wicked life. And along with rulers, I would include the directors of the public press, as being of the general class of "leaders of the people." Even while you boast of the potency of this engine of the nineteenth century, you have allowed it to fall in many cases into most incompetent and dangerous hands. See who have held this responsible lever in our land in these latter days! Some are honorable and patriotic; but more are unreliable; some mere half-educated youths, without any stake of family, estate, or reputation in the community; some fiery denouncers, some touching the springs of public affairs with a drunken hand, and many the open advocates and practitioners of the duellist's murderous code—these men you have permitted and even upheld and salaried, in your easy thoughtlessness, to misrepresent, misdirect, and inflame the public sentiment of the nation!

There are many reasons which demand of every God-fearing citizen that he shall sustain, directly or indirectly, none but honest and prudent men in places of influence. When you elevate a bad man, you give to him a hundred-fold more power of example to corrupt your sons, and your neighbors' sons, by his evil acts. Those acts are a hundred-fold more conspicuous and more weighty to attract notice and imitation, than if you had left him in his deserved obscurity. When you delegate your money, influence, or civic power, to a bad man, you make his wicked official acts and influence your own; he is your chosen agent, and acts for you, and be assured a jealous God will not forget to visit the people for the guilt thus contracted.

But especially should you remember, at such a period as this, the boundless mischief wrought by the habit of reckless vituperation, and the political violence, in which bad and foolish or inexperienced men indulge, to further political ends. It is this which chiefly has created our present unhappy dangers, by misrepresenting each section to the other. You have heard descriptions of the *reign of terror* in the first French Revolution, and perhaps as you saw the frightful and murderous violence of political factions there displayed, you have exclaimed: "Were these men or devils?" They were men, my brethren; "men of like passions with us." Read the narrative of the philosophic *Thiers*, and you will learn the source of these rivers of blood. Unscrupulous leaders of parties and presses, in order to carry their favorite projects and overpower political rivals, resorted to the *trick* of imputing odious and malignant motives to all adversaries; democrats denouncing Girondists and royalists as traitorous plotters of foreign invasion, and national sack; royalists denouncing democrats as agrarians and robbers, till by dint of bandying the outrageous charges backwards and forwards, all minds were gradually embittered and prepared to believe the worst. Hence the bloody political proscriptions; hence the frightful butcheries of the *Septembriseurs;* because misguided men were taught to believe that no less trenchant remedy would anticipate the treason designed against the country.

Now I say to you in all faithfulness, that the reckless and incapable men whom you have weakly trusted with power or influence, have already led us far on towards similar calamities. They have bandied violent words, those cheap weapons of petulant feebleness; they have justified aggression; they have misrepresented our tempers and principles—answered, alas, by equal misrepresentations and violence in other quarters—until multitudes of honest men, who sincerely suppose themselves as patriotic as you think yourselves, are really persuaded that in resisting your claims, they are but rearing a necessary bulwark against lawless and arrogant aggressions. Four years ago, an instance of unjust and wicked insolence was avenged, on the floor of the Senate of the United States, by an act of violence most unrighteous and ill-judged. And now, not so much that rash and sinful act of retaliation, but the insane, wicked, and insulting justification of it generally made by Southern secular prints, directed by reckless boys, or professed duellists—a justification abhorred and condemned by almost all decent men in our section, is this day carrying myriads of votes (of men who, if not thus outraged, might have remained calm and just towards us) for the cause whose triumph you deprecate. Thus the miserable game goes on; until at last blood breaks out, and the exhausted combatants are taught in the end, by mutually inflicted miseries, to pause and consider, that they are contending mainly for a misunderstanding of each other.

Now I well know, my brethren and fellow-citizens, that if I should speak to you in private, you would all concur in my honest reprobation of this folly and injustice: I know that I have but expressed the common sentiments of all good men among us. Yet, in your dislike to be troubled, in your easy good nature, you let things take their course, under the wretched mismanagement of the hands into which they have fallen; you even permit your money and your influence to go indirectly in support of these agents of mischief and misrule, who thus misrepresent your characters, and aims, and rights. If the public interests cannot arouse you from this good-natured sin, let me see if I cannot touch you more nearly. Whereunto can all this mutual violence grow? Do not the increasing anger and prejudice, which seem so fast ripening on both sides for a fatal collision, tell you too plainly? And when these rash representatives of yours, in our halls of legislation and our newspapers, shall have sown the wind, who will reap the whirlwind? When they have scattered the dragons' teeth, who must meet that horrent crop which they will produce? Not they alone; but you, your sons, your friends, and their sons. So that these misleaders of the people, while you so weakly connive at their indiscretions, may be indirectly preparing the weapon which is to pierce the bosom of your fair-haired boy; and summoning the birds of prey, which are to pick out those eyes whose joy is now the light of your happy homes, as he lies stark on some lost battle-field. For God's sake, then—for your own sakes, for your children's sake, arise—declare that from this day, no money, no vote, no influence of yours, shall go to the maintenance of any other counsels than those of moderation, righteousness, and manly forbearance.

Last: Every Christian must study the things which make for peace. All must resolve that they will demand of others nothing more than their necessary rights, and that in the tone of moderation and forbearance. Yea, that they will generously forego all except what duty forbids them to forego, rather than have strife with brethren. We must all be magnanimous enough to forbear the language of threatening and reproach, (language which evinces no courage,) to acknowledge the excesses of ourselves and our friends, and to make reparation for it, whether such reparation be offered on the other side or not. Instead of complaining in vindictive and bitter spirit of the extravagances of misguided men on the opposite side, each man should inquire whether there are not sinful extravagances on his own side; and when it is necessary to remonstrate, do it in the tone of wounded love, rather than of insane threatening. In one word; let each one resolve to grant all that is right, and ask nothing else; "and lo, there will be a great calm."

GOD'S PRESENCE WITH THE CONFEDERATE STATES.

A Sermon Preached in Christ Church, Savannah, on Thursday, the 13th June, being the Day appointed, at the Request of Congress, by the President of the Confederate States as a Day of Solemn Humiliation, Fasting, and Prayer:

BY THE RT. REV. STEPHEN ELLIOTT.

Not unto us, O Lord, not unto us, but unto Thy name give glory, for Thy mercy and for Thy truth's sake. Wherefore should the heathen say, Where is now their God? But our God is in the heavens: He hath done whatsoever he pleased.—*Psalm* cxv. 1, 2, 3.

THE devout proclamation of our President invites us to give to-day a public manifestation of our gratitude for the clear proofs of the Divine blessing hitherto extended to the people of the Confederate States, in their efforts to maintain and perpetuate public liberty, individual rights, and national independence. At the same time it calls upon us to humble ourselves before God in this, our time of peril and difficulty, to recognize His righteous government, to acknowledge His goodness in times past, and to supplicate His merciful protection for the future. It is a day to be devoted to mingled gratitude and humiliation—to thanksgiving for great mercies and to a confession of our unworthiness of them—to acknowledgment that unto Him alone belongs the glory of our present condition, and to supplication that He will continue to be our shield and strong tower of defence. This direction which the proclamation of our Chief Magistrate has given to the devotions of the day will require a review of our civil affairs from the commencement of our constitutional struggle, in order to point out to you the overruling and directing hand of God in all our movements. May His Holy Spirit rest upon me and preserve my pen from bitterness, and my tongue from evil speaking, and may that same Spirit enlighten your minds to perceive His presence in all that is past, and sanctify your hearts to keep it there through all that is before us.

For many years past, God has permitted us, as a people, to be deeply humiliated. While we have enjoyed great material prosperity, and have, in a certain sense, maintained our position under the forms of the Constitution, we have been systematically slandered and traduced, in public and in private, at home and abroad, in a way such as no free and independent people has ever before so quietly submitted to. Because of the maintenance of an institution inherited from our fathers, which the rest of the world was pleased to consider as incompatible with civilization and with Christianity, we have been made, through every form of literature, a by-word among the nations of the earth. The lecture-room, the forum, the senate chamber, the pulpit, have all been used as the instruments of our denunciation. The newspapers of the Northern States and of Europe have vied to express their abhorrence of our social life and their contempt for ourselves. The grave statesman, the flippant poet, the sentimental novelist, the critical reviewer, the witty satirist, has each in turn singled out our homes as the targets of his falsehood, and our mothers, wives, and daughters, as the objects of his insult. In many of the religious bodies of the United States, their communicants from the slaveholding States were excluded from the participation of the sacrament of the Lord's Supper, and the Southern ministers from brotherly interchange of service. We had committed an unpardonable sin in doing what Abraham, the friend of God, had done, what Philemon, the dearly-beloved fellow-laborer of Paul the aged, had not been ashamed to do. All this abuse and misrepresentation was borne according to the temper of men; by some with the patience of Christians, leaving their justification in the hands of God, by others with contempt for an hypocrisy which could see the mote in a brother's eye but not the beam in its own eye; by not a few with arrogant defiance and words of bitter scorn. So far it had been a war of ideas, but leaving, nevertheless, rankling wounds behind. Gradually it passed from literature to politics, and we were soon made aware that a deep-laid scheme, resting upon the double basis of fanaticism and interest, was closing in upon us, which was to reduce to overt acts the ideas which had been so assiduously impressed not only upon the minds, but upon the feelings, of a whole generation. We were to be humbled, not simply by being held up to the scorn of the noble and generous all the world over, but by being virtually disfranchised, even while retaining the forms of constitutional liberty, and being permitted to keep up the appearances of equality. This scheme was devised by a far-seeing statesman, now occupying a position of commanding influence, who laid his plans with consummate skill, and has pursued them for twenty years with undeviating firmness, through good report and through evil report. He advanced from point to point with the steady pace of inevitable destiny, drawing his lines closer and closer around his fluttering yet unresisting victim. He educated, through the press and through the pulpit, a whole generation, and the two ideas which he has made the ideas of the times are, the irrepressible conflict, under democratic institutions, between freedom and slavery, and the utter inability of slavery to maintain itself in the face of freedom. The one idea combined into a great party the fanatic, the laborer, the foreigner, the farmer, the manufacturer; the other idea gave confidence and fearlessness to his followers. When this powerful and ever-growing host was thoroughly prepared for its work, he decided, after a calm survey of all the chances of the conflict which he was about to inaugurate, that success was inevitable. He perceived that there was but one movement that could defeat his plans—a dissolution of the Union—and he maintained that to be an impossibility. He believed that party divisions could keep the South so distracted—could separate her statesmen by such lines of bitterness—that no combined resistance to his sure but steady advances could ever be brought about. Had all his followers been as prudent as himself, and had not God been on our side, nothing could have saved us from slow but inevitable destruction; for it was not his purpose to strike any blow that might alarm or arouse the South, but to achieve all his purposes through seemingly constitutional movements. He well knew that the rapid growth of free territory, filling up with a foreign population of the most radical description, would surely give him what he aimed at, and that gradual changes in the Constitution, or plausible interpretations of it, would cover all his advances with the forms of law, and render any opposition difficult which proceeded beyond the limits of legislative or judicial resistance, of which he had no fear. And then he looked upon the section he was devoting to ruin, and perceived that she was engaged in a fierce Presidential strife, even while he was closing his toils around her; well might he have supposed that his game was a sure one and that time only was needed to make his triumph complete. At this moment, in the confidence of his heart, he might well have asked, "Where is now their God?" and our answer could only have been, "Our God is in the heavens: He hath done whatsoever He pleased." But just at that moment, when he considered us deserted and doomed, commenced a series of events which have brought us this day to the altar of the living God, to ascribe the glory of our deliverance not to ourselves, but to Him, to confess our unworthiness of all this unmerited goodness, and to pray Him to continue to bless the work which He has thus far so graciously favored—"Not unto us, O Lord, not unto us, but unto Thy name, give glory, for Thy mercy and for Thy truth's sake."

By that mercy of God, our greatest difficulties have been successfully passed through, I do not say our greatest privations, or our keenest sufferings. We may yet have before us years of self-denial and of self-discipline—we may be called to suffer in our fortunes and in our homes—our chambers may be clothed in mourning, and our hearts may be lacerated with sorrow, and yet, with all this, it may be true that our greatest difficulties as a nation have been already met and overcome. The severest trials through which a movement such as ours is forced to wade are those which arise in its inception and in its organization. The work which we had undertaken to accomplish was in many respects a novel one. It was not a revolution against intolerable ills—it was not the casting off of a foreign tyranny which had ground us to the dust—it was not even rebellion against the forms of the Government under which we had lived, that we might substitute for them other forms, but it was the withdrawal from a Union which had given us, in spite of its abuse and corrupt administration, a large share of material prosperity and social happiness, and which was associated with all our anticipations of national greatness. The love of the Union was deeply ingrained into the hearts of the nation, and into no part of it more deeply than our own Southern section. We were proud of it as that which gave us dignity abroad and advancement at home. The people considered its freedom to be the envy of the world, its Constitution the *ne plus ultra* of political wisdom. Our most prominent statesmen had held it up before the nation as the bond of our greatness, and as the hope of the human race. Webster had consecrated it in the Northern mind by that master-piece of eloquence which, as a rhetorical effort, has not been surpassed in ancient or modern times. Clay had surrounded it with all the charms of his fascinating personal popularity, and had identified it, all through the West, with his wide-spread political opinions. Jackson had added to the influence of this idol of the West the idea that the Union had been once preserved by him, and that he had left its continued preservation as a sacred legacy to his followers. Even Calhoun, while advocating the doctrines of State sovereignty, had pressed them most earnestly as the means whereby alone the Union could be maintained. But, above all, Washington—the personification of American constitutional liberty—had committed it, in his dying words, to the people as the central idea around which the future should forever revolve. It seemed impossible ever to overcome this idea, and yet the question had become one, in the minds of many, no one knew how many, between the Union and a passive subjection to the yoke which had been so skilfully preparing for our necks. Again and again had disunion been attempted and had failed, in some cases with ignominy, with hopelessness in others. The Union was fast absorbing every thing in the popular mind and becoming the devouring idol of the nation. Before it the Constitution had changed its whole scope and meaning—before it liberty was fast becoming a mere word—under its sanction an irresponsible majority was transferring power, prosperity, and wealth from one section of the country to the other. The cry of Union had become a sanction for every irresponsible decree, a war-cry against all opposition that promised to be effectual. The greatest danger of the South was, lest her people should permit this idea to overlay every other consideration and to rise superior to every constitutional infraction. There was no overt act of tyranny to rouse the people to madness—no action on the part of the Government to render resistance immediately necessary—nay, the Government had, in a certain way, been in the hands of those who were willing to concede to the South her constitutional rights. It was necessary to meet the deeply-laid and far-reaching scheme of which we spoke just now, by an equally far-seeing and prospective opposition; and the difficulty was, lest the people should not see, with any degree of unanimity, the necessity for immediate action. All saw that the time was coming—all looked shudderingly at the prospect of civil convulsion which seemed drawing nearer and nearer—but hope was strong in many of our most devoted Southern hearts—men who are now standing with their swords in their hands and their shields clasped over the bosom of their mother in the very front rank of battle—that God might yet avert the evil, and postpone, if not defer forever, the stern necessity. Secession was urged more upon what was before us in the future, than upon what had actually taken place. Coming events had, to be sure, cast their ominous shadows before; but as yet there was no act which had come directly home to the cottage and fireside. The raid into Virginia in 1859, had, at the time, produced a deep sensation; but as that mother of States had treated it lightly herself, having been satisfied with the punishment of the wrong-doers, it had died away. Under these circumstances, the most sanguine feared the issue of the question between Secession and the Union. They believed that a majority in certain States would sanction an act of separation, but they dreaded such an opposition in each State as might neutralize the action and impair its whole moral effect. Any thing like a nearly equal vote in the States would have created a nucleus of opposition which would have rendered the whole proceeding inefficient. But thanks be to God, He gave us among ourselves a more remarkable unanimity than any one had dared to hope for, and what was lacking in ourselves was supplied by the blunders of our adversaries. Instead of supporting those who were not prepared for separation, by granting their moderate demands of constitutional amendment, they struck blow after blow upon an already over-excited country, with a folly that was inconceivable. Every plank upon which the Union men of the South desired to stand was successively struck from under them, and the unanimity which the merits of the question failed to produce, their stubborn obstinacy rendered inevitable. Instead of meeting the advances of the Union men of the South with a lofty magnanimity—a magnanimity which a victorious party can always afford to exhibit—they met them with a defiant arrogance. They showed evidently by all their actions that they considered the struggle as at an end, and that they were commissioned to walk as conquerors over a subjugated territory. One by one, all their friends were driven from them, and thus has been produced a union of the South which was scarcely hoped for when the struggle first began. And, thanks be to God, their folly still continues; and if, with humble hearts, we bow ourselves before God, and ascribe this important result not to ourselves, but to His overruling and protecting providence, we shall see still greater wonders worked for us, and new stars rising to take their place in our constellation, and nations coming to our aid who were supposed to be bound to the North by the strong bonds of sympathy and fanaticism. "Not unto us, O

Lord, not unto us, but unto Thy name give glory, for Thy mercy and for Thy truth's sake."

Another danger which threatened us, and which is the *experimentum crucis* of all new nationalities, was the adoption of the permanent Constitution under which we were to live. It is always a moment of critical peril. It was the rock upon which Cromwell's successful usurpation crumbled to the dust. So long as he lived, his genius sustained the civil arrangements which he had substituted for the English Constitution; but with his death things flowed back into their ancient channel, and the nation returned joyfully to the monarchical government, even of the Stuarts. It was the rock upon which the European revolutions of 1848 all split. Theorists took up the question of government, and inexperienced professors and fantastic poets were deputed to arrange constitutions, and to mould the necessities of a practical world. It ended, just as any man of common sense might have foreseen that it would end, in the usurpation of a clear-headed man of practical experience. In the formation of the Constitution of 1789, that which we have just amended, there was a large diversity of opinion, and much time was consumed ere it could be made satisfactory to the thirteen States. The leading men of the country were forced to exert all their influence to secure its adoption. Washington talked for it—Madison, and Hamilton, and Jay, wrote for it—the heroes who had illustrated the war of the Revolution, prayed for it as the seal to their bloody triumph. And yet, with all this array of influence, it was very reluctantly adopted by several of the States, and one distinguished gentleman of South Carolina said, during the debates upon its adoption in the Convention of that State, "I desire no other epitaph to be written upon my tomb than this: "Here lies the man who voted against the adoption of the Federal Constitution." How wonderful, then, that in a few weeks a Congress of gentlemen, who had differed all their lives upon questions of national policy, who were just warm from heated discussions of principles as well as men, who were yet reeking with the sweat of one of the bitterest Presidential elections which have ever distracted the country, should have submitted to the people of the Confederate States a Constitution of the most conservative character, in which many grave errors of the old Constitution had been amended, and new features introduced of the highest moral and religious import. They entered that Congress with several questions ominous of evil pressing upon them—questions upon which, if they had erred, their cause must have been shaken to its centre. Among these were the reopening of the African slave-trade, the change in the value of slave representation, and that question which had once before disturbed the Union—the proper scale of duties upon imports and exports. A false step upon any one of these three questions would have been, in our then condition, almost irretrievable. The reopening of the African slave-trade would have disgusted Europe and produced great dissatisfaction at home. A change in the value of slave representation would have disaffected that large population of our mountains and pine barrens who own no slaves, and would have thrown them at once into the hands of demagogues. Too high a tariff would have checked the sympathy of England and France, and too low a tariff would have forced us to resort to direct taxation, which a people must be educated to bear. Marvellous, then, was it in our eyes that these gentlemen should have laid upon the altar of their country all their private views and all their public differences, and should have adjusted every point with such nice discrimination, with such wise and Christian moderation, with such a happy conception of the necessities which surrounded their States, that an almost unanimous shout of applause should have arisen from a delighted constituency. And afterwards that seven conventions, composed in a like manner of men of every shade of opinion and of every party in politics, should have so quietly and so unanimously accepted their work, can be attributed to nothing else but the overruling spirit of God. All these bodies entered upon their duties with fasting and prayer—they all acknowledged God every day in prayer—they placed Him in the forefront of their Constitution, and they recognized Him as the Supreme Ruler of the Universe, and we therefore can truly say again, "Not unto us, O Lord, not unto us, but unto Thy name give glory, for Thy mercy and for Thy truth's sake."

The next trial through which the Confederate States were called upon to pass, arose out of the regulation of its financial affairs. Napoleon is reported to have said, blasphemously enough, that battles were decided by the heaviest artillery, and the world is fast coming to the conclusion that the longest purse is the arbiter of war. Granting this to be in some measure true, we yet acknowledge most humbly the presence of God with our Government in this most important matter. The most arrogant boast of the North was of its own abounding wealth and of our exceeding poverty, and so long had this assertion been made, and so persistently had it been adhered to, that both sides were fast becoming to believe it. The North and the South were both losing sight of the unalterable principles of political economy, and had become confused amid the complications of commerce, and trade, and exchange. In a conflict like this, wealth must be looked at from a different stand-point from that in which it is viewed in a time of peace. At its commencement, the North has most accumulated money, because its great cities have been the converging centres from all parts of this widely-extended country, but accumulated money is very soon expended in a war like this, and the ability to continue it will depend far more upon the available income of each section than upon its money capital at the outset. The wealth of the North depends upon manufactures, upon trade, upon commerce, and the North-West furnishes a very abundant supply of food. Analyze this wealth, and you will perceive that its results depend upon the ability to find consumers and to furnish an exchangeable value upon which to trade. Unless manufactures find a market, they remain a drug upon the hands of the manufacturers, and are a loss instead of a gain. Unless trade finds purchasers as well as sellers, it very soon becomes bankrupt in the face of rents, and living, and the taxation of a war such as this will be, if it goes on. Unless commerce has something to export as well as to import, it must necessarily come to an end, for one cannot buy, as the world goes on now, unless he has something to sell. The North has no great export of its own which is a necessity to the world. Now and then the failure of a grain crop in England or upon the Continent, creates a demand for corn, and then, for a season, the West can furnish a value that is exchangeable. But this is an exceptional case, and the commercial men of the North have never placed any permanent dependence upon it. It has rested its exchanges upon the cotton and tobacco of the South, and it has obtained possession of these by flooding our States with its manufactures and nicnacs of every description, and by acting as the commercial broker of the South. And besides selling our valuable staple for trifles like these, which we could as well make for ourselves, we have annually distributed much that remained of these staples upon hotels and watering places, in steamboats and railroads, in shops of luxury and temples of fashion, and upon what is facetiously called education and accomplishments. And by the time that the cotton and the tobacco were made, it no more belonged to us than did the manufactures of England, and we were compelled in common honesty to let it go where it was really owned. At a very moderate calculation, the exchangeable value thus furnished the North in return for its manufactures and its climate and its fashion, amounted annually to between one and two hundred millions of dollars. But all this is now changed; we have seen the last of it, at least during the war, and a year or two will show that the subtraction of this amount from the one side, and the addition of it to the other, will make a marvellous difference in the aggregate of wealth. And while the withholding of this immense sum of money from the North will cripple its resources, it will be put in circulation among ourselves, and add to the income and resources of our own citizens. For there is no truer principle in political economy than this, that the distribution of money has as much to do with the wealth of a country as its production. God seems to have endowed our financial officers with the wisdom to seize the strong point of our economical position and our people with the patriotism to receive and adopt it. They have made our great staple to supply for them the place which gold and silver supply for the banks. As they issue paper money upon the coin which they possess, so will the Confederate States issue paper upon the cotton which it will accumulate by the exchange for it of Confederate bonds, and thus, instead of a currency depreciating continually like the old continental money, we shall have a currency always at par, because the cotton, which is its basis, is always wanted, and receives no injury of any material consequence from being piled up during a blockade. If a currency keeps at par, and it will always keep at par when it is known to represent an actual value, nobody will care to have it redeemed, especially so long as he may be hemmed in from intercourse with any except those whose currency it is. And besides furnishing a bank capital for the Confederate States, it becomes in the hands of the Government an instrument of great power for the regulation and control of foreign alliances. Refusing to permit its export except through our own seaports, it will soon bring all the nations who use our cotton face to face with the question between us and our enemies. It is not that cotton is king, but that God has given our statesmen wisdom to use a great advantage aright, and the people self-denial to acquiesce in the arrangement, and to stand manfully by it. "Not unto us, O Lord, not unto us, but unto Thy name give glory, for Thy mercy and for Thy truth's sake."

And in this very matter our God does seem to have smitten our enemies with judicial blindness. Just when they most needed sound wisdom, they have inaugurated a financial system which must cripple their resources. A prohibitory tariff, and one which they will find it difficult to repeal, because it was given as a sop to particular States, just when a nation needs both friends and money, is the very height of folly, and a system of borrowing at a heavy discount is a poor beginning for a people boasting of its wealth and arrogant about its resources. The commercial men of the North perceive this weakness, and therefore it is that they cry out for quick measures and a short war. They know that they cannot bear a long one, and very soon will they begin to murmur at any commander-in-chief who desires to move slowly and surely, and will either hurry him into measures which will ensure his defeat or force him to yield his marshal's baton into bolder, because more ignorant, hands. Truly does God seem to have ordered every thing for us, and to have made every thing work for the security of our cause. How can any one distrust Him or be faithless enough to ask with our enemies, "Where is now their God?"

If we turn from the financial to the military affairs of the Confederate States, we perceive the same visible presence of God in our concerns. In the beginning of this movement we appeared to have no resources wherewith to meet the immense preponderance of power that was against us. They had armies, navies, armories, manufactories, every thing that could conduce to their strength—fortresses bristled in our midst, and aimed their guns against the people they had been built to protect—a large, well-ordered army stood upon our Texan frontier quite in a condition to have invaded and embarrassed us—a large armament was fitted out to strike at the heart of South Carolina, which was considered the soul of the rebellion—a navy yard of immense resources, filled with arms, and ammunition, and ordnance, supported by the strongest fortress in the Union, and defended by men-of-war armed with guns of the heaviest calibre, lay upon our northeastern frontier. A hastily-raised militia was all we had to depend upon in the conflict. But in a moment every thing seemed changed in a way more than natural. Skilful officers sprang from every direction into the arena. Armed men arose as if from the dragon's teeth which the Abolitionists had been sowing for years. And fear seemed to fall upon our enemies—unaccountable fear. Officers who had never quailed before any living man—soldiers who had borne the old flag to victory wherever it had waved over them—navies which had moved defiant over the world—all, all seemed paralyzed. That large border army surrendered to militia without a blow—that gallant armament, made up of the same fleet which had run in the revolution into the Thames, which had defied the Algerine batteries, which had brought Austria to terms in the Levant, which had spit its fire into the face of the almost impregnable fortress of St. Juan d'Ulloa, stood inert and saw a gallant soldier, who was upholding their own flag, beaten out of his fortress by sand batteries and volunteers. That immense navy yard, with its vast resources, with its great power of resistance, with its huge fortress at its back, with its magnificent men-of-war all armed and shotted, was deserted in an unaccountable panic because of the threats of a few almost unarmed citizens, and the rolling during the night of well-managed locomotives. And nowhere could this panic have occurred more seasonably for us, because it gave us just what we most needed, arms and ammunition and heavy ordnance in great abundance. All this is unaccountable upon any ordinary grounds. But two days before, a naval officer of very high rank had reported to head-quarters at Washington that this navy yard was impregnable. Is not this very like the noise of chariots and the noise of horses, even the noise of a great host, which the Syrians were made to hear when the Lord would deliver Israel? "And they said one to another, Lo, the King of Israel hath hired against us the King of the Hittites and the Kings of the Egyptians, to come upon us. Wherefore they arose and fled in the twilight and left their tents and their horses, and their asses, even the camp as it was, and fled for their life." "Not unto us, O Lord, not unto us, but unto Thy name give glory, for Thy mercy and for Thy truth's sake."

And now, my beloved people, after such tokens of God's presence with us in all the departments of our civil affairs, need we be afraid of man's revilings, and man's threats? If God be with us, who can be against us? Shimei's cursings did not hurt David; they only returned upon his own head. And if any be presumptuous enough, in the arrogance of their wealth and in the pride of their numbers, and in the presumption of their Pharisaism to ask "Where is now their God?" we can humbly answer "Our God is in the Heavens: He hath done whatsoever he pleased." Nay, more, we can tremblingly rejoice and point to His presence with us upon earth. He is too manifestly with our people, giving them unanimity and patriotism—with our rulers, giving them wisdom and moderation and a proper sense of their dependence upon Him—with our armies, shielding them in the hour of conflict,—for us to acknowledge it. We should be as brute beasts before Him if we did not perceive His presence and humble ourselves before Him. God loves to be honored in the assemblies of the saints, and he delights in the praises and thanksgivings of his people. There is no surer mode of driving Him from us than by refusing to acknowledge His presence among us. It is not humility to be blind to the tokens of God's goodness towards us, it is faithlessness—it is not vain boasting to enumerate his glorious acts in our behalf, it is giving Him the honor due unto His holy name. Read the Psalms of David, and note how frequently he enumerates in long and elaborate verse the wondrous acts of the Lord, closing each stanza with the triumphant refrain, "For His mercy endureth forever." And surely he knew how God loved to be praised. Let us not be afraid or ashamed to see the hand of the Lord in every thing, to believe firmly that He does manifest himself for the right, and to be a praying and a thanksgiving people, as well as a fighting people. "Some trust in horses and chariots, but we will trust in the Lord our God."

But while we render thanks unto the Lord for all His benefits towards us, how deeply should their reception humble us! For we have been utterly undeserving of them. They are the tokens of unmerited mercy. If God were only strict to mark iniquity, which of us could stand? As a people, how little have we done for his cause! how poorly have we fulfilled the great mission intrusted to our hands! What wretched stewards have we been of the treasures committed to our keeping! How polluted our land has been with profaneness, with blasphemy, with Sabbath-breaking, with the shedding of blood! What violence and recklessness, what extravagance and waste have manifested themselves as the normal condition of our people! What an idolatry to fashion has disfigured the ancient simplicity of our people! What a high value has been put among us upon all those qualities which are the very opposites of the graces of the gospel, upon pride, upon self-reliance, upon animal courage! How inordinately has wealth been sought after and valued! How honor, falsely so called, has been exalted and almost defied! And if with all these hateful sins cleaving to our national skirts, God can yet manifest His presence with us, what might we not hope for, if we lay down those iniquities at the foot of Jesus' Cross and cry for mercy? Let us begin to-day, and, with deep humility of spirit, confess our unworthiness and pray the Lord that He will not turn His face from us, but will still enable us to say "Our Lord is in the Heavens."

We are engaged, my people, in one of the grandest struggles which ever nerved the hearts or strengthened the hands of a heroic race. We are fighting for great principles, for sacred objects—principles which must not be comprised, objects which must not be abandoned. We are fighting to prevent ourselves from being transferred from American republicanism to French democracy. We are fighting to rescue the fair name of our social life from the dishonor which has been cast upon it. We are fighting to protect and preserve a race who form a part of our household, and stand with us next to our children. We are fighting to drive away from our sanctuaries the infidel and rationalistic principles which are sweeping over the land and substituting a gospel of the Stars and Stripes for the gospel of Jesus Christ. These objects are far more important even than liberty, for they concern the inner life, the soul and eternity. Let us be strong and quit ourselves as men—strong in the strength of Jesus, strong in the presence of the Lord of Hosts. Let us, in all our efforts, in all our successes, say unceasingly, "Not unto us, not unto us, O Lord, be the glory." Let us in all our reverses still praise the Lord and in all humility reply, "Our God is in the Heavens: He hath done whatsoever he pleased."

OUR PERIL AND OUR DELIVERANCE:

A Sermon preached Sunday, October 20th, 1861, in the South Reformed Dutch Church, New York City,

BY REV. ROSWELL D. HITCHCOCK, D. D.

It is written: Man shall not live by bread alone, but by every word that proceedeth out of the mouth of God.—*St. Matthew*, iv. 4.

Two things are absolutely indispensable to human life; and only two. These are, generically, food and drink, whose simplest and best specific forms are bread and water. Bread we call the staff of life. This familiar imagery is as ancient at least as the time of Abraham. To the three angels, one of them the mysterious Angel of the Covenant, who appeared to him as he sat at the door of his tent in the plains of Mamre, the hospitable patriarch said: "I will fetch a morsel of bread, and stay ye your hearts." Moses, when he threatened the people with famine in punishment of their sins, described it as the breaking of their staff. Isaiah also warns the inhabitants of Jerusalem and Judah, that the Lord of Hosts will take away the stay and the staff, the whole stay of bread, and the whole staff of water. Bread was what the famished Bedouin craved, when he caught up so eagerly the bag he found lying by a fountain in the desert, and flung it down again so quickly in despair, exclaiming: "Alas! it is only diamonds." Water is what the wounded soldier begs for so piteously with his dying breath.

These two appetites of the body were both made use of by our Lord in commending to human acceptance the divinest blessings of the Gospel. In the synagogue at Capernaum, during the second year of His ministry, He called Himself the bread of God, sent down from heaven to give life unto the world. And again, in the temple at Jerusalem, on the last great day of the Feast of Tabernacles, the autumn before he suffered, he stood and cried: "If any man thirst, let him come unto me and drink."

These incidents suffice to rescue from the contempt of a fastidious criticism, what some might otherwise have looked upon as too homely an illustration of spiritual truth. Such fastidiousness is nowhere countenanced in the Scriptures. The Maker of our bodies never speaks scornfully of their normal, innocent necessities. Human life, in the lowest sphere of its merely animal functions and wants, is invested with a sort of sacredness as the workmanship and husbandry of God. Since the days of Noah, the law of "blood for blood" has been its divinely appointed shield from murderous violence; while the countless and varied forms of human industry and enterprise, required to furnish the needed comforts and ornaments of life, have nowhere been more highly commended, not to say more strictly enjoined, than in the writings of those men who spake as they were moved by the Holy Ghost. Even wealth finds endorsement in the Proverbs of Solomon, who has told us that "the hand of the diligent maketh rich." Our Lord's injunction: "Labor not for the meat which perisheth," is not an absolute, but only a relative interdiction of human industry. It is only an exclusive, or a disproportionate devotion to material pursuits, which is here forbidden. Even in our text no slight is put upon the ordinary supports of human life. Our Lord, after forty days of fasting, had been challenged by the Tempter to make demonstration of his divine Sonship by turning into bread the stones which were underneath his feet. His answer was, in language borrowed from Moses: "Man shall not live by bread *alone*, but by every word that proceedeth out of the mouth of God." As though He had said : I do not deny the desirableness of bread for the body, although even bread is not always a necessity, since man has also a higher nature, which must take its nourishment, whence the body itself may also be nourished, from the lips of God.

Thus may our text be understood as adjudicating the question always and everywhere at issue between the two natures of man. From both sides of the Jordan, out of both economies, from the lips at once of Moses and of Christ, the decision comes, that while the lower nature may not be crushed, the higher nature must not be smothered. In effect, if not in form, the injunction is: Fail not to make prudent provision for the body, but be sure you make still better provision for the soul. Be diligent in all proper worldly business. Let the bosom of the earth be tilled, and its bowels searched for treasures. Let the sea also be ploughed and sounded. Let the very ends of the earth resound with the hum and stir of human toil and traffic. And let the whole life of man be enriched and adorned with the spoils and trophies of an ever advancing,.triumphant material civilization. But through, underneath, and above all this, let there be a yet keener diligence in matters pertaining to the soul. Let its fields also be ploughed and dressed, till they wave with the goodly harvests of knowledge and grace. Let its heights be climbed, and its depths sounded. Let the wisdom which is from above, and unto life eternal, be more precious than gold or rubies. Let the kingdom of Christ be more real, and of more account, than all the kingdoms of the world. In fine, let there be a grand spiritual civilization, underlying, pervading, and electrifying the material, till the rebellious Titans are all subdued, and the knowledge of the Lord fills the earth, as the waters cover the sea.

It is of this momentous struggle between the material and the spiritual, as now in progress on our own continent, and underneath our own eyes, that I propose to discourse to-day. Lend me, then, your attention, while I consider:—First, what our peril is; and, Secondly, what our deliverance must be.

I. We are first to consider what our peril is:

In one word, it is the peril of an overmastering materialism. A peril not different in kind from what has always beset the race; which, in a new degree beyond all historic precedent, we share in common with the whole of Protestant Christendom; and yet, for obvious reasons, a peril peculiarly our own, sharper, and hurrying more swiftly to its crisis, than has befallen the experience of any other nation upon the globe.

A little more than three hundred years ago, the leading nations of the earth were launched all at once, and with tremendous impetus, upon a new career. The feudal disintegration, which followed the dismemberment of the empire of Charlemagne, had given place by degrees to the well-defined and well-compacted nationalities of modern Europe. One by one, and yet all of them within a narrow compass of time, these nationalities stood forth solidified, centralized, and panoplied. Italy was the only exception; Italy, and to some extent also Germany. All the rest were unified, and thereby clothed with power. The Papacy, which had easily managed the discordant multitude of petty feudal princes, now began to tremble in the presence of kings and emperors, each with a newly consolidated nationality behind him, just beginning to be conscious of its strength and jealous of its rights.

While this decisive change was rapidly going on in the sphere of politics, there was, in the sphere of practical life, an equally rapid succession of most important inventions and discoveries, which smote the sluggishness of mediæval Europe like so many galvanic batteries. These were: First, the mariner's compass, known in China more than seven centuries ago, but not known in Europe till after the Crusades, and not rendered available for an adventurous commerce till it reached the Occident. Second, the invention of gunpowder, or rather the application of it to gunnery: an art not known to the Chinese, who, though they manufactured the compound about as well as we do now, had never used it in war. On the battle-field of Crecy, in 1346, artillery thundered for the first time in history, ushering in a new era. Third, the art of printing, also known in China, at least nine hundred years ago, but not known in Europe till invented, as we say, by Guttenberg, possibly in pursuance of a hint borrowed from the Orient, about the middle of the fifteenth century. Fourth, the discovery, in 1486, and the doubling in 1497, of the Cape of Good Hope, which gave Europe an easy highway to the Indies, and beckoned her fleets out beyond the Pillars of Hercules, to whiten all the oceans of the globe. And fifth, the discovery of our own continent of America, which has touched to the quick every nation of Europe.

Such a series of triumphs over time and space, over mere brute strength in the masses, over isolation, ignorance, and prejudice, must in any case have revolutionized society. But, followed up as they were so closely, and subsidized by the Lutheran Reformation, they became doubly rousing and revolutionary. Commerce, the mechanic arts, and an improved agriculture became, in no long time, the special allies and badges of Protestantism. Papal Italy, it is true, gave to the world Columbus, Vespucius, Verazzani, and the elder Cabot; but she herself took no part in the great enterprises of maritime discovery, and reaped no advantage from them. Papal Spain and Portugal, not so much corrupted by sudden and enormous revenues, as radically weakened and wasted by causes long at work upon their spiritual constitutions, soon fell behind in the general rush for wealth and empire, leaving their sturdier Protestant rivals to snatch the better part of the newly-discovered territories, inaugurate a more industrial, thrifty civilization, and so command eventually the markets of the world. Even France, constitutionally so mercurial, aggressive, and versatile, spurning the Reformation offered her by Lefévre and Calvin, committed the stupid blunder of exiling her ingenious Huguenots, made enemies of those who should have been her helpers, and was hunted by the red flag of England from the rising to the setting sun. Thus it was that Protestant Europe took on the character which she wears to-day. Purer in doctrine than Papal Europe, and, in most respects, no doubt, purer also in morals, more intelligent, more industrious, more enterprising, and consequently more prosperous, Protestant Europe is nevertheless in the heat of a raging fever, her very vitals burning with the lust of gain. England especially suffers under the ravages of this vehement disease. For generations has she been applauded by the grateful nations as the bulwark of Protestantism, and the dauntless evangelist of freedom. But look on England to-day—the England that speaks to us through Liverpool and Manchester, through Cabinet and Parliament; her stout hand not upon her heart, but upon her pocket; cold towards us, who were but recently so warm towards her; icy cold towards us in our desperate struggle with the most wantonly wicked rebellion on record in history, sneeringly indifferent to the triumph of law, order, authority, and right, anxious only about the cargoes of cotton which are to feed her whirling spindles. If this be our Protestant brotherhood, this the fellowship of nations which have stood together for the freedom of the world, well may we hang our heads in bitter shame as we remember even the Crusades of the Middle Ages. These, at least, were a gallant frenzy, a generous fanaticism, while we have fallen upon times of most ignoble selfishness and greed. Tell us, ye British statesmen, tell us, ye sordid sons of heroic sires, are constitutions only parchments? Are nations only herds of farmers, artisans, and traders? Are our fathers' graves only mounds of earth, and our children's cradles mere upholstery? Is chartered freedom only sounding rhetoric? Is duty only a name? Is honor dead? Has the Almighty abdicated? And is there nothing for us, in this nineteenth century, but to delve, and spin, and trade, to clutch and hoard, to eat, and drink, and bloat, and die, and make no sign?

But while we thus upbraid Protestant England, leading the van of Protestant Europe, let us not be blind to our own misdeeds. We are radically the most Protestant of Protestants. We came over here, most of us, as fugitive dissenters; the Irish Catholic, not less than the English Puritan. We came here in quest of a freedom denied us beyond the sea; freedom to worship God, each in his own way, and freedom to govern ourselves in the fear of God. For a time, we kept step to the music of the grand old Christian Psalms, with which we first waked the echoes of the forest. But presently, as we took vigorous root here on the virgin continent, we began to imbibe its rankness. So vast a stretch of vacant fertile territory never before solicited the husbandman. Such mountains of iron and copper, anthracite and gold, never before allured the miner. Such a system of lakes and rivers never before floated harvests to market. Never before was landless labor invited to such a paradise. That subtle instinct of our nature, which renders ownership in the soil so intense a luxury, has found here its keenest stimulant. Alike from Southern plantation, from Western prairie, and from the golden gate of the Pacific, there have broken notes of challenge and of welcome, which have maddened our bounding blood.

New kings have arisen, which know not Joseph, nor Joseph them: cotton in the South, corn in the North, and gold on the Pacific shore. Obedient to their call, we have rushed on headlong over vast territories, planting States, as other nations have planted only colonies; while far along ahead of the advancing wave of population we have flung a spray before us, spattering the wilderness with hamlets too meagre, and cabins too scattered, to permit the church and the school-house promptly to follow them. And so have we conquered the continent,—leaping from the Atlantic to the Mississippi, from the Mississippi to the Pacific. With such a basis laid for wealth in the products of our soil and the treasures of our mines, we have advanced rapidly in the mechanic arts, already, in the greenness of our youth, rivalling the oldest industry of Europe. Equally rapid has been the growth of commerce, encouraged by our midway position between the great continents, till now we are the most eager and ubiquitous of the modern Phœnicians. Every sea is vexed with our bold and hurrying keels, every climate rifled of its products. We boast of having gone the farthest towards the arctic and the antarctic poles. We alone, almost, of the nations, hunt the whales of the Northern Pacific. We find new islands for the geographers. We hang with fluttering pinions upon the jealously guarded coasts of China and Japan.

Consider, also, what our blood is; not English, or Irish, or Scotch, or German, or Dutch, or Scandinavian, or French, or Spanish, or any other, but all of these, and many more, from almost every land and language under the cope of heaven. And, what is not to be lightly thought of, these manifold contributions have not been slowly distilled into the veins of our national life, but have come almost like invading armies, forcing upon us an amalgamation of races such as no nation has ever before experienced. If Europe throbs and flushes under the pressure of her diversified and exuberant life, as the chafing races struggle together within her bosom, much more may we, who have the blood of all these races mixed in our boiling veins.

Add to this the unexampled elasticity and freedom of our civil institutions, institutions as elastic and unfettered as the wild air we breathe, and you have before you the elements of the stupendous problem of our destiny now hastening towards its solution.

Need I tell you what we are, and where we stand to-day? Behold and see. A vast continent underneath our glowing feet; and we boastful of its gigantic proportions, as if great territories must needs breed great souls. A continent rich on its surface with the gathered fatness of centuries, rich beneath its surface with all that toughens the sinews of nations; and we straining every muscle to make them ours. On one side of us the Atlantic, thundering in our ears of Europe and Africa; on the other side of us the Pacific, whispering of Asia and Australia; and we, with eager ears open to both. With a form of government, the more sagacious of whose founders feared might be wanting in force; and yet over all the continent, in the riot of our youthful impatience of restraint, we are shouting back and forth to each other, from the Lakes to the Gulf, and from ocean to ocean: "That is the best government which governs the least."

Verily, the millennium has dawned; but it is the millennium of a rank and rampant materialism. We are mad after gain; madder than we know. It is the one great passion of the continent, poisoning our social life, poisoning our politics, poisoning even our religion. Just now the very life of the Republic is menaced by a rebellion, in its atrocity matched only by the rebellion of Lucifer, in its meanness matched only by the rebellion of Absalom, but having its root, when we come to the last analysis of causes,—having its root, I say, in nothing else than this accursed greed of gain. It is the institution of slavery, as all admit, which is now striking so frantically for the dominion of the continent. And who does not know that the inventions of Arkwright and Whitney, enhancing the value and stimulating the demand for cotton, have done more than all other influences combined towards making slavery the unscrupulous, insolent, and hateful power that it is? Who does not know, that a long series of Northern concessions, inspired in part by a generous patriotism, but also in part by the natural timidity of commerce, had begotten in the minds of the Southern conspirators an assurance, now so happily falsified, that the industrious and opulent North would never take up arms in defence of the imperilled Union. Suppose we crush this rebellion, as I am sure we shall, unless, by our folly in withholding the blows which are most dreaded by our enemies, we provoke the stars in their courses to fight against us, as they fought against Sisera of old, what will be gained if, when the war is ended, we propose to return to our idols, and go on just as we went before? What will be gained? Only a respite; by no means a deliverance. We shall only swell again with pride, and again make the world ring with our boastings. We shall only gorge ourselves with our gains, and be fattened like bullocks for the slaughter.

II. This brings me to speak of what our deliverance must be.

Deliverance is what we want; not mere respite, which only adjourns the conflict, lifting the agony from our spirits to lay it over upon our children; deliverance, complete and final. What avails it in a raging fever, rapidly nearing its crisis, that we comfort ourselves with cooling drinks, while the disease is striking boldly at our vitals? What avails it even in health, that we breathe the purest air of the mountain, if we take no food?

In the sentence chosen for our text, we read either our doom or our deliverance, just which we will; our doom, if we are foolish, our deliverance, if we are wise. It is written, written in God's word, and written in all the history of the race: "Man shall not live by bread alone, but *by every word that proceedeth out of the mouth of God.*" Such is the divine regimen for the nations. They live, if they live at all, by no felicity of position, soil, or climate, by no abundance of material good, but by the living word of the living God.

In our case, duty is as plain as the path of the sun along the firmament. The triumphs of our material civilization are not to be thrown away, nor its splendors diminished. So long as our land is fertile, so long shall we reap and garner its harvests. So long as our mountains stand, so long shall we sink our shafts into their shaggy sides. So long as coal burns, or iron melts, or gold is purified, in the furnace, so long will the furnace roar. So long as our lakes sparkle in the morning light, or our rivers run laughing to the sea, so long shall we float our produce to its marts. So long as the restless ocean heaves, so long shall we ride upon its billows. It is simply preposterous to say that such things ought not so to be. Who says it? Surely not nature, whose every growing tree, whose every flowing stream, whose every breathing breeze, is eloquent of life and power. Surely not the God, either of nature, of providence, or of grace, of whom it was said by his only begotten Son: "My father *worketh* hitherto."

Work then we must, and shall, and should. And work will bring us wealth, and wealth will bring us power. What then? Need wealth be idolized, or spent upon our lusts? Need power be vaunted and abused? If so, we perish; perish, as Tyre and Sidon perished; perish, as Carthage perished; perish, as, according to the Indian legend, the last of our gigantic mastodons perished, smitten down by the hot thunderbolts of the Great Spirit. Thank God, it need not be so. There is no necessity laid upon us that we curse God and die. Nor is it our task to lay our ineffectual finger upon this vast revolving wheel which carries the whole machinery of our earthly life, and bid it pause. It is not our task to slay this giant of our material prosperity, and stretch his huge corpse out across the continent. We are called to no such service. Ours is the far grander task of teaching the giant wisdom, and subduing his earth-born energies to Him who hath told us, that "*Man shall not live by bread alone.*"

How, then, shall men and nations live? "*By every word that proceedeth out of the mouth of God.*" So reads our text. The Hebrews in the desert had no need of bread; they were fed with manna from the skies. But our Lord proved that there was no need even of manna. It was enough for him as the Son of man, that he had faith in God. On this he feasted, while he fasted, the forty days. It was God's commandment which he obeyed in fasting, and this commandment, thus obeyed in faith, was the bread he ate. The commandments of God, then, are the bread of life for the nations.

These commandments, it can hardly need to be said, are all embodied in the Gospel of his Son. What was written on the tablets of stone at Sinai, what was announced by prophets, what is written on the fleshly tablets of the heart, all that God has ever spoken, whether in thunders, or in whispers, is here gathered up for its final, decisive utterance. And this is our deliverance; neither more, nor less, nor other than the glorious Gospel of the blessed God. Our fathers brought it with them across the sea. They grounded their civil polity upon it. By it they squared, or aimed to square, their whole life, private, social, and public. They went to battle in the strength it ministered. They buried their dead in the hopes it kindled. They died themselves in the triumphs it taught them. By this our Christian birth, our Christian baptism, and our Christian history, we are a Christian people; and none who join us from any quarter of the globe, Buddhists, infidels, or idolaters, may be permitted to reverse this verdict.

If a Christian people, then must we be loyal to our calling, baptizing our unexampled material prosperity into the name and service of our Lord, dedicating our wealth, with a wise and eager generosity, to Christian uses. Wealth we have, and wealth we shall have more and more. The Mediæval Church, which preached from all its pulpits: " Blessed are the poor," has given place to a better Church, which preaches the preaching of its Lord: " Blessed are the poor in spirit." The Gospel has no curses for the rich, if only they be rich also in faith and love. Its grand ideal, its one great lesson, is not self-crucifixion, but self-control, not voluntary poverty, but industrious and faithful stewardship. *Goods in trust for Christian uses:* this describes all property, real or personal, in the possession of a Christian man. What we have comes not by purchase, but by gift; and it is given to us, that we may give it back. How far we now are from obedience to this Christian law of property, how far even from consciously assenting to this law as justly in force over us, I need not say. But only take the measure of our estates and incomes, and then the measure of our charities, and tell me, whether even the Hebrew tenth, scorned by the Christians of the first three centuries as beneath their privilege, tell me, whether even the Hebrew tenth is realized among us. Or compare our stinted gifts, large as they may sometimes seem to be, with what we lavish upon ourselves, and tell me, whether the ratio is quite creditable to our Christian name. I cannot, of course, prognosticate the life of the Church during the Millennium, for which it prays and waits; but sure am I that the Millennium itself will never come till the Church has revised, not to say completely and radically revolutionized, its whole economy of giving. More, vastly more, must find its way into the treasury of the Lord, before the work of the Lord prospers.

And now, if God spares the life of the nation in answer to our prayers, let us as a Christian people solemnly resolve, that we will not suffer ourselves to be launched again upon such a surging tide of worldliness as that from which, by the fiery judgments of God's hand, we have just been snatched. Even now, in the midst of civil war, we are in the midst of material plenty. Our stores are almost bursting with grain, our vaults with gold. But with returning peace, there will be returning traffic, such as the country has never known. We shall presently hear the roar of it in our docks and along our streets. And may God have mercy on our souls. While yet upon the dizzy brink of this new prosperity, let us tremble, and let us pray. Let us dedicate ourselves, with all our property and all our power of making property, anew to the God of nations. Let us appreciate the spiritual grandeur of the new era which Providence is preparing for us. This new era must needs be more Christian than the one now closing in fire and blood,—more Christian in its fidelity of unselfish stewardship, or He who sitteth in the heavens will not suffer it to be at all. We have gone on just as far as we can go in our insane idolatry of material good. From this hour onward, we must elaborate and wield our fortunes in the interest of a far loftier and more beneficent civilization. A Christian people, opulent and thrifty as we have been, should certainly have more to show for it in our achievements of Christian charity. Our institutions of mercy for the poor, the sick, the fatherless; our institutions of learning and religion; our mission schools and churches in the poorer and more crowded districts of our larger cities, in the more sparsely peopled portions of our widely extended territory; our societies which have in charge the printing of Bibles and religious books, the equipment of an accomplished and zealous ministry, and the sending forth of missionaries throughout our own and into foreign lands,—these ought all of them to be far stronger and more efficient than they ever have been. The measure of our achievements in the past, will not suffice as the measure of our achievements in the time to come. The destiny of the continent is now suspended in awful scales, whose beam trembles among the stars. It is indeed a noble continent, noble in outline, in resources, and in boundless possibilities of good; but it belongs to Christ by a far more sacred title than it belongs to us. His name, not ours, is engraved upon it. For the interests of his kingdom has it been colonized. And he is looking now, in this sharp crisis of our history, for a loyal Church; a Church which shall understand its mission, and subdue the continent, in all its forces and with all its treasures, to thoroughly Christian ends and uses, running up the standard of the Cross over all its fields. In our closets, and on our knees, let us await the coming baptism of a new confession. A baptism of fire it must be, but not sent to burn us, only our dross. Let us not fail to recognize our proper Sovereign, although in his advent flames go before him, and darkness is underneath his feet. Let Mammon no longer be worshipped within our borders. Let us make less haste to be rich. Above all, let us renounce, now and forever, the groundless claim to our earnings as our own; and let us accept the better office of an honest Christian stewardship as at once our only safety and our highest honor.

Our political life in all its spheres, municipal, state, and national, is likewise in desperate need of mending. For a long time back, the so-called better classes among us, and especially our Christian citizens, immersed in gainful business, or else engaged in more congenial enterprises of individual and organized beneficence, have retreated from the political arena, leaving it in the hands of hungry adventurers and partisans. The votes which good men carry to the polls are too often dictated by bad men, whom no prudent merchant would ever think of trusting with his property. The *caucus*, so honorable in its origin, has become the basest of engines, managed to defraud the people of their honest choice, so that the very term is losing its place in classic usage. Statesmen are hunted down by demagogues in pursuit of the spoils of office. Our largest popular conventions are theatres of intrigue, such as pure-minded patriots may well blush to encounter. Even our chambers of legislation have opened their doors to bribery, and become the veriest chambers of wickedness. Hence the acknowledged rottenness of our whole political system, brought about in no small degree by the shameful remissness of multitudes of patriotic and Christian citizens, who are too deeply engrossed in their own private pursuits to stand forth as champions of the common weal. Politics are no longer a science, but a trade. Things have come to such a pass, that it matters too little what party is in the ascendency; there are soldiers of fortune, in mischievous abundance, ready at any moment to march their squadrons from one camp to another, just as the eagles of victory may lead the way.

Here, too, let us now make our stand. These abominations have flourished and rioted quite long enough. As Christian citizens, there is a solemn duty laid upon us to elaborate, in its grandest proportions, a Christian state. We must be done flattering the masses. Men are no better in the aggregate than they are as individuals. The voice of the people, when the people are corrupt and reckless, is any thing but the voice of God. Let us remember the profane shout of the Cæsareans in the courts of Herod, and how God smote the inflated tyrant and gave him as food to worms. God's voice is in his Providence, and not in us, except as we are the wise interpreters and the willing ministers of that Providence. But more than all, God's voice is in the volume of his word, and we must listen for it there. Nations are not cradled and reared to maturity, that they may trample on the Divine authority. A righteous judgment presides over their fortunes. They are set in their places, that they may execute the eternal decrees of justice and mercy. If they fail in this, they are stricken down. If they scorn the weak, oppress the poor, and shut their ears against the sighing of the captive, they are doomed to perish. The Persians have a proverb, that the cry of the orphan rocks the throne of the Almighty. The God we profess to serve, chooses to be known in the earth as the friend of the friendless and the avenger of the oppressed. He sees his own image in every child of want and sorrow, and woe to the people who defile or despise that image. Woe to the nation which seeks its own aggrandizement by the conquest of weaker nations. Woe to the race which seeks the heights of power by setting its ruthless foot upon the necks of weaker races.

The roots of our life as a people are in God; and our God is the God in Christ. There is no law of history more absolute than this: that nations rise or fall, flourish or decay, according as they help or hinder the kingdom of Christ our Lord. The kingdom of Christ, I say: not that amount of intelligence and virtue, which an infidel civilization may succeed in diffusing among the masses of men; but the kingdom of Christ as an organized society, built upon the foundation of Apostles and Prophets, and maintained in the world by the preaching of the word, and the observance of Christian ordinances, and the administration of the Christian sacraments. Our hopes for the future of our imperilled institutions of civil government must therefore all centre in the Church. It is the one thing of all others on this continent most dear to the heart of God. Our first duty is to save it from reproach. Infidel interpreters of Scripture, desecrating the sanctity of Christian pulpits, if such interpreters there be, must be frowned into silence. Learned Doctors, abusing the Scriptures by trying to make them abet oppression, must be indignantly rebuked. Those who come among us from the continent of Europe, especially from Germany, prejudiced against Christianity itself by reason of its connection with oppressive political institutions at home, must here be taught that the kingdom of Christ, though in the world, is not of it.

Five righteous men, as we read, would have saved the cities of the plain. But then they must have been righteous men, thoroughly righteous, profoundly fearing God, and diligently keeping his commandments. So may Christ's Church on this continent, now trembling beneath the tread of nearly a million of armed men, save us. But this Church must be worthy of its Great Captain, radiant in its graces, energetic in its evangelism, holding forth in its simplicity and purity the word of life, multiplying its converts, grappling boldly with our national sins, and subduing all things to itself. Our great work will not be done; it will only just have commenced when the war in which we are now engaged has ended in victory. For the present we struggle only to re-assert the national authority, and restore the integrity of the national domain. This will be, indeed, a magnificent achievement, worth immeasurably more than many thousands of lives and many millions of money. But this accomplished, there will still remain the far more difficult achievement of thoroughly subduing the continent, as it never has been subdued, to Christ. For long years, with all our patience and with all our might, shall we have to struggle with the gigantic task of making ourselves more positively and more entirely a Christian people. The principal impediment now disputing our progress, can hardly need to be named. We see it inscribed upon the rebellious banners which now challenge us to battle. It is *Slavery*, an institution which we may tolerate as our fathers tolerated it, but which must never rule us in the future as it has ruled us in the past; an institution which has revealed its essential hatefulness, and aroused against it the indignation of our most conservative and moderate thinkers, by giving birth to a brood of atrocities which the tenderest Christian charity can hardly hesitate to pronounce Satanic. Providence will probably see to it that this barbarous institution shall be so crippled by the war it has wantonly provoked, as never again to raise itself in rebellion against our flag. But though crippled, this institution bids fair to survive the present conflict, passing over, with all its embarrassments, to become one of the chief problems of a better Christian future. What shall be done with it, no human wisdom can as yet determine. But this at least is clear, that we must cover the continent, not merely with the shadow of our victorious flag, but also with the shadow of the Cross. The church and the school-house must enter every settlement, and unto all the people must be carried the Word of God, which alone giveth life to the nations.

ABSALOM'S REBELLION.

A Sermon preached in Christ Church, Philadelphia, Thursday, September 26, 1861, on occasion of the National Fast, recommended by the President of the United States, at the request of both Houses of Congress.

BY BENJAMIN DORR, D. D.,
RECTOR OF SAID CHURCH.

"And the King said unto Zadok, Carry back the ark of God into the city; if I shall find favor in the eyes of the Lord, He will bring me again, and show me both it and his habitation. But if He thus say, I have no delight in thee; behold, here am I, let him do to me as seemeth good unto Him."—2 *Samuel* xv. 25, 26.

I KNOW of no portion of Scripture, my friends, more suitable for our meditation and instruction at this time, than these words of David. They express that deep humility of heart, that entire resignation to God's will, that implicit trust in his mercy, goodness, and power, which the solemn services of this day are designed to awaken and cherish in ourselves. That we may enter into the spirit, and so profit by the teachings of the text, we shall do well to review that painful page in the history of God's chosen people, of which it is a part,—THE REBELLION OF ABSALOM; a rebellion which, for sinfulness and folly, had never before a parallel.

Let us look at it. Absalom was the third son of David; born in Hebron, once the capital of the kingdom of Israel, where David was crowned, and where he reigned seven years. He enjoyed opportunities and advantages as a prince of the tribe of Judah, which, had they been properly improved, might have rendered him a happy and useful man. But he became vain, crafty, ambitious, and revengeful, and these vices led him on to murder and treason. In a fit of revenge, he slew his elder brother, and fled from his home and country. Through the solicitation of Joab, David permitted him to return to his house in Jerusalem, but he was not allowed to come to the palace, nor to see his father's face for two whole years. When, however, the indulgent parent received him into his presence, it was with full pardon for all the past. He took him to his bosom, as his best beloved son; and Absalom gave such outward proof of respect and reverence, as would lead to the belief that his repentance was sincere. "He came to the king, and bowed himself on his face to the ground before the king, and the king kissed Absalom." But all this was a mock humility; a hypocritical device to conceal from his father his infamous designs.

The very next chapter records his rebellion,—how he planned, and how he executed it. In the first verse we read "that Absalom prepared him chariots and horses, and fifty men to run before him." "He rose up early, and stood beside the way of the gate," where causes were heard, and the laws administered, "so that, when any man who had a controversy came to the king for judgment," he seized the opportunity of poisoning his mind against the wisest and best of kings, and that king his own father. "See," he said, to each person who approached the gate, "thy matters are good and right,"—but you will gain nothing, though justice be on your side, for "there is no man deputed of the king to hear thee;" and then, with canting hypocrisy, he adds,—"Oh that I were made judge in the land, that every man which hath any suit or cause might come unto me, and I would do him justice." "And when any man came nigh to do him obeisance, he put forth his hand, and took him and kissed him." Thus did he, by false pretences, and arrogant boastings, "steal away the hearts of all the men of Israel who came to the king for judgment." If I were ruler in the land, if I were set in the judgment seat, how happy and independent would this people be!—and so the infatuated men of Israel thought;—better have Absalom than David for our king!

And when this wild and wicked prince had so fastened upon them this miserable delusion, and so corrupted their minds and consciences, that they were ready to join him in open revolt, he again approaches his unsuspecting and too indulgent father with the deceivableness of Satan transformed into an angel of light, and says to him, "I pray thee, let me go and pay my vow, which I have vowed unto the Lord, in Hebron. For thy servant vowed a vow while I abode in Geshur in Syria, saying, If the Lord shall bring me again indeed to Jerusalem, then I will serve the Lord. And the king said unto him, Go in peace. So he arose and went to Hebron." He leaves his father's presence with the name of the just all-seeing Jehovah on his lips and the most detestable treason in his heart. Immediately on going out from the king, with the avowed intention of performing a religious act in his native city, and with that parting blessing of his pious father yet sounding in his ears, Go in peace; "he sent spies throughout all the tribes of Israel, saying, As soon as ye hear the sound of the trumpet, then ye shall say, Absalom reigneth in Hebron."

Tidings were soon brought by a messenger to David that "the hearts of the men of Israel were after Absalom," that "the conspiracy was strong," and that it "increased continually." The wisdom and prudence, as well as the meekness, humility, and resignation of the aged king are strikingly displayed on receiving this astounding intelligence. "Arise," he says to his household, his servants, and his chosen captains,—to all, indeed, who "were with him at Jerusalem;"—"Arise, and let us flee; for we shall not escape from Absalom;—make speed to depart, lest he overtake us suddenly, and bring evil upon us, and smite the city with the edge of the sword." He saw that a hasty flight was the wise and prudent course, as that alone would probably save the holy city from destruction.

His friends and followers express their willingness "to do whatsoever their lord the king should appoint." "And the king went forth, and all the people after him" down the valley of Jehoshaphat, across the Kedron, "toward the way of the wilderness." The chief captains of his armies, Joab, Abishai, and Ittai were with him; the priests also, Zadok and Abiathar, were of the company, and all the Levites with them, bearing upon their shoulders the Ark of the Covenant, the symbol of the divine presence, lest it should fall into the hands of the rebels and be destroyed. But David requests that it be replaced in the sanctuary, and there left to the divine protection; and he expresses the humble hope that God would take him also into his holy keeping, and restore him to the city and tabernacle on Mount Zion,—the place where his honor dwelleth;—but, if not, he would submissively resign himself to God's will. "And the king said unto Zadok, Carry back the ark of God into the city. If I shall find favor in the eyes of the Lord, he will bring me again, and show me both it and his habitation. But if he thus say, I have no delight in thee; behold, here am I, let him do to me as seemeth good unto him." What an example of meekness, and humility, and submission is this!

David, with his numerous attendants, fled beyond Jordan to the city of Mahanaim, one of the cities of refuge in the land of Gilead. Absalom took possession of Jerusalem, set up his rebel standard there, and, shortly after, gathered unto him all rebellious Israel, from Dan even to Beersheba, and in his own person led forth the mighty host to battle. He also encamped in Gilead, near to Mahanaim, where David was. In the mean time, the king, and his men of war, were not inactive; nor was he, or they, intimidated by the number and strength of their adversaries.

The great calamity which came upon him so suddenly humbled him indeed in the very dust, but it aroused no feelings of revenge. We hear no passionate expressions of anger, or hatred, towards his unnatural son;—his sorrow and grief were too deep for that. He bows his head in meek and patient submission to the chastisement, as the dispensation of One who doeth all things well.

His grief did not overpower his reason, nor end in gloominess and despair. He prudently quitted his capital, on the first outbreak of the rebellion, not from any personal fear, but to avoid unnecessary bloodshed in the capture of the city by the conspirators, and to take the most effectual and speedy measures for suppressing the rebellion.

He unfurled the royal standard at Mahanaim, and all the men of Judah, his loyal subjects,—aroused like a lion, the emblem of their tribe,—hastened to the rescue of their king and country. Nor was it an undisciplined host that he purposed to send against the rebels. He placed over them "captains of thousands, and captains of hundreds," and arranged the whole army in three grand divisions, each of which was commanded by one of his most experienced men of war. The history tells us that "David sent forth a third part of the people under the hand of Joab, and a third part under the hand of Abishai, the son of Zeruiah, Joab's brother, and a third part under the hand of Ittai the Gittite. And the king said unto the people, *I will surely go forth with you myself also.*"

The same fearless spirit with which, in youth, he encountered and slew a lion and a bear, the same invincible courage with which he met the giant Goliath of Gath in single combat, armed only with a shepherd's sling and stone, the courage which, in after years, and in many a battle, nerved his arm for the cause of his country and his God, now prompted him, at the age of more than three score years, to unsheathe his sword against his rebellious son and subjects,—enemies more wicked than the Philistines, more cruel than the lion and the bear. "I will surely go with you," is his noble resolve. "But the people answered, Thou shalt not go forth; for if we flee away, they will not care for us; neither if half of us die will they care for us; but now thou art worth ten thousand of us; therefore now it is better that thou succor us out of the city. And the king said unto them, What seemeth you best I will do." Another instance, this, of meek submission. Yet his heart still yearns for his son. Wicked as that son was, and all unworthy of parental pity, he ventures to plead with the captains of the hosts in his behalf. "The king stood by the gate side, and all the people came out by hundreds and by thousands. And the king commanded Joab and Abishai and Ittai, saying, Deal gently for my sake with the young man, even with Absalom. And all the people heard when the king gave all the captains charge concerning Absalom. So the people went out into the field against Israel; and the battle was in the wood of Ephraim."

The rebel troops are utterly routed and "slain before the servants of David, and there was there a great slaughter that day of twenty thousand men." The infamous traitor, the head of the conspiracy, the leader of the rebels, fled for his life; but justice speedily overtook him. He is caught and suspended by the neck in the branches of an oak, is thrust through the heart with a spear in the hands of Joab, his dead body is cast into a pit in the wood where he was slain, and "a very great heap of stones is laid upon him." Thus perished Absalom the traitor, reaping the reward of his iniquity, a miserable death and a dishonored grave. His deluded followers, who escaped the slaughter of the twenty thousand, "fled every one to his tent," and the rebellion was at an end. But the record of his treason and its punishment, has been handed down in the Bible, as a warning to all who are tempted to sin like him.

It is a fact worthy of note here, that Absalom himself, by an act which he intended should redound to his honor, helped to perpetuate his own infamy. The verse following that which records his inglorious death and burial, tells us that "Absalom in his lifetime had taken and reared up for himself a pillar, which is in the king's dale; for he said, I have no son to keep my name in remembrance." He had once three sons; but, happily for them, they died before their father's disgrace. "And he called the pillar after his own name; and it is called unto this day, Absalom's place."

The monument which he reared for himself, and which he probably thought would be his tomb, still stands, if tradition be true, "in the king's dale," as it stood three thousand years ago. "And often," as one well remarks, "it must have served among the Israelites for a salutary warning to sons who were disposed to be undutiful, to subjects who were tempted to rebel."

The structure now known as Absalom's tomb, or place, is a massive monument hewed out of the solid rock, standing near the Jews' Cemetery in the valley of Jehoshaphat, between Mount Zion and the Mount of Olives. Whether this be, or be not, the pillar mentioned in Scripture as the one which Absalom reared for himself, has long served, and still serves, to "keep his name in remembrance;" for neither Turk nor Jew passes by, without casting a stone at it, to testify his abhorrence of Absalom's unnatural sin. By the Jewish law, as you remember, the punishment for a rebellious son was death by stoning. "All the men of his city shall stone him with stones, that he die; so shalt thou put evil away from among you; and all Israel shall hear and fear."

Never before was there a rebellion so monstrously wicked as this of Absalom, and never, until now, has it had its parallel for iniquity.

Absalom lived under the best government upon earth, a government of God's own appointment, with a king at its head whom God had specially raised up for that purpose. In all civil, social, and religious privileges and blessings the Jews were immeasurably superior to any other nation. They enjoyed the largest liberty, and the highest measure of prosperity, that is ever given to any people. They were God's own peculiar people whom He had chosen for himself. He had delivered their fathers from oppressive servitude in Egypt, had wrought miracles in their behalf in the land of Ham and during their wanderings in the wilderness. He had given them victory over all their enemies, cast out the heathen from before them, and given them quiet possession of the Promised Land. He had framed their constitution, laws, and religion, the wisest and the best that mankind had ever known; and under these, during David's reign, the nation had attained its highest prosperity; "for the Lord had given him rest round about from all his enemies." And so it might have continued, had not the selfish, ambitious, unscrupulous Absalom coveted the throne, and determined to make himself king. To accomplish this, he must overturn the constitution, the laws, and the religion of the land; and this he will do, though the nation be ruined, his family and kindred slain, and his own hands be bathed in his father's blood.

All wickedness is folly; and in this case the folly is as glaring as the sin. Had he succeeded in his iniquitous schemes, what would he have gained? Nothing but the empty title of a king over a ruined nation, with a father's and a brother's blood and the blood of countless thousands, whom he had been instrumental in slaying, crying aloud for vengeance; and the great God of heaven and earth, whose government, and laws, and religion he had trampled on, armed against him.

But he might have come to the throne peacefully, and at no distant day, had he been a dutiful son; for he was, if not the oldest living child, certainly next to the oldest, and being a special favorite, David would without doubt have gladly made him king. He would then have secured to himself the benefits and blessings of the constitution, laws, and religion of the land; he would have reigned over a prosperous, happy people; and, more than all, he would have had the Almighty, ever-living and true God for his guide, protector, and friend. But in his madness and folly he cast all these aside, rushed headlong to his ruin, and when he thought to grasp a crown, he found only a traitor's grave. And now, brethren, let us inquire into the cause of this great calamity. Why was all this evil brought upon the Jewish nation? This is a question which no one would venture to answer with absolute certainty; but it is one which all may reverently consider; especially in its bearing on ourselves, and on the solemn services in which we, as a nation, are this day engaged. We may say generally, that sin was the occasion of all their distress, and that it is the cause of ours also. Indeed, all suffering is the consequence of sin. But, in the instance before us, we find evidence in the sacred records that this great rebellion was a judgment on both king and people for their sins. The nation itself had, in its prosperity, become proud, self-confident, and forgetful of God; and not only deserved chastisement, but needed it for its reformation. Its gross corruption is manifest from this, that one wicked unprincipled man like Absalom could so easily and suddenly steal away the hearts of so many thousands, and engage them to join him in this conspiracy. A people that would do this must be corrupt to the core, and expect nothing but God's righteous indignation against them.

But the rebellion and its punishment were also a consequence of David's former sins, especially that one great sin, which over-shadowed all the others. True, years had passed since its commission, and David had humbled himself in deepest penitential sorrow, as his fifty-first Psalm will show. True, God also, who desireth not the death of a sinner, but rather that he should turn from his wickedness and live, had remitted the sentence of death against him, and instructed the prophet Nathan to say to him, because of his repentance, "The Lord hath put away thy sin; thou shalt not die." But inasmuch as the sin was so fearful, it brought such dishonor upon himself, his family, his people, his religion,—it gave such occasion to the enemies of God to blaspheme,—the Lord declared that he should never, in this world, cease to suffer for it. "Behold, I will raise up evil against thee out of thine own house; and the sword shall never depart from thine house." And so it came to pass. The close of his life was embittered by domestic troubles, and he was literally "chosen in the furnace of affliction," as prophecy had foretold. The rebellion of Absalom was the severest trial, and contributed, more than all the others, to "bring down his gray hairs with sorrow to the grave."

But he could say, "I know, O Lord, that thy judgments are right, and that thou, in very faithfulness, hast caused me to be troubled." "Before I was afflicted I went astray; but now have I kept thy commandments." His sorrows and trials wrought in him "repentance unto life, not to be repented of." They drew him more closely to the great Fountain of light, and life, and love; they made him more and more "a man after God's own heart." They fitted him more and more for his heavenly inheritance. It is written, "God resisteth the proud, and giveth grace to the humble." He "humbled himself under the mighty hand of God, and he was greatly exalted in due time." "Clothed with humility on earth," he is "crowned with glory" in heaven.

Where is there a brighter example of humility, and patience, and resignation, than he presents to us on first hearing of his son's conspiracy? Where is there, in all history, a scene more touching than his flight from Jerusalem, with numbers of his loyal subjects, his household servants, the chief officers of his army, the priests of the sanctuary,—all anxious to show their fidelity to him, and their sympathy in his distress;—the king weeping as he went, with bare feet and covered head,—going from the gate of Zion down that painful path, which God's own beloved Son, David's Lord and ours, afterwards trod,—across the Kedron, past Gethsemane, and up Mount Olivet. "And all the people that were with him covered every man his head, and they went up, weeping as they went." It was a grievous mourning.

But the king was not so absorbed in his own great sorrow as to be unmindful of other matters. He saw that the priests, in their zeal for the preservation of the ark, which had sometimes fallen into the hands of their enemies, were bearing it away from the holy city, and he desired Zadok the priest to restore it forthwith to its place in the sanctuary. "Carry back the ark of God into the city; if I shall find favor in the eyes of the Lord, He will bring me again, and show me both it and his habitation; but if he thus say: I have no delight in thee; behold, here am I, let him do to me as seemeth good unto Him."

Behold, then, in David's humility, repentance, and faith, an eminent example for ourselves; for our magistrates, our rulers, and for all the people of this land. He, the divinely appointed sovereign of the greatest nation upon earth, humbled himself in the very dust, on account of his own grievous sins, and the sins of his people. He acknowledged the wisdom, and justice, and goodness of God in all his dealings with them, and expressed his perfect confidence that the Judge of all the earth would do right. "If I shall find favor in the eyes of the Lord, He will bring me again and show me His habitation," the place where His honor dwelleth; but if not, "here am I, let Him do to me as seemeth good unto Him." That humility inclined Him who hath respect unto the lowly, to take David "out of the deep waters, to set his feet upon a rock, to order his goings, and to put a new song into his mouth, even a song of salvation unto his God."

Shall we not take David for our pattern in this respect, now that we are placed in circumstances so like to his? The rebellion which he had to meet was, as we have shown, without just cause—to accomplish no good end,—plotted and carried out by his *own familiar friend, whom he trusted, who did eat of his bread*,—even the son of his bosom. Yet, wicked and sinful as the rebellion was, it stole away the hearts of a large portion of Israel, and armed them against the best constitution and government in the world. Has not that rebellion a parallel in the one which is upon us now? And where shall we turn for help but unto David's God, who is our God? And how shall we obtain His aid, but by bowing ourselves before His mercy seat in penitence and prayer? We have come hither for that purpose to-day. "The President of the United States, moved by his own sense of duty, and by the request of both houses of Congress, has designated this as a day of humiliation, prayer and fasting, for all the people of the nation. He earnestly recommends that the day be observed in all families and churches with religious solemnity, and with a deep sense of our sins as a nation, of our sore distress and danger in this hour of trial, and of our intimate dependence upon the divine care and protection."

If our devotions this morning, my friends, have been sincere, we all of us have done just what David did, under like trials and difficulties. We have uttered the same confessions of sin, the same supplications for grace, the same expressions of sorrow and grief for our manifold transgressions, the same trust, and confidence, and hope in God, and all in the self same words that he uttered three thousand years ago. His own inspired penitential Psalms, which flowed from the inmost depths of his soul, when bowed beneath the weight of sorrow, suffering, and sin,—which, from his time until now, have been used by all God's people in giving utterance to the anguish of a broken and contrite heart,—have furnished us with a formulary for to-day.

If our lips have expressed the real feelings of our hearts, then we cannot doubt that God's blessing will rest upon us, and upon our cause. The cause, we know, is a righteous cause; the warfare is a holy warfare, for the protection of our lives, our property, our homes, our liberty, and our laws. It is for the preservation of that glorious constitution, to obtain which, our fathers pledged their lives, their fortunes, and their sacred honor,—yea, many of them sacrificed their best heart's blood. Shall we do less to defend it than they did to purchase it?

A civil war is a tremendous evil, but the surrender of all the blessings that our fathers bled and died for, without an effort to save them, would be a more tremendous evil. All the loyal States are united on this point. "We may differ," as one of our wisest and best statesmen* has said, "as to many things in the past, we may differ as to many things in the future, but we must *act* for the present. And for the present there is but one course for us all. Our misguided brethren of the South have left us no alternative but to fight. Our capital must be defended. Our flag must be sustained. The authority of the Government must be vindicated. The great experiment must be fairly and fully tried of restoring the Union upon its old constitutional basis. And whatever is necessary for these ends must be promptly and thoroughly done. God grant that the struggle may be successful, and that the rights of the North and the South may once more be found compatible with that condition of 'unity, peace, and concord,' which belongs to us as a Christian people."

So spake one of Massachusetts' noblest sons; and his words find a response in all loyal hearts. We are all of one mind now. Sectional differences are forgotten. The demon of party, that evil spirit which has done so much to demoralize the nation, is exorcised; cast out into the abyss, never, we hope and trust, to revive again. The trumpet now gives no uncertain sound. The hearts of the people are moved, as the heart of one man, for "upholding the supremacy of law, and the cause of justice and peace." In the name of our God we have set up our banner, and He will defend the right. The watchword is, "Liberty and Union, now and forever;"—The Constitution as it is, perpetual, unchangeable. May the God of battles and of nations "give us wisdom to discern, and faithfulness to do, and patience to endure, whatsoever shall be well pleasing in His sight." "May He have pity upon our brethren who are in arms against us, and show them the error of their way." May He incline our hearts to pity them, and never permit us to forget that, though in rebellion, they are our brethren still; many of them once near and dear to us as Absalom to David. Our hearts need constant watching, lest hatred and malice creep in and hold possession there. We must not suffer our abhorrence of this great crime to crush out the finest, holiest instincts of our nature. We must see to it that our hatred of the sin does not obliterate all compassion for the sinner. Think how many hundreds, nay, thousands of families in our land are divided among themselves, by reason of this terrible war. In how many instances that we hear of, is the parent against the child, and the child against the parent. Each is to the other as a member of his own body; dear as a hand, and valuable as an eye. But when an eye or a hand must be sacrificed for the preservation of life, may we not lament its loss? Many of the truest patriots in our land have brothers or sons in the rebel army. When they hear of the death of one of these, may they not express their grief in some such words as those of David, on a like occasion? "O Absalom! my son! my son!" Most of you can probably call to mind a companion, or relative, whom you greatly loved, who is also there. And should you hear that he is slain in battle, surely you would be not less a patriot, and you would be much more a Christian, if you shed a tear to the memory of your erring brother.

This is the feeling which we should cultivate in our hearts. It is, I believe, the prevalent feeling among us at the North. One whose opportunities for judging have been greater, perhaps, than those of almost any other man,—that eminent orator and statesman, Mr. Holt, of Kentucky, says: "I have everywhere found the most healthy and the most encouraging state of public opinion in reference to the prosecution of the war. I have nowhere found any exasperation against the people of the South. Strong and brave men, while speaking to me of our unhappy distractions, have wept in my presence, and I have honored them for it; for, if a brave man cannot weep over the overturn and ruin of such a country and such a government as this, where is there a catastrophe that can touch his heart?"

We may, and should, pray for those who are armed against us, as our divine Redeemer prayed for His enemies,—even as He prayed for us, when we were rebels against Him,— "Father, forgive them, for they know not what they do!"—As holy Stephen prayed for his murderers; "Lord, lay not this sin to their charge." When any one of them repents and amends, and expresses a desire to return, we should welcome him back with open arms, as a friend and brother, who was dead to us, but is alive again; who was lost, but is found.

If such be the temper and disposition of our hearts, then will the Lord be on our side. And "If God be for us, who can be against us?" No weapon formed against us shall

---

* The Hon. Robert C. Winthrop.

prosper. He will, we may humbly hope, restore unity and concord to our borders; and so order all things, "that peace and happiness, truth and justice, religion and piety, be established among us to all generations."

Hasten it, heavenly Father, in thine own good time, for the sake of Jesus Christ our Lord. Amen.

THE NATIONAL WEAKNESS.

A Discourse delivered in the First Church, Brookline, Mass., on Fast Day, Sept. 26, 1861.

BY REV. F. H. HEDGE, D.D.

Let not him that girdeth on his harness boast himself as he that putteth it off.—1 *Kings* xx. 11.

WHEN President Lincoln, five months ago, put forth his Proclamation, announcing a combination against the laws of the land too powerful to be suppressed by ordinary methods, and calling for seventy-five thousand troops to meet this exigency, there mingled, with the grief and indignation awakened in us by the treason which necessitated such an appeal, a thrill of patriotic joy at this demonstration of a new energy on the part of Government, after so many months of passive submission. We gloried in the prospect of a speedy solution of our national difficulties by a vigorous assertion of the Federal authority. Our spirits, which had settled into sullen gloom, almost despair of our country's future, were raised to a pitch of jubilant expectation, as we felt, through all our bones, the shock of national consciousness which that manifesto communicated to the loyal States.

The States were not slack in acknowledging the appeal. Massachusetts, true to her historical primacy, with promptness worthy her illustrious pedigree, responded to the call. Her Governor's word gave back the President's like its echo; a regiment of her sons, equipped and on the march in less than six days, was the echo to that; and a second 19th of April, dated with her blood, initiated and auspicated the new conflict. The seventy-five thousand were mustered and sent; and to these were added as many more. Our hearts were established: we were not afraid. The prevalent expectation was, that a three-months' campaign would suffice, if not to heal all difficulties, and reinstate the shattered Union, at least to crush the power of the rebels, and make it impossible for them to pursue their disorganizing course and to carry out their nefarious design.

So we girded on our harness with some boasting. With what result? The three-months' campaign, inaugurated with so much enthusiasm, after some less important engagements, terminated with the battle of Bull Run. The three months expired,—five months have elapsed,—and the rebel power is still unsubdued. "The harvest is passed, the summer is ended, and we are not saved." The rebels are not crushed, nor even so weakened as yet to despair of final success, or to manifest the least inclination to recede from their position. So far as they are weakened at all, it is by want of means, by their straitened economy and financial embarrassment, and not by the triumphs of the Federal arms. The Federal arms have not triumphed in any important engagement, except when opposed in overwhelming force to a weak resistance on the part of the enemy. And, although the disaster at Bull Run cannot be regarded as a victory on the part of the rebels, it added greatly to their confidence, and therefore to their strength; while it terribly rebuked our own overweening confidence in ourselves, and proved to us how little enthusiasm and patriotic determination will avail, without military discipline,—without wise conduct, prudence, and self-control. An army of brave men,—for such unquestionably they were,—by mere conceit of approaching danger, not real, imminent peril, overtaken with a panic which dissolves all bonds of military organization, almost of human fellowship, and converts a body of warriors into a herd of frightened deer, flying at the top of their speed when none pursued, never halting to ascertain whether any just cause existed for their alarm, utterly bereft of counsel and reason, and given over to a passion of insane terror,—this, after all the noisy demonstrations, the congratulations and harangues, the receptions and parades, which solemnized the setting forth of these hosts, though not an uncommon occurrence in war, and though no worse than a hundred panics recorded in history, is still a shame and a tragedy, which sadly illustrates the difference there is between promise and performance, between girding on and putting off.

Meanwhile, the pirates of the new Confederacy, in defiance of the public sentiment of

Christendom, are pursuing their prey, and snatching their plunder, on all our seas. Hundreds of vessels, with large amounts of value, have been seized by these bold buccaneers, who have thus far eluded all attempts to arrest their career.

Such, then, is our position at the present time. With vast resources and superabundant strength at our disposal, we have not as yet, for want of headship, of adequate organization, unity of purpose, and harmony of counsel, succeeded in applying those resources and that strength with decisive effect. The enemy in our borders, whom a well-directed effort might crush into dust, is still unsubdued, undaunted,—still mocks us through our own indirection. The fact is humiliating, and, like all humiliations, a salutary lesson to such as are willing to be instructed by it,—a lesson of weakness which it much concerns us to lay to heart. As a nation, we are proudly conscious of our strength: it were well we understood our weakness also, our national infirmities and faults. Of some of these, I propose now to speak.

One element of weakness is our self-conceit, —the vain-glorious persuasion that we are, on the whole, the greatest people and the wisest that ever occupied the earth with their labors, or tracked it with their footprints. One can pardon some degree of self-importance to a great and prosperous nation: I suppose there never was one without it. Let a people think well of their ability, and cherish a high sense of their providential mission. We accept it as a sign of national health. But let the conceit bear some proportion to the fact, and let it respect the national calling rather than the national merit; else it is a sign of morbid development, great superficial expansion, with no proportionate increase of substance. We Americans not only arrogate to ourselves a great destiny, in which, if we are true to our opportunities, we may be right; but we boast of great doings, in which we are certainly wrong. We confound prosperity with merit; we mistake a growth which is partly due to natural laws, partly to rare opportunities, and partly to a certain shiftiness of constitution, for a proof of greatness; we plume ourselves on our expansion; we give ourselves airs on the strength of a rapid, perhaps unexampled, increase of population, and a corresponding success in trade. When I hear such boasts, I cannot help recalling what an English cynic says of our pretensions: "Brag not yet of our American cousins. Their quantity of cotton, dollars, industry, and resources, I believe to be almost unspeakable. But I can by no means worship the like of these. What great human soul, what great thought, what great noble thing, that one could worship or loyally admire, has yet been produced there? None! The American cousins have done none of these things."

I cannot help remembering that the little republic of Athens, while yet in its youth, with its limited territory, population, and means, produced, within a century after the Persian wars, the immortal works which are still the chief boast of letters and art; and, what is more, the immortal men whom the world still honors as little less than divine. The most that we can say of ourselves is, that we have occupied a large territory with our civilization, such as it is, and invented some ingenious contrivances for the expedition of business, and the merely mechanical intercourse of life. Mechanical ingenuity, directed to material ends, is, thus far, our chief distinction as a people. And even here our merit is not supreme. The steamship is a great addition to the sum of human means; but the ship itself, which preceded it, is incomparably greater. The electric telegraph is a cunning invention; but the art of writing, about which little noise was made at the time, was a greater advance in civilization, and a greater blessing to mankind.

The real and most important achievement, and therefore the true test of a nation, is the national character. Tried by this standard, the American people can claim no preëminent rank among the nations. Here our weakness is painfully evident. It is true, the national character is not yet fully developed, and must not be too severely judged. True it is also, that the national character has many excellent and noble qualities, among which I may mention generosity, kindliness, and daring. But these are offset by fatal defects. Chief among these is a certain looseness which pervades the intellectual and moral life of the nation, debilitating its mental capacity, and vitiating all its action.

Intellectually, this trait appears in the superficiality, the crudeness, the want of discipline, of thorough and effective training, which characterize American life; and are due, in part, to the very constitution of our republican society, in which the facilities afforded for a certain kind of success, the chance of a prosperous career, to mere self-assertion, with little or no culture, and no laborious preparation of any kind, tend to lessen the demand for thorough education, and consequently reduce its standard and restrict its means. Where a hasty education will suffice for social and political success, the greater part will seek no other. To an American, the last criterion of merit, and the supreme mark of his calling, is to get the most votes; and, in this, it is not the best educated that succeed best, but the most unscrupulous and the most importunate. Accordingly, our public men, as a general rule, are worse educated, worse trained, and worse mannered, than those of any other civilized nation. A thoroughly taught and cultivated American gentleman is proverbially a rare phenomenon, and nowhere more so than in public life. The men who represent us in the courts of Europe, represent, too often and too faithfully, our ignorance and ill-breeding. With no knowledge of the language of the country to which they are sent, or of French, (the language of courts,) with no tincture of polite or diplomatic learning, with no one qualification for the post they occupy but the service rendered in procuring the election of the chief who sends them, they seem rather to have been accidentally cast ashore in those strange lands, than delegated thither as the plenipotentiaries of a great nation. There are splendid exceptions, I know, extending through all our history,—instances like those of Irving, Wheaton, Everett, Bancroft, and that of the accomplished ambassador who now represents us at the court of Vienna; but such has been the prevailing type. How, indeed, can it be otherwise? How should we be better abroad than at home? The representation is according to the constituency. The same want of thoroughness appears in the home-departments of State, whose incumbents are mostly and grossly deficient in knowledge and tact, equal to no exigency requiring brain and heart instead of routine. A great crisis like the present finds them incompetent and unprepared.

Viewed in its moral aspects, the looseness of which I speak is manifest in the want of reverence and subordination, which forms so conspicuous a trait of our nationality, and proves, at the present juncture, so serious an obstacle in our military operations. The American is not taught by the genius of the civil polity under which he lives, as other nations are by theirs, to respect and obey his superiors. On the contrary, the lesson he learns from his political experience is, that he has no superiors, —a lesson of equality, which, unless counteracted by domestic training or corrected by his own good sense, he is apt to interpret as a right to his own way in every condition and relation of life: a principle of action utterly incompatible with military discipline. It is difficult for him to admit the idea of a superior, much more to submit himself with unquestioning obedience to one who is placed in authority over him. Subordination is the first and fundamental principle, not only of military organization, but of social order. This lesson the American citizen has yet to learn; and, if the war shall serve to enforce it, it will prove a providential school of a very important civil virtue, as well as of a moral and Christian grace.

The same looseness appears in the moral indifference, which, not content with mitigating, has gone far to abolish, the criminal code, or the application of it in practice; which overlooks the gravest transgressions in public men, if associated with popular qualities; which tolerates bankruptcy of the most aggravated and fraudulent kind as a mercantile mishap, not compromising the social position of the offender;—an indifference to which the audacious filibuster is as worthy a hero as Scott or Kane; and which views criminality in general rather as an interesting variety of human nature, than as damnable guilt. Suppose our national difficulties settled, the rebellion suppressed, the Union restored: I fear that the leader in this conspiracy, whose crime against this country is unsurpassed in the annals of treason, so far from receiving his deserts on the gallows, would become the popular hero of the day. Should he visit the loyal States, I fear he would be received with public honors, and would be as likely as another to be elected President of the United States. We may certainly claim, as a people, the merit of extraordinary freedom from vindictiveness; but we must also plead guilty to a most extraordinary degree of moral indifference.

One other element of national weakness I will mention; and that is our present system of political administration, which has come to be a regular quadrennial revolution, extending through all the departments of State, and including every Federal office in the land. No sooner has any functionary become sufficiently versed in the duties of his station to discharge them with credit to himself and with profit to the nation, than immediately he is ejected, and his place supplied by a novice, who, mindful of the brief and precarious tenure of his position, is chiefly intent on making the most that can be made, in the way of pecuniary gain, of the opportunities it affords. The mischief arising from this source is incalculable. Not only are character and talent of the highest order almost necessarily excluded from the service of the State by a system which makes office the reward of successful demagoguism, but a lottery is opened with each Presidential term to hungry adventurers, whose only idea of office is that of a prize in the game of politics, with opportunity of plunder. If occasionally men of the better sort, who might excel in some honorable calling, are tempted by the hope of political preferment to mix in this arena, they do so at the expense of their morals or their time; for this is a race in which merit, self-respect, and scrupulous integrity, are sure to be distanced by importunity, chicanery, and brazen-faced impudence. Can they condescend to tamper with electors, and to foul their hands with low intrigue? If not, let them stand aloof from the game, and renounce all hope of success in that direction. This is a system which throws to the surface the dregs of our American civilization, and opens an impassable gulf between merit and political eminence. The present century has witnessed a steady decline in the character of our public men. Where shining ability and high-minded patriotism were once the rule, they have come to be the exception. To the Jeffersons, the Adamses and Clays, has succeeded a race of jobbers and hack politicians. Such are the results of this deplorable system of quadrennial rotation in office. This has made us, with all our prosperity, our rapid growth, and extended commerce, a byword and a hissing among the nations.

Since the throne of the world was sold at auction to the highest bidder, there has been nothing in its way so base as American politics. So demoralizing, so disorganizing, is the tendency of this system, that even the rupture of the Union, at the prospect of which we startle and are now so distressed, could bring us nothing worse than our own chosen and established methods were all these years preparing for us. All this must be reformed, or we slide to inevitable ruin, from which, hitherto, our ample territory and vast material resources alone have saved us. The quarrel between North and South which now agitates the land is but an anticipation of (unless it shall prove, as I trust it may, our deliverance from) greater evils that were threatening us before this outbreak, and that must have arrived, independently of the present crisis, by the natural termination of the course we were pursuing. We were rushing, with a speed unexampled in the history of nations, to the civil dissolution which precedes despotism in the natural order of history. The war now enkindled by sectional conflicts, with all the evils and miseries attending it, will prove, in the end, the greatest of blessings, if it serves to arrest this downward tendency; if it opens our eyes to our political errors and vices, and puts us in the way of reforming them; if it raises to the supreme power a truly wise and independent man, with an eye to discern what is needful, and strength of will, in spite of precedent and popular clamor, to enforce it,—a man who, without respect to party, shall put the right men in the right places; retaining the competent and faithful of former administrations, and fearlessly ejecting the incompetent of his own; and whose influence, backed by Congress and the nation, shall avail to make that practice the law of the land. I see no salvation for this people, no way of redemption from political ruin, until the principle is established of permanence in offices whose term is not prescribed by the Constitution, nor necessarily affected by the exigencies of State,—a permanence limited only by the competence and good behavior of the incumbent. Such a system of administration would tend to make office no longer the reward of electioneering and the prize of demagogues, but the fit investment of intellectual and moral worth; it would tend to take the affairs of State out of the hands of jobbers and pettifoggers and bar-room politicians, and commit them to those who are equal to the trust; it would tend to stop the mouths of the orators of the stump, to abate the nuisance of the popular harangue, and to purify the national speech; it would make the annual and quadrennial elections a safe and peaceful process, instead of the hurly-burly it now is, inflaming the passions, setting friend against friend, dividing households, and imbittering all the intercourse of life; it would help to do away with this periodical Walpurgis, this uncovering of the hells of wrath and strife; and, finally, it would make politics with us what they are in other lands,—a science of civil and international relations, instead of a trade and a trick, which none can be concerned in and not be defiled; it would give us counsellors instead of speculators; magistrates whom we can sincerely respect, instead of available ciphers; and make, in the good old Bible phrase, "our rulers peace, and our exactors righteousness."

I shall not speak of slavery in connection with this subject of the national weakness; not because I do not feel it to be the great weakness of the land,—the head and front of our offending, but because the subject has been so thoroughly discussed as to need no comment of mine, and, at present, no further ventilation. Those who do not see it to be the crowning evil of our polity are not likely to be converted by any illustration which I can give it.

The faults and vices I have named, if not the immediate cause of our troubles, are yet, in so far as the head and heart and hand of the nation have been weakened and its action vitiated by them, the true source of the mortifications, the disappointments, and all the bitter experiences, of this year of sorrows. God grant these experiences—"his chastisements," as our Chief Magistrate calls them—may work in us the good work of discipline and reform,—may open our eyes and bring back our hearts to forsaken truth and violated law!—that we may learn wisdom and learn obedience by the things we suffer, and rise from the humiliation of this affliction, a purified people, "zealous of good works."

And now, fellow-citizens, it befits us to consider what is needful and good for the present distress. Here we are, committed to a war whose term no mortal can predict, whose issues defy all human calculations; a war which will cost us hundreds of millions of money, and, it may be, hundreds of thousands of lives; a war which will beggar our commerce, check our industry, decimate our cities, dismember our households, ingulf our beloved, and wring our hearts with unspeakable anguish. What shall we say, in view of these horrors? what policy embrace? what course pursue? I know but one counsel in this emergency. One thought is uppermost in my heart; one word gushes up to my lips. It is hard to say it, in the face of all this tribulation and woe; but I know of nothing better: that word is, Onward!—onward, while a dollar remains in our treasury, and a regiment in the field!—onward, with due caution, but with unabated zeal and indomitable hearts! We have girded on our harness; and cursed be he that would bid us put it off until one of two issues arrives to our arms,—until we have quite conquered the enemies of our peace, and driven rebellion into the sea, or we ourselves are so far conquered as to have no means and no hope left; until it becomes evident, and is forced on our reluctant minds, that we have undertaken an impossibility, and are fighting against God, and must needs submit to his decree and the stronger foe, and accept the rupture of the Union as the bitter end and the heavenly doom! There are times when the cry of peace is the voice of treason, frightful and hateful as war ever is. Precious is peace; but liberty and right are more precious still: and liberty and right are at stake in this contest,—the liberties and rights bequeathed to us by our fathers, and bought with their blood. For certain it is, that if we fail to conquer the rebels who have lifted their parricidal hands against the common mother of us all, the National Union, they will eventually conquer *us*, and exercise a deadly dominion over us, if not by force of arms, by the surer weapons of political intrigue,—by insidious tampering with our commerce, by fell collusion with traitors on this side, by sowing dissension in our counsels and strife in our ranks, till province after province is added to the new Confederacy, and, piece by piece, what remains of the old Union is broken up. For the hydra of Secession is a monster that will not cease to ravage and destroy until the life is burnt out of it by the searing application of loyal arms. There will be no drawn game in this warfare: our only alternative is to conquer or succumb.

The cry of peace has been raised, here and there, by those whose political prospects or material interests are imperilled or impaired by the war. What would they have? what kind and conditions of peace would they propose? Shall the North—that is, the Federal Government—lay down its arms, and say to the rebels,

"We have erred: we repent. Go your way; do what you will: we oppose you no longer"? If such be their meaning, let them declare it, and see how many they can draw to their side. But no: they would have a convention for mutual adjustment. Suppose the convention assembled: what is there to adjust that the Constitution has not adjusted? Will the South accept that arbiter? The seceding States have already disowned it. For the North to offer more than the compromises of the Constitution, would be saying to the rebels, "We submit to your will: put your feet on our necks." May I never live to see the day when that concession shall take effect! Better a war of extermination than such adjustment.

The demand for peace has hitherto, so far as I know, been confined to the North, the party aggrieved and assailed,—the party acting in defence of the Union and the Constitution. It must come from the other side of the Potomac; the cry must go up from the ranks of Secession, and be accompanied by return to the old allegiance,—before our warfare can be accomplished.

Great are the difficulties attending this struggle for nationality. There never was a conflict so complicated and embarrassing as ours. Had we only the known, declared, and open enemy to encounter, our task would be comparatively light. But we have to contend with secret foes; our enemies are partly those of our own household; Treason lurks in our own ranks in league with Rebellion outside and furthering its cause. If we fail at last, it will be the treachery that walketh in darkness, not the destruction that wasteth at noonday to which we succumb.

But we will not admit the thought of failure with such an overweight of means and forces as falls to our side, with such issues as hang on our success,—the interests of civil society, the cause of order the world over, the cause of liberty for all time. Let us rather think, with such interests at stake that Nature herself is in league with us; that the stars, in their courses, fight on our side; that humanity travails with the burden of victory. Let us think that the shades of our fathers look solemnly down on this solemn struggle to preserve what they gave. And, with these, let our piety connect the more recent memories of those who have fallen in this campaign,—the proto-martyrs of our cause.

High among these, shines the honored name of Lyon, than whom no braver ever led the van in the field of death. He sleeps well: his memory is blest.

"There is a tear for all who die,
A mourner o'er the humblest grave;
But nations swell the funeral cry,
And Triumph weeps, above the brave."

And so let the day of public humiliation be to all the people of this Union a day of new consecration and new hope. May He who weighs the nations in his balance find this nation true to his word, and trusting in his name, in war as in peace! May those who gird on the harness of battle wear it without boasting, but with cheerful courage and unfaltering trust; and, when in due season we shall put it off, may our boasting be not in ourselves, but in God, who giveth us the victory!

NATIONAL LAWLESSNESS, AND ITS CURE.

A Sermon Preached in the Madison Square Presbyterian Church, New York, the Sunday after the Fourth of July, 1861.

BY WILLIAM ADAMS, D. D.

In those days there was no king in Israel, but every man did that which was right in his own eyes.—*Judges* xviii. 6.

THE period of Hebrew history which is thus described, was that which followed the death of Joshua. Though the incidents which illustrate this state of anarchy are recorded in the appendix of the book of Judges, and not at its beginning, with which they synchronize, yet it is agreed by the best chronologists, Jewish and Christian, that the incidents themselves took place in the year 1406 B. C. The exodus of the Hebrew people from Egypt under Moses was in the year 1491 B. C. Then was it that Moses and all Israel chanted that song upon the shores of the Red Sea, which will stand to the end of time, like a monumental shaft, in honor of a great deliverance. Subtracting the one date from the other, we find the result 85 years, precisely the same number which have passed since the Declaration of American Independence in 1776, to this its anniversary in 1861.

It seems to us incredible that a people so distinguished by the favor of Divine Providence; so recently delivered out of Egyptian bondage, with signs and wonders so extraordinary, and guided into the occupancy of the fair land which for so long a time had been promised to them and their fathers; should so soon, if at all, relapse into lawlessness, and irreligion, and heathenism. We should have supposed that with such memories as those which characterized their national history; and these so fresh and recent, that they would have been sure to adhere to all those political and religious laws which were their security and honor and blessing. With what nation had God dealt as with them? Yet twenty years only had passed since the death of Joshua—the leader of the nation, the viceroy of God, who had been a personal witness of all the marvels which had signalized their history from the date of the exodus; scarcely a decade of years had been finished since the last of those venerable men had died, who had participated in the scenes of the Wilderness, and the occupation of the national domain; when the whole people, as if smitten with frenzy, cast away their eminent prerogatives, secured to them at such a cost, and, like swine trampling on priceless pearls, abandoned themselves to anarchy and idolatry. Then ensued that terrible period of Jewish history which is thus briefly described: "In those days there was no king," no magistracy in Israel, "but every man did that which was right in his own eyes." Then occurred those scenes of rapine, and violence, and wrong, and carnage, which fill the closing chapters of this Book—scenes of barbaric cruelty, terminating in most fierce and bloody wars between tribes once linked in firmest concord, which cannot now be read without a blush for human shame and sighs for human folly.

The method, as it would seem, from this episode of history, as well as from the whole drama of history itself, by which the Almighty educates nations for a high civilization, is to allow them to experiment, for themselves, according to their own ways and devices. There is a shorter, easier, and more economical method within the reach of all, if they would but adopt it: even to regard the requirements of God, with implicit faith and obedience. But when men will bolt out of the right way, and will do that which is right in their own eyes, though it be antagonistic to the will of the Supreme, there is but one way, even that they should make trial of their evil courses, and be made to feel, in their own experience, how evil they are, and how tremendous the consequences of every infraction of the divine code. Such was the result of this portion of Hebrew history. It was well, both for themselves and for the world, that a nation, bent on the experiment, should make one trial of what it was to be without any lawful magistracy. It was not necessary that the experiment should be repeated. The lesson was burnt deep and ineffaceable into the national convictions. Sensualism, brutality, internecine wars, barbaric invasions, so far prevailed, that at length necessity, the instinct of self-preservation, suggested various remedies. Persons remarkable, at first, for physical strength and courage presented themselves as rallying points for the assertion of right, the vindication of justice, and the protection of the innocent. Such were the "judges" of Israel—Othniel, Ehud, Deborah and Barak, Gideon, Jephthah and Samson—rude compounds, as we should say, of the warrior and the magistrate, yet the offspring of necessity, and the strong helpers of the people, out of the morass of anarchy, into somewhat of order and law, gradually shaped into permanent magistracy, and culminating at last in the splendor of the Hebrew monarchy.

Why should not every man be allowed to do that which is right in his own eyes? Why should not mere *will* and *feeling* be a sufficient authority for the actions of individuals and communities? We all have an intuitive apprehension that such a state of things cannot be allowed; that it would be sure, if tried, to bring about a general wreck and ruin of the race. Yet all may not be able to give such an answer to this question as would satisfy one who forms his opinions, and regulates his conduct, on ethical and religious grounds. It is on such grounds alone, that the question comes within the province of the pulpit, as a teacher of *Christian morals.*

The question is invested with special importance, in our own times, and in our own land, because of the tendency here to defy the ideas of *personal rights, personal freedom*, and *personal independence.* Every thing in our institutions, in our literature, in our manners, has long tended to stimulate these ideas to the utmost. We have had any number of discussions and treatises designed to prove that individual opinion was the highest arbiter of truth and duty, and that every man's own intuition was the ultimate standard of what is right. It will be conceded by all that the whole tendency of our national life and thought is to foster this spirit of personal liberty and independence. Nor are these qualities to be spoken of with disrespect. They are most essential elements in the grand compound of human civilization. Combined with certain other elements of law and order, they form the very highest development of humanity. What are the other elements so essential? What are the limitations which must be fixed to the exercise of personal freedom? This is the very gist of the question. This is only proposing, in another form, our original problem: Why may not every man do that which is right in his own eyes?

Man is not an independent existence, but a part of a living organism, which we call society, by which he is connected with other individuals in indissoluble relations. This is a necessary condition of things, dependent not on our choice, but without our choice, on the will of the All-Wise. We hear much of the *social compact*—an expression used by those who have reasoned concerning the origin and laws of human society and civil polity; and since we must have terms to represent ideas, there is no objection to this phrase, if we use it with a discreet perception of its import. The point to be guarded in the use of the word *compact*, or any of its equivalents, in the definition of society, is this: organized society is not the *voluntary* concourse of individuals, but a providential necessity into which we are born, without our knowledge or consent. It is not of his own will that every child enters the world subject to an authority higher than his own. He is introduced, at his birth, into a social state which necessitates his subordination to a pre-existing order, in the shape of parental government. In like manner, without his consent at all, he is born into the civil polity, a condition of things which depends, not on the voluntary associating of men, but on absolute necessities imposed by the Being who has given us an existence. Without this beneficent organization, which we call *Society*, the State, the Government, I will not say the human race, could not exist at all; but certainly it could not exist with any possibility of civilization, and culture, and development, and progress, and happiness. The State represents the great ideas of order, security, right, justice, and humanity, as the necessary condition of all morality. There must be order as the basis of all right relations; and order consists in obedience to positive laws, in a necessary condition, ordained by the Almighty. It is in this sense that the Bible defines the *powers that be*—that is, civil government—as ordained of God; asserting that resistance to this (without just cause) is resistance to God himself. In asserting this, the inspired Word does not represent that government is a cast-iron, immovable, unchangeable power, to exist in all ages and all countries in one and the same form. It has itself applied spiritual and reformatory power which tends to make governments better, more just, and more humane. It instructs those who govern that they too are under divine obligations to act without wrong, or cruelty, or oppression; and the great problem of society, through solemn centuries, has been so to adjust these two forces, the freedom of the individual and the order of society, as to secure the greatest amount of all that is right, and just, and peaceful, and happy. In the progress of events, it has sometimes happened that the one force or the other has been in excess; that there has been an uprising and outbursting of popular liberty, which has overturned superincumbent authority, creating, for a season, confusion, disorder, and revolutionary violence, till government could readjust itself on a better and wiser basis; while, on the other hand, the Ruling Power has often asserted itself with such vigor and severity as to bear down all personal liberty, forbidding all motion, or peeping, or protesting, till stimulus, hope, and life have died out of the individual man.

Amidst all these alternations there has been an actual progress through these compound forces of *freedom* and *order*. The pendulum has swung to and fro, and the index finger on the clock of time has been moving on and round. It has been our *boast*—or if the word suggests too readily the national fault of self-complacency—it has been our sober belief that, as the result of all preceding experiments, and the general improvement of the race, under the auspices of education and religion, in our own land, at length, there had been attained a form of government which secures, in happiest combination the world has ever seen, the largest amount of personal liberty, with the most reliable expression of order, protecting property and person and life. If either of these forces has been in danger of running to excess, it surely has not been severity on the part of the Ruling Power. The theory of our form of civil government is the right of free men to govern themselves by laws which they have, from their own intelligent choice, themselves enacted and recognized. This peculiar form of social polity exists under what is called a *constitution:* a written constitution—that is, a system of rules, and principles, and ordinances by which the government shall be administered, and these adopted by the people themselves, and not a gift conferred by a monarch; and to guard against all sudden caprices, the whims and passions of an hour, these rules and ordinances are engrossed in an instrument, which prescribes the orderly method by which at any time the document itself may be altered and improved. The principle which underlies a government so constituted is, that the people themselves are so intelligent and virtuous that they can be trusted with the power of self-government. Whether this be true, in fact, of our own population is the very experiment which we are trying before the gaze of the world. The theory itself, whatever the issue of its first great trial, what does it leave to be desired? What could man ask more than this: the right to prescribe for himself the rules and ordinances by which government shall be administered, and the order of society shall be secured? Could the imagination of man go farther than this? Is it not in advance of all which is possessed by other nations? The Constitution of the British Realm is not a written instrument, in the hands of the people, to be read in schools, for it consists in an accumulation of historic precedents, of established usages, which are recognized as fundamental law. The Constitution of England is not *written* at all. For what has France been struggling through all her dynasties and revolutions, but that there should be granted to her some *octroyée* through imperial favor, which would secure to her citizens more of personal right and freedom? What more would Italy desire, torn by faction, sighing for unity, oppressed by the worst form of despotism, than the permission to govern herself according to a written constitution. I will not speak of Spain and Austria, where the genius of order has reigned so long and so tyrannically, that individual freedom and courage are almost smoth-ered out; but how would Hungary and Poland, in which the seed-thoughts of our Protestant faith have been planted so deep, prolific already in noble purposes and struggles, how would they clap their hands for joy, if, at last, they could only attain their long-lost, long-sought right of prescribing and administering their own constituted government!

This privilege, which has made us the admiration and envy of the world, was no sudden attainment, but the fruitage of a long, slow, deep-rooted growth. It is the issue of historic causes. It has been purchased at a great price. We who enjoy it might think that it had always been in existence the same as now. In fact it is of recent origin. At what a cost of time, and heroism, and martyrdom, and suffering, and blood has it passed into our hands. Consider what has already been accomplished under its auspices. It has secured all which is implied in order, with the least possible restraint, consistent therewith, on the freedom of the individual. It has wronged no man. It has oppressed no man. It has never brought one man to the scaffold or the prison unjustly. It has secured to a vast population all their rights. Through this large domain, any man, any woman, could travel unmolested, unquestioned, without espionage, without passports, and without a suspicion of harm. All forms of lawful business were protected, and a vast nation had started forth in a career of unprecedented prosperity, with no kind of restraint save what they had imposed on themselves for their own peace and comfort, as if to show to the world, at last, what a people could be and do under the auspices of freedom, industry, education, and religion.

Surely, if ever there was a people under any conceivable obligation to love their country, to obey its laws, to be loyal to its Constitution, it is the people of these United States. Bear in mind the principle of our national life; that which has been smelted out of the fires and battles of past ages; that which is the peculiar gift of our country to the general history of the race—the ultimatum, as we should say, of human hope and desire—*the right of self-government;* personal liberty unrestrained save by those limitations of order which thoughtful liberty has imposed on herself. If the Word of God, fresh from its inspired origin, abounds with commands to "honor the king," to "obey

www.ingramcontent.com/pod-product-compliance
Lightning Source LLC
Chambersburg PA
CBHW030258170426
43202CB00009B/801